THE TROUBLE
WITH
Post-Blackness

THE TROUBLE
WITH
Post-Blackness

EDITED BY

Houston A. Baker Jr.
and
K. Merinda Simmons

Columbia University Press　　New York

Columbia University Press
Publishers Since 1893
New York   Chichester, West Sussex
cup.columbia.edu

Excerpt from "Gwendolyn Brooks" in *Don't Cry, Scream* by Haki R. Madhubuti (Chicago: Third World Press, 1969), reprinted by permission of Third World Press © 1969 Haki R. Madhubuti

Excerpt from "What Color Is Lonely" in *Songs of a Blackbird* by Carolyn Rodgers (Chicago: Third World Press, 1973), reprinted by permission of Third World Press © 1969 Carolyn Rodgers

Excerpt from "Someone Leans Near" in *Five Poems* by Toni Morrison (Las Vegas: Rainmaker Editions, 2002), used by permission © Rainmaker Editions. All rights reserved

Library of Congress Cataloging-in-Publication Data

The trouble with post-Blackness / edited by Houston A. Baker and K. Merinda Simmons.
    pages cm
Includes bibliographical references and index.
    ISBN 978-0-231-16934-9 (cloth : acid-free paper) — ISBN 978-0-231-53850-3 (e-book)
    1. African Americans—Race identity. 2. African Americans—Intellectual life. 3. African Americans—Social conditions—1975-. 4. Social change—United States. 5. Identity politics—United States. 6. Post-racialism—United States. 7. African American philosophy. 8. United States—Race relations. I. Baker, Houston A., editor. II. Simmons, Merinda, 1981– editor.

E185.625.T76   2015
305.800973—dc23   2014013811

Columbia University Press books are printed on permanent and durable acid-free paper.
This book is printed on paper with recycled content.
Printed in the United States of America

c 10 9 8 7 6 5 4 3 2 1

Jacket design by Noah Arlow.
Jacket Image: © Hank Willis Thomas, Crossroads, 2012. Hank Willis Thomas in collaboration with Sanford Biggers. Courtesy of the artists and Jack Shainman Gallery, New York.

References to websites (URLs) were accurate at the time of writing. Neither the author nor Columbia University Press is responsible for URLs that may have expired or changed since the manuscript was prepared.

CONTENTS

ACKNOWLEDGMENTS

The editors wish to thank those who helped make the present collection a reality. We are grateful for the tireless efforts of Natalie Baggett, program coordinator and administrative assistant at Vanderbilt University. Every aspect of the project has benefited from Natalie's efficiency, communication skills, and indomitable organization. We thank Stephanie Li of the University of Rochester for conceptualizing a symposium bearing the title of the present volume. Professor Li secured travel and accommodation funds and honoraria from the Humanities Project of Rochester for all the volume's contributors. She then orchestrated an exciting one-day intellectual exchange at the university on April 11, 2014. It goes without saying that Stephanie Li and Natalie Baggett worked in tandem on some important logistics. Vanderbilt University English Department graduate student Andrew Hines encountered our project at its inception. His archival skill and shrewd analytical competence provided a fine inaugural bibliography for our work. At a later phase Andy was indispensable in resolving documentation anxieties. Our colleagues at the University of Alabama and at Vanderbilt have been generous and encouraging. We extend special gratitude to colleagues in the Department of Religious Studies at the University of Alabama, the Culture on the Edge research collaborative, and to those in the departments of English and African American and Diaspora Studies at Vanderbilt. Our indebtedness to our editor, Jennifer Crewe, and Columbia University Press is unbounded. Jennifer encouraged our project from the outset. Her publishing team is a professional assembly to be envied.

While we have been fortunate in all our institutional navigations, we could not have achieved such a fine collection without the individual graciousness, punctuality, and brilliance of our contributors. They represent the best standards and practices of collective intellectual enterprise. We cannot praise or thank them enough for making our job so seamless and rewarding.

Finally, we extend sincere and personal thanks to Vanderbilt University professor Charlotte Pierce-Baker, who invited us into her home to work. She advised us on the construction and tone of our enterprise. She shared insights and critique that made our collaboration more astute. We also benefited personally from the kind support and company of Nathan Loewen and Arlo Simmons-Loewen.

If we have overlooked anyone who helped and inspired us to complete the present project, we apologize.

THE TROUBLE
WITH
Post-Blackness

Introduction

The Dubious Stage of Post-Blackness—
Performing Otherness, Conserving Dominance

K. MERINDA SIMMONS

> There is no such thing as identity, only operational acts of identification.
>
> —Jean-François Bayart, *The Illusion of Cultural Identity*

> Intellectuals are holders of cultural capital and, even if they are the dominated among the dominant, they still belong among the dominant. That is one of the foundations of their ambivalence.
>
> —Pierre Bourdieu, "The Myth of 'Globalization' and the European Welfare State"

I should make one thing clear from the outset: this volume is not *about* Touré. His recent *Who's Afraid of Post-Blackness? What It Means to Be Black Now* did give rise to a productive conversation between my co-editor and me, one that sowed the initial seeds toward thinking about a collaborative project addressing this topic. And while many of the essays in this volume—this introduction included—directly address Touré's text, they do so in order to make broader claims about the implications of a "post-black" rhetorical schema. Touré and his ideas about "what it means to be black now" are useful data, to be sure, as problematic metonyms for the complex discourses on identifications of something called "blackness" in this present digital age. His book, then, offers an occasion for the contents of this collection: namely, a multiperspectival conversation that traverses a variety of genres and investigates the ever-shifting classifications of culture and capital where domains of "race" are concerned.

Who's Afraid of Post-Blackness? is thus but one symptomatic indicator of a larger discussion on race and politics in America. Many like to think that the discussion is about naming and reality—how should we identify ourselves in a new context of a black president? Fifty years after the March on Washington, how are we to take account of King's dream but articulate a different vision for what it "means" to be an African American in a globalized, technologically determined society? Those who quickly and rightly critiqued claims of a populace that had enjoyed a "post-race" environment since the election seemed to have the answer. People of color did not have to live in a delusionary white fantasy of post-racialism. That was obviously an insulting proposition. Instead, well-intentioned talking heads suggested that we begin thinking of a society that is clearly not post-racial but *is* just as clearly *post-black*. But I'm getting ahead of myself.

Not too long ago I found myself in the midst of a debate among a few colleagues about race, essentialism, strategy, and discourse. It began after one of them wrote a blog post in which, taking up the Bourdieu quote above (which came from a 1996 address published in *Acts of Resistance*), he discussed what he takes to be the ambivalence of intellectuals—the structural privilege necessary for the seemingly progressive work of recovering voices thought to be silenced. He gave an example of a scholar who places herself in the camp of Spivakian strategic essentialists in order to talk about racial otherness (her specific interest lying in the category "Asian American"). I shared a link to the post with my own online community (the blog itself is composed of a group of scholars, myself among them, writing about acts of identification), with the following quote from the piece: "In other words, what sort of essentialism, upon analysis, is *not* strategic?" What my colleague was getting at was the way in which so many scholars of identity and race leave untroubled the dominant category—in this case white hegemony—that they are attempting to subvert by strategically essentializing other marginalized voices. In other words, we should take pains to view whiteness (any mode of "dominance," for that matter) as itself a constructed and highly contingent space. This, put simply, is the trouble with post-blackness: in the attempt to analyze and describe—and thus bring awareness to and advocate for—particular modes of performing something called "black identity," the discourse on post-blackness keeps up and running an untroubled category of whiteness against which it demarcates itself.

The back-and-forth that ensued after my sharing the post was an interesting and telling one, occurring mostly between my colleague who wrote the piece and a scholar of race studies whose work is becoming well-known in spheres of both academe and popular culture. Without belaboring the intellectual twists and turns of the conversation, I do find the basic emphasis of the disagreement to be indicative of the kinds of discursive moves that surround the conversation about post-blackness and that the essays in this volume address through various channels and case studies. The race theorist suggested that there are essentialisms and then there are essentialisms. Those normative claims that hold (or have historically held) dominant or colonizing status are, the scholar claimed, qualitatively different and distinct from those coming from racially marginalized voices. The response by the original post's author suggested that what required interrogation is not the right or accurate label to use for this or that group, nor is it which essentialism is *really* reductive. Rather, what we should examine is the impulse to treat race as a necessary signifier of difference while leaving whiteness alone as a cohesive whole.

At issue ultimately was a fundamental difference in the way that each scholar talked about discourse—whether to see it as an academic novelty that does not take account of daily lives and the experiences therein or as a necessarily constitutive framing structure of how we understand those lives and experiences in the first place. It has become easy shorthand to lament the "limits of discourse" or the implications of talking about identity as "merely a construction." After all, we can talk all day long about race as a discursive trope, but we are left staring in the face the obvious realities of how inequity and power are manifested through racial designations. Aren't the respective fates of Trayvon Martin and George Zimmerman enough to make us see this? Perhaps. But I would submit that it was not "blackness" in itself that killed Martin or acquitted Zimmerman. Rather, it was the complex interplay of various classifications at work: categories of race, safety, danger, defense, and masculinity around which very exacting boundaries were drawn by certain players in the trial who were able to gain credibility with the jury—itself a space worthy of the debate and critique it has received. Credibility, of course, is its own operating signifier here, too. We need look no further than the response to Rachel Jeantel. She was berated by the defense and pitied (though with little sympathy or complexity) by the jurors, her usage of the English language often being at issue. The fact that her first language is Creole—that she speaks Spanish and English too, and is thus trilingual—was not something that made her appear exceptionally talented, as it would and does routinely for others. Instead, her linguistic "skills" were cast as degrees of separation, keeping firmly in place an easy line between "us" and "them" for the jurors.

Invisible, of course, were the ways in which the jurors, defense team, and prosecutors were firmly ensconced in linguistic codes and shifts of their own: precise and specialized languages of legal precedent and protocol, not to mention those of the specific roles each group was assigned to play within the context of a courtroom. It is not "blackness" that makes the difference but rather the meaning and value attributed to it by various social actors, each with interests that allow race to perform and come to mean a certain thing for that person or group. In this sense, then, if we take discourse analysis and constructionism seriously, there's nothing "mere" about them. Discourse is an organizing rubric for making sense of and categorizing identities and experiences around us. In this manner, our interest should lie not in what is unique or different about a particular identity group but in what kinds of interests or motivations we bring to the table in order to classify that group as particular or "othered" in the first place. Where the rhetoric of post-blackness is concerned, the concentrated focus on how African Americans perform their blackness too often gets presented as a reflection of Touré's subtitle: *what it means to be black now*, rather than these performances being necessarily coterminous with the discursive rubrics that identify them as distinct or signifying of "what it means to be black" at all.

I am taking a cue here from cultural theorists who discuss discourse as an organizing tool. The emphasis on difference as a *thing* to be either ignored or celebrated depending on one's pursuits is dropped in favor of thinking about the systems and processes of knowledge that prompt us to organize and mark various human behaviors and signifiers as "difference," demarcating individuals and groups as unique in this or that way. Thus, racial performance is not the kind of ultimately liberated and empowered moment of agency that Touré would have us believe. Modes of behavior and identification occur within structured, discursive frameworks of societal organization that offer us scripts for understanding racial acts of identification. This is not to say that we are zombified automatons with no say in our performances whatsoever. It is to say that when we make choices and exact a certain degree of agency, we do so from an up-and-running discursive context where economic, historical, and linguistic particularities (just to name a few) reside.

In that sense, we might call to mind Stuart Hall's notion that race works more like a language than it does a demarcating description of physiological difference. He has famously called it a "floating signifier," unattached trans-historically and always at once limited and constitutive in its construction of "inside" and "outside." While academicians have by and large traded notions of race as a biological fact for ones that see it as a social construction, many now are comfortable breaking the rules of poststructuralism because of how well-versed they are in those very tenets. Along with the increasingly popular phenomenon of "public intellectuals"—a term that stacks up a false dichotomy between public and private knowledge and space—there has been an increasing emphasis on a new materialism, ostensibly getting us back to the brute facts of race and racism on the ground. In this mode, academics want also to be activists, staying "real" in the zone of what seems to many the illusory world of intellectual navelgazing. After all, this train of thought would suggest, there is a world of experience out there, with realities often violent and even fatal for racially marked bodies. So many so-called public intellectuals and proponents of the materialist turn in race studies point to what they see as the "real" consequences to discursive turns and, in so doing, critique any analytical focus on discourse or the contingency of categories as failing to take account of the material realities of people of color. Cornel West and Tavis Smiley, for example, have practically made second careers out of writing and speaking together on the actions that they believe need taken in poverty-stricken pockets of African American society. I may well agree with many of their political persuasions and ideals, but the focus on a "real world" of "lived experience" when describing domains of blackness seems to leave a category called white privilege—even while critiqued—naturalized, obvious, and undisturbed. The focus on discourse that poststructuralist strands of cultural theory (like that represented by Hall) have been asking us to hold for decades suggests that the question of whether there "really" are or are not particular differences in the world is not the point. Rather, any meaning or value given to those differences is the product of various systems of classification. In that sense, what we should analyze and be curious about are the ways in which certain signifiers of difference get codified or treated in certain ways.

The irony of a position that would hold white hegemony as more problematic than essentialism launched from a so-called black perspective is that it resorts to a seemingly untouchable space of personal experience. After all, how can one offer any response to the *point finale* of how another person experiences this or that identity marker? In this way, however, a quick and easy reading of the old feminist adage "the personal is political" gets adopted. This reading takes the idea to mean that processes of identification (the personal) are political ends in themselves, inarguable facts of a phenomenological matter. They are, then, unquestionable and yet simultaneously uniquely belonging to the one articulating that personal domain. However, I see the concept as suggesting that these acts of identification are invariably and unavoidably political acts—nothing more or less—and thus a subject of inquiry or piece of data we might study, like anything else. They are, as such, their own discursive moments, not transcendent or exclusive spheres.

Touré's venture into the question of what it means to be black now is profoundly indebted to the idea of the dominion and ultimate autonomy of the individual. As such, his paradigm of personal self-possession and authorship is working well within the codified framework of the so-called American Dream. And because he does not wish to see this trope as a rhetorical device alone (thus complicating his need for being able to write and perform one's own blackness), he instead leaves it completely unscrutinized. *Who's Afraid of Post-Blackness* is interested in the ways in which contemporary African Americans understand and enact their blackness and their American-ness. To discuss this, Touré talks about personal experience—his as well as those of the 105 "luminaries" he interviews. What is puzzling is the idea that the sphere of personal experience might help us launch critiques of authenticity. Personal experience is what so many people use to lay claim to the very authenticity that Touré wants to problematize. In an attempt to dispel the myth that economic privilege (with accompanying tastes, experiences, and interests) and blackness are mutually exclusive, he takes pains to show how his own means—financial, educational, or otherwise—make him no less black than anyone else.

To this end, the critiques he continues to answer to throughout the book are the claims leveled against his blackness—that he "ain't even black." To do so, though, even as he suggests that he is "a real and authentic Black man," he talks about blackness as something that people have to transcend or get beyond (75). Otherwise, it might hold them back. This is the case early on for Michael Eric Dyson's depiction of Barack Obama's being "rooted in but not restricted by his blackness" (xiii). When Touré talks about his skydiving experience, for example, he casts it in the following language: "If I'd let being Black hold me back from skydiving I would've cheated myself out of an opportunity to grow as a human." So, while he says that "to be born Black is an extraordinary gift bestowing access to an unbelievably rich legacy of joy," he nonetheless assures his readers that "to experience the full possibilities of Blackness, you must break free of the strictures sometimes placed on Blackness from outside the African-American culture and also from within it" (4). Thus, somehow, though the "possibilities of Blackness" are endless and variant, one can find ways to experience them fully. What's more, blackness is cast as a deeply personal journey of self-discovery—certainly not a discursive device orchestrating the various modes by which one might describe or identify oneself. Thus, his recollection of being accused of not being black prompts him to proclaim the following:

> It was the most humiliating moment of my life but also one of the best moments of my life, because it forced me to take a searingly painful look inside and figure out exactly what it means to me to be Black. It led to a liberating epiphany and being at peace with who I am. That moment started me inching down the mental road that would lead to this book. The world had before that told me I wasn't Black, or wasn't their vision of Black, but subtly, never that bluntly. It was for me a sort of nigga wake-up call. (75)

Blackness, then, is for Touré a profoundly individual and subjective process of self-identification. I don't disagree. However, the insistence on this personal space as one beyond discourse and impervious to question or critique is what I find less than compelling.

Cast as wholly personal, performing one's blackness in a particular way is for Touré the epitome of what constitutes a post-black act. But if we take up the earlier discussion of all essentialisms being strategic, working for different ends with different means, we might also consider the inverse: that all strategies are, in fact, also essentializing. Thus, when Touré identifies three "dimensions of blackness," offering descriptions of "the multiplicity of ways to be Black," he nonetheless blankets black experiences into three domains of possible performance (9). While three ways may be two steps ahead of one, introducing new categories does little to complicate the dominant structure of classification that Touré purports to critique. Michael Eric Dyson (who also writes the foreword) helps him define these "three primary dimensions of blackness"—its own interesting rhetorical moment, as they are not discussing three primary performative acts but rather dimensions of blackness, implying an identifiable whole that contains those three modes.

Dyson labels the categories "accidental," "incidental," and "intentional." Touré recasts them as "introverted," "ambiverted," and "extroverted" (9). Citing Clarence Thomas and Condoleezza Rice as examples, he suggests the first is "a perhaps more private relationship with Blackness," where one's blackness is an accident of birth (9). The second "refers to having a more fluid relationship with [blackness]" in which it is important to folks without dominating them (9). The third, then, is a more deliberate or motivated brand of blackness along the lines of what Malcolm X, Martin Luther King Jr., and Jay-Z represent (10). Dyson claims, "Black people have different modes of Blackness and when we need to be each of those varieties of Blackness, we exercise them. We vacillate among the modes depending on what we need. When you deal with multiple audiences you have to pivot around different presentations of Blackness" (11). For Touré, then, "The ability to maneuver within white society—and how high you can rise within white power structures—is often tied to your ability to modulate. Black success requires Black *multi-linguality*—the ability to know how and when to move among the different languages of Blackness. . . . There are many ways to be Black in all Black people" (11). In this sense, these three ways of being are like different cards we play depending on our needs at a certain time. People exercise the different modes of blackness depending on their needs or desires, intelligently modulating between all the blacknesses we have inside.

Here's the thing. To talk about such modulation as a black phenomenon, to break blackness down into general and specific taxonomic categories is still to imagine that we can describe with aptness and clarity what constitutes it—no matter how interchangeable, and no matter how subject to personal manipulation. Further, it is to forget that dominant groups are no less contingent. Whiteness is likewise forged from consistently changing boundaries and is made up of its own scripts and codes that people perform. So, as progressive as his stated motivations may be, Touré creates something of a bind. Specifically, he casts black social linguistic mobility wholly within a context of what he calls "white power structures." That these structures are not themselves fixed or stable is not at all addressed in a sophisticated or critical way. Instead they are left alone to be simultaneously the dominant sphere to which African Americans in Touré's model aim to aspire as well as the knowable space of identity (rather than an act of identification like any other) that we need not question because of its clear cohesiveness.

Touré makes this evident at the earliest moment in the book, in fact, when he offers the following author's note concerning why he capitalizes "Black" but leaves "white" lowercased:

> I have chosen to capitalize the word "Black" and lowercase "white" throughout this book. I believe "Black" constitutes a group, an ethnicity equivalent to African-American, Negro, or, in terms of a sense of ethnic cohesion, Irish, Polish, or Chinese. I don't believe that whiteness merits the same treatment. Most American whites think of themselves as Italian-American or Jewish or otherwise relating to other past connections that Blacks cannot make because of the familial and national disruptions of slavery. So to me, because Black speaks to an unknown familial/national past it deserves capitalization. (ix)

Thus, in attempting to cast "Blackness" as a space rich in variation and diversity—offering the three multifaceted ways to perform it—he nonetheless undermines his own project by stacking up a "real" difference between the availability of heritage or tradition to "whiteness" and "Blackness," respectively.

Code-switching is all well and good, often cast (as Touré discusses it) as a subversive means of deconstructing a categorical, monolithic "right way" to be black. It is a way, such a line of thought would have us think, to dismantle the master's house using our own tools. What gets lost in this configuration, however, is the way in which dominant (white) power structures are reified by the moves thought to be critiquing and deconstructing them. And, actually, demonstration of proficient use of the proverbial master's tools has tended to be a prerequisite for any sort of social mobility (Frederick Douglass's pivotal reading instruction, or Toussaint L'Ouverture's literacy and use of ideological claims from the French Revolution, to name just two examples). So scholars tend to see the nondominant as crafty in the undoing or reappropriation of dominant codes, but such acts are invariably (perhaps necessarily?) cast in light of that dominant structure, thus reifying its seeming neutral and obvious privilege.

In various discourses of identity studies, scholars have talked about the privilege embedded in what they identify as an "invisible norm." Masculinity studies emerged in part as a response to the assumption that, if we're talking about "gender," we must be talking about women (because women are marked by their otherness). Whiteness studies has a similar story. In *Playing in the Dark*, Toni Morrison draws our attention to whiteness as an invisible norm, describing her attempt to get us to look critically at whiteness as itself constructed by and contingent upon certain actions, certain scripts that people who identify as "white": "My project is an effort to avert the critical gaze from the racial object to the racial subject; from the described and imagined to the describers and imaginers; from the serving to the served" (90).

What does this have to do with code-switching among various ways to perform blackness? The norm or dominant set of behaviors or patterns—basically, what we're thought to be shifting *from* (or are trying to switch toward)—is thought somehow to be uncoded. That is, we don't see ourselves as performing a role or series of codes when in our "normal" or dominant context. Thus, moments of code-switching typically refer to performances within nondominant spaces. This is where the problem comes in. If we start looking at that dominant context as its own manufactured space (as approaches like whiteness studies and masculinity studies have begun to do), "code-switching" only perpetuates the faulty idea that the dominant space is neutral and without a code of its own. It suggests we look at some variant outside the norm . . . when the norm—the white power structures against and still inside of which Touré positions himself—is all variance in the first place.

It is in this way that George Zimmerman's defense team read Rachel Jeantel's linguistic norms—as a space of irreducible difference—a move that simply normalized dominant linguistic and cultural codes by implicitly suggesting that only some languages or cultures are in fact "creole." But scholars and public intellectuals—certainly the post-blackness adherents—make a similar move. We do not talk about English being a creole language after all . . . but isn't it? Aren't all languages creolized? In that sense, there is no culture not creolized, not heterogeneous or hybrid in some way. So whose variation must count as variation? No matter what qualitative value or lack thereof might be given to the supposed code-switcher, there still seems to be a problem of how we maintain the very hegemonies that seemingly progressive scholars studying identity like to think they are disrupting.

What's more, even though the dominant seems without or beyond codification, it also provides the irreducible language or system to which other codes translate back. So while the dominant enjoys invisible norm status, it nonetheless dictates a very specific and managed set of rules to aid in the translation or conversion of nondominant codes. For example, when I taught writing composition courses a few years back in an English department, I talked with my students about the rules that governed the system of standard written English. This system was taken as a given and basically obvious format to which their writing had to conform, and students consistently acquiesced to the Modern Language Association rules I taught them. Of course, the debates over whether sentences really can end in prepositions have been heated ones among grammarians. The rules are not at all thought to be stable or ends in themselves. Further, scholars of rhetoric and composition (not to mention politicians at times) continue to disagree over whether and how to incorporate other codes (African American Vernacular English, Spanglish, web lingo, etc.) into the course content. Do we allow other modes of discourse to "count" in such settings? Should a student be able to write in her own dialect or linguistic system? By way of pacifying students, teachers often use the adage, "You've got to know the rules before you can break them." But that's just it—right there, we admit that there are rules (and again, very specific and hotly contested ones, if we're talking rules of grammar) to the dominant system but nonetheless treat it as the obvious and neutral norm.

Touré's discussion thus keeps up and running a stable and hegemonic whiteness that is left untroubled and underarticulated. There's a universal "humanness" that, implicitly throughout the book, he casts as transcending the particularities of race-based discourse. However, this realm of intellectualist universalism is not some all-encompassing orb of meaning and presence. It is a rhetorical device that disallows the very thing he purports to do in his book—namely, undermine black authenticity and present blackness as ever-shifting and self-determined. The kind of basic human condition to which Touré appeals helps make sense of his early skydiving anecdote. After brushing off the comments of the men who intimate to him, "Brother, Black people don't do that," he embarked on a near-death experience that allowed him to get closer to God, he suggests, and to understand that he was but a miniscule presence in a greater plan (1). In his description of the experience, he positions blackness as the space to overcome en route to that realization: "If I had let being black hold me back from skydiving, I would have cheated myself out of an opportunity to grow as a human" (4). His critique of the men's version of blackness that would have held him back is not an isolated one. Not only is his ideological or experiential standpoint in clear contradistinction from theirs but his age (while not significantly younger than they—he was in his thirties—he takes pains to describe them as middle-aged) and his status (they were working in the restaurant and recognized him from TV) are as well. Thus, while the men were not so much older than he, their philosophy of blackness was problematically dated, as far as he was concerned. Touré's critique, then, is one launched against a sort of blackness performed in an older generation—one that he sees as having held itself back from the kind of access that he has been able to enjoy.

In his critique of the "dream" articulated in the rhetoric outlining Civil Rights–era priorities, Touré asks us to think about a more "fluid" and complicated blackness. Progressive as this may seem, the move nonetheless trades a critique of one dream with the embrace of another—specifically, the vague ubiquity of "the American Dream" that cloaks ambivalence and contingency with a blanket of unanimity under which American citizens might all claim a common point of access and agency, no matter their contexts. In this vein, he closes the book with two culminating chapters: "How to Build More Baracks," followed by "We Are Quintessential Americans." He suggests about a vague African American collective: "We are American. And we are so American that rejecting this country means rejecting part of ourselves. . . . One day many years ago Barack Obama decided he was going to be president and he wasn't going to let being Black keep him from his dream" (199). The other, less productive response to America, Touré suggests, is one of structural critique. The outcome was Afrocentrism:

> I think it's our awareness of being Americanized and our deeply conflicted emotions about that—our righteous unhappiness with America—and our intense desire for a tangible connection with an alternate national identity that led us to Afrocentrism. We craved a relationship with Africa, we have needed to be from and connected to some other place because our relationship with this country is very problematic and we feel so unrooted here. But Africa, too, is an unrequiting lover because it is a long-distance lover—long-distance temporally. By that I mean we haven't lived there in a very long time. (193)

The metaphor of unrequited love marked by temporal long distance is a clumsy one. In this formulation, Afrocentric pursuits amount to little more than immature Freudian fantasies of filling a void in the subconscious. For this reason, he has no trouble dismissing it as a revolutionary dream that does not stand up against the possibilities available in co-opting the American Dream.

This is most evident with the way he closes his final chapter, offering an unapologetic assimilationist vision for African American "progress":

> We progress by getting as much education as we can and launching ourselves into corporations and entrepreneurialism and politics and finance and real estate. We need more and more Blacks sitting at tables of real power. Let's be like Barack. Let's get what we want from America in spite of racism. Let's buy into the promise of America and get what we deserve. Let's come home. You can fight the power, but I want us to be the power. (201)

The ideal performance of blackness is to "be like Barack"? Touré asks that African Americans simply go get a piece of the pie, apparently forgetting

the structural constraints that inhibit the sort of self-made-man arche-
type he promotes. He insists on the personal agency to which he and his
fellow luminaries have access, ignoring the intensely complicated system
of economic access that allows for the luxury of his call to individual
agency. Further, there is a clear and "real power," identifiable and stable,
even while the blackness that might gain entry into it is multifaceted and
refuses a label of its own authenticity. Post-blackness would thus ask us to
move beyond double consciousness but yet entertain a double standard,
positioning itself as a fluid and contingent space while not seeing white
dominance or "real power"—identified by corporate finance and entrepreneurship—as constituted by the same kind of flux.

Touré and I start from the same premise—"there is no black authenticity"—but we arrive at very different conclusions. His is a self-privileging of
a neoliberal inclusivity. My own conclusion is one that suggests there is no
a priori blackness, no blackness removed or separate from the discourses—
and imbedded interests—naming it. When we think of code-switching and
racial performativity as innocuous or objective terms used to describe certain
actions within a universe of personal experience, we forget that all descriptions are situated and decidedly *not* neutral. In this manner, code-switching
as a category might be thought of as normative, even imperial. After all, what
is interesting is not the thing itself but the describer's relation to the thing
(or category or what have you). So how might we talk about blackness and
performance in complicated ways, troubling the notion of post-blackness
for a number of different reasons and from a number of different perspectives? The essays that follow in this volume offer some challenging and productive responses to this question. The layers of inquiry in this collection,
while multifaceted, are grouped according to five main types of critique,
the first two of which both offer direct engagements with Touré's text.

BLACKNESS IN AESTHETICS

Margo Natalie Crawford and Stephanie Li offer readings of *Who's Afraid of
Post-Blackness* with etymological emphases on creative and artistic impulses.
These modes of expression are themselves forms of black identification,

according to these essays. In "'What Was *Is*': The Time and Space of Entanglement Erased by Post-Blackness," Crawford engages specifically in an analysis of the Black Arts movement in the 1960s and 1970s. During this time, she argues, black aesthetics was a domain for improvisation, abstraction, and performance in ways that get ignored by proponents of post-blackness who want to see the concept as a wholly new and unique thing.

Then, asking "what does post-blackness mean for black creative writers," Li chastises the notion of post-blackness for what strikes her as "a dangerous abdication of history" in her essay "Black Literary Writers and Post-Blackness." She takes up a reading of Toni Morrison's *Desdemona* as an opportunity to invite creative and literary traditions into the conversation on race and performance.

BLACKNESS IN TIME AND TECHNOLOGY

While Crawford and Li look to literary and visual aesthetic emphases that fuel particular identifications of blackness, the critiques of Touré's text from Greg Thomas, Rone Shavers, and Riché Richardson focus on the "post"-ness of Touré's post-black trope, taking up chronology and contexts of time that are so conspicuous in this so-called digital age. Working with themes of history and identity and taking them into rubrics of nation, exchange, and market forces, Thomas offers his "African Diasporic Blackness out of Line: Trouble for 'Post-Black' African *Americanism*." In it, he speaks to what he sees to be the monocultural tendencies of "post"-based rhetorics, suggesting that "an unexamined politics of 'African Americanism' lay at the bottom of 'post-Blackness.'" Taking seriously the implications of ideology and identity as outgrowths of the modern nation-state's matriculation of capital, his essay offers us a deft and deep examination of those very politics that found particular resonance in 1960s and 1970s black liberation movements.

In "Fear of a Performative Planet: Troubling the Concept of 'Post-Blackness,'" Shavers offers Afro-Futurism as a method of problematizing the idea that a progressive way ahead involves the dissolution of race and erasure of racial performativity. Then, in her timely essay "E-Raced:

#Touré, Twitter, and Trayvon," Richardson takes up a conversation on social media and the Trayvon Martin case—using what many perceive to be a dismissive Twitter post from Touré about the killing as a starting point—to critique the intellectual and ideological implications of post-blackness.

BLACKNESS IN GLOBALIZATION

Along with digitized networks of communication and identification, of course, have come new emphases on global diasporas—departures and presumed returns—and constructions of personhood in those contexts. The essays by Heather D. Russell and Bayo Holsey shine two different lights on this common set of interests. The access provided in the globalized framework that Twitter and the digital age offer is the platform from which Russell rightly asks us to consider what counts as something called "black experience" in her chapter "Post-Blackness and All of the Black Americas." Taking up some of the roles played by Afro-Caribbean identifications, she offers an analysis of the ways in which nation, empire, and questions of diaspora complicate discussions of an imagined "black identity."

Holsey then follows by discussing the formation of blackness as defined by one's individual experience with or relationship to an imagined (often romanticized) Africa in "Embodying Africa: Root-Seekers and the Politics of Blackness." Reading Alex Haley's *Roots* as having popularized this formation, Holsey goes on to show how such nostalgia is received and reworked by African governments and sociopolitical development strategies on a structural level. The continued emphasis on a diasporic subject as an individual on a quest to return symbolically to Africa, Holsey argues, is one of the higher costs of present-day capitalism.

BLACKNESS IN AUTHORSHIP

Holsey's interest in how individual subjectivity and notions of "home" intersect is at work—though in a very different genre—in the essays by Patrice Rankine, Erin Aubry Kaplan, and John L. Jackson Jr. These texts take experience as their starting point, offering varying applications of argumentation by way of personal anecdote. Like Russell and Holsey, Rankine is interested in global contexts of blackness, specifically taking up hip-hop and ghettoization. However, these issues come into the fore through the local environment of Rankine's own geographical ambivalence. With readings of Charles Taylor's thoughts on secularism, hip-hop, and his own institutional setting, Rankine, in "'The world is a ghetto': Post-Racial America(s) and the Apocalypse," confronts blackness in a career change that brings into relief the ways in which the boundaries around spheres called "personal" and "political" are nebulous indeed.

Kaplan and Jackson present their own troubles with post-blackness with personal and anecdotal retrospection. In "The Long Road Home," Kaplan remembers her own coming of age in the 1970s and critiques the rhetoric of post-blackness as being universalizing, reducing institutional and structural realities facing black Americans into an abstract concept that streamlines black experiences and renders them invisible. Meanwhile, Jackson recounts in "Half as Good" his familial phenomenon of being expected to always be far above average in school (what he calls the "twice as good" rule), describing mediocrity or "normalcy" as a luxury of white schoolchildren. Jackson carries this into a conversation about black academics, noting that great prestige and laud are still no recipe for feeling appreciated or respected in an academy still plagued by what he calls "race-based stigma."

BLACKNESS IN INSTITUTION

Dana A. Williams and Ishmael Reed bring to the table perspectives on notions of blackness among African Americans in institutional and political contexts of modern-day America. Williams's "'Whither Now and Why': Content Mastery and Pedagogy—A Critique and a Challenge" uses Howard University as an intellectual staging ground to discuss the relationship between "blackness," diaspora, and the Humanities (a zone of discourse that many now describe as threatened or at least under attack). In so doing, she asks the difficult question of where institutions like Howard will go in academe vis-à-vis their commitments to global interfaces and identifications. To begin rounding out the volume, Reed brings us back to a conversation about how these issues and questions play out in "Obama's America." In his unapologetic and provocative piece, "Fallacies of the Post-Race Presidency," Reed confronts us with the political pathologizing of blackness on the part of President Obama, who talks about "it" not only as stable and self-referential but also as a trigger of various social ills. In this manner, blackness is often presented politically as mutually exclusive to legitimate sociopolitical positionality.

Finally, taking the opportunity to trouble post-blackness in poetic form, Emily Raboteau mixes imagism and ideology to think through blackness and perspective in "Thirteen Ways of Looking at Post-Blackness (after Wallace Stevens)." She takes a cue from Wallace Stevens's "Thirteen Ways of Looking at a Blackbird" as well as her experiences in the classroom with multiple perspectives looking at a singular object in order to complicate the stabilizing impulses of post-blackness.

Editorial candor can never (nor should it) forestall reader responses that note a project's limitations. Still, as editors, we think it allowable and honest to note that we have not aspired to produce a volume that offers the definitive and final word on the trouble with post-blackness. Our domain is principally—and in broad definition—"cultural." In-depth social, political, and economic analyses do not form part of our bill of fare. Nor are there detailed world systems or global considerations of the ravages of a neo-liberalism that traces its dominion to fifteenth-century trade and commerce among Europe, Africa, and what W. E. B. Du Bois calls "the islands of the sea." That is, the systemic cast of ideological, economic, religious, and political determinants of post-blackness is rather assumed by the present essays than "scientifically analyzed." We are committed most fully to raising what have been called the "specters of the Atlantic" to discursive worlds of popular media, cultural criticism, personal reflection, literary history, and pointed critique. There are a great many excellent monographs, essays, and journals that take other directions, and we are enormously grateful for their wisdom. We do not, however, expect the present collection to be our only collaboration, and in future we would hope to broaden the disciplinary scope of our attention to the discourse on post-blackness.

We set out to provide a critique of a notion, but what we found was that the notion engendered even bigger questions: What is the place of literature in the domain of racial performance? What is the efficacy of language as a preserve of creative expressive modes? How do identifications of the modern nation-state fit in to readings of blackness? How does the flow of media capital serve as a reflexive picture of global neoliberal capitalism at its institutions? How do we discuss blackness and identity without resorting to experiential authority and race phenomenologies? Our questions remain and continue. Our intention in putting together this collection was to assemble a group of voices to help us to start the conversation on blackness, politics, and performance with more useful terms than those used in simply calling ourselves and this sociopolitical moment "post-black." While the writers whose work is included here come at the notion of post-blackness in various ways and with different—at times competing—analyses of the problems such a notion presents, they are, when taken together, a conversational starting point that helps us trouble post-blackness.

REFERENCES

Morrison, Toni. 1992. *Playing in the Dark: Whiteness and the Literary Imagination*. Cambridge, MA: Harvard University Press.

Touré. 2011. *Who's Afraid of Post-Blackness: What It Means to Be Black Now*. Introduction by Michael Eric Dyson. New York: Free Press.

I

"What Was *Is*"

The Time and Space of Entanglement
Erased by Post-Blackness

MARGO NATALIE CRAWFORD

To this day I have a strong aversion to cramped spaces like those that
nearly destroyed my youth. But I am even more terrified by the literal, material, open ground of white enemy territory.

—Houston A. Baker Jr., *Betrayal: How Black Intellectuals
Have Abandoned the Ideals of the Civil Rights Era*

Don't call me *out* my name.

—Everyday Afropessimistic Afrofuturist

Amiri Baraka's introduction in his short story collection *Tales of the Out
& the Gone* (2007) begins with the following words: "What should be
obvious in these tales are the years, the time passing and eclipsed." Baraka
then wonders, "What is left of what has left" (9). This play with what
changes and what remains (in this introduction to a collection of short
stories written from 1974 to the twenty-first century) is one way to understand the pulse of black post-blackness. This feeling does not emerge *after*
the 1960s and 1970s Black Arts movement (BAM); the notion of "black
post-blackness" is a way to understand the continuity between the BAM
and twenty-first-century African American aesthetics.

At the 2012 Modern Language Association conference, a special session was devoted to Kenneth Warren's *What Was African American Literature?* (2011). One of the presenters, Sharon Holland, deftly used William Faulkner's words "what was is" as she framed her response to this book.[1] Warren's book is one version of a current post-black discourse that cannot be homogenized due to the many approaches and forms. The trouble with many performances of post-blackness is the failure to remember Ralph Ellison's temporal dimension of invisibility—the "different sense of time," that time that leaps ahead and backward.[2] These performances fail to realize that "black is" and "black ain't" (Ellison's underground tutelage) (1952, 9). Post-black advocates' claims about the lack of room for experimentation, abstraction, and play in 1960s and 1970s black aesthetics are faulty. When we uncover the productive play and fierce experimentation during the BAM, we see that even texts that are more subtly post-black (such as Darby English's *How to See a Work of Art in Total Darkness* and Kenneth Warren's *What Was African American Literature?*), texts that are *not* a part of the "post-black" public intellectual writing, still flatten or simply ignore the complexity of the BAM.[3] A more honest engagement with the BAM would force these advocates of the post-black representational space (Darby English) and "post–African American literature" (Kenneth Warren) to admit that the impulse to envision a next step (after a collective racial enterprise or representational art) is not new and not distinct from the project of a nonassimilationist black aesthetics that first gained the shape of a movement in the 1960s.

During the BAM, outer space, abstraction, and the eccentricity that Larry Neal simply referred to as the "weird" were steadily invoked but they were not imagined as being post-black. The BAM pivoted on a dialectic between collective mirrors and collective collages that layered and gave blackness depth. This depth was a spatial and temporal strategy of resistance that insisted on blackness as the past, present, and future. Black aesthetics' time of entanglement (echoing Achille Mbembe's words) is what the post-black performances erase. Post-black advocates fail to understand black abstraction, black improvisation, and, even, *black* post-blackness. The irony of the post-black critiques of essentialized blackness is that the current emerging post-black "marketing" is obscuring the transnational motion that was created when "Black" was mobilized as such a powerful unifying concept full of layers and different temporalities. Post-blackness is stuck in a misunderstanding of black aesthetic movement.

I first started thinking about the relation between the neologism "post-black" and "post–Black Arts movement" when I read Thelma Golden's introduction to the catalog of the 2001 *Freestyle* exhibit at the Studio Museum. In this framing of the exhibit as "post-black," she pauses at one point in order to say that "post-black" may be shorthand for "post–Black Arts" movement.[4] The notion that this elision is sometimes shorthand (not any attempt to erase the significance of the Black Art movement to post-black) competes with many other circulations of the term "post-black" that do not cling, in any manner, to the words "black arts" or the "black aesthetic." In the United States, the words "black aesthetic" first begin to circulate widely as a way of thinking and seeing during the 1960s as the BAM begins. The movement was often the black aesthetic movement as people engaged in a constant theorizing about the black aesthetic. In the pages of the most central archive of the movement (Hoyt Fuller's *Black World*, first named *Negro Digest*), there is a steady attempt to flesh out the meaning of the words "black aesthetic". This steady need to figure out what the neologism is differs from the current circling around "post-black" and its performance of the unnaming.

The key problem with many of the post-black frames now being set up is the celebration of unnaming for the sake of unnaming (not very different from the art for art's sake that the BAM critiqued). As the whispers and murmurs about the post-black slowly turned into television interviews of "post-black" Touré unpacking Obama's administration, we saw that the nonrevolution will be televised. Gil Scott-Heron's iconic poetic song still resonates, but now the question becomes, how does the nontelevised nature of the cultural revolution that produced so much reflection on the black aesthetic and black self-determination enable the current dominant culture industry to televise its distorted version of black consciousness raising as it markets post-blackness. Scott-Heron's iconic critique of televised blackness and the Black Power movement's critique of Blaxploitation reveal the movement's great understanding of the market forces eager to reduce Black Power to a televised brand. In the novel *The Nigger Factory* (1972), Scott-Heron situates the problem of "televised" cultural revolutions as the problem of a certain generation's inability to really know the struggle because they did not live it. But the key tension that we often fail to realize is that Scott-Heron and others locate this post-knowing in the 1970s; they begin to think about the "post" generation as the movement is about to end. Just as Blaxploitation films do not really start after the movement, the worry about the black counterrevolutionary and the post-movement lack of understanding happens *during* the movement. Scott-Heron, in *The Nigger Factory*, depicts post-movement consciousness as a certain process of gathering and responding that does not shape one era into an ending and set up the other as a beginning. This is the challenge of black post-blackness. This is the challenge facing those of us who want to resist the recent performances of the end of black aesthetics.

There is, of course, no way of knowing the first utterance of "post-black," but Thelma Golden's 2001 explanation of the affect tied to the term lingers. The affect is comparable to a nod. It is the feeling of just taking something for granted and therefore not needing to remain defined by that term. It could be also likened to a wink. The affect of the wink is exemplified in the following performance (by a performance artist and curator) that could easily be understood as "black post-blackness": "Lowery Sims: Are you still black? William Pope.L: Obviously. Of course not" (Bessire 2002, 62). The wink here becomes "black post-blackness" in the space between "obviously" and "of course not." In the definitive space (with the period mark), the wink makes the name "black" seem less important than the "obvious" issues of antiblack racism that "still" make being black, for the majority of blackened subjects, an experience of racial and economic terror. This is the note of the "obvious" structural racism that limits the significance of any individual embrace or rejection of the name. This questioning of the usefulness of names has a long history in African American critical thought. At the end of Bayard Rustin's 1971 essay on the historical trajectory of names used by African Americans to name themselves, he writes, "The problems confronting Negroes are formidable, and they will not be solved by altering a name, or by dressing differently, or by wearing one's hair in a new way. We should not be fooled by names or appearances. The real problems lie beneath the surface" (1989, A25).

Rustin wrote these words during the era of the BAM (as this self-naming movement was beginning to end). This essay is best read not as a Black Arts / Black Power movement manifesto but rather a reflection on black cultural nationalism written by someone whose political sensibility is produced by the Civil Rights movement. When Rustin sets up the question about names as, finally, a question about surfaces as opposed to the depth of the lingering problems facing African Americans, his tone matches the tone of the iconic hip-hop song "99 Problems." As Jay-Z says, in this song, "I've got 99 problems," but the next Rustin-inspired line is: "But a name ain't one." The surface and depth tension is at core of the post-black and black tension. Post-black (when it leaves Thelma Golden's and William Pope.L's initial affect of the wink—the black post-blackness) becomes a dangerous surface, a surface that pretends to have the depth and enlightenment that blackness seemingly cannot contain. Rethinking the hard-core thinking about black abstraction and black improvisation during the BAM may be the only way to demystify the dangerous surface, the nascent reification of "post-black."

GESTURES AND NAMES

Gestures were always about to turn into definite action. In the meantime, people learn that style has substance and that something powerful happens when people discover "the essential gesture" of blackness. This dynamic abounds in the literature and visual art of the BAM. The words "essential gesture of authentic blackness" are used by Kimberly Benston in *Performing Blackness*. The force of this notion that the BAM broke the false boundaries between gesture and essence explodes when we couple Benston's theory of "essential gesture" and the BAM principle of "mimesis at midpoint." The African Commune of Bad Relevant Artists (AfriCobra) used the phrase "mimesis at midpoint" in their manifestos, as they explained their aesthetic sensibility. In a 2012 interview, Gerald Williams, one of the AfriCobra artists explained:

It was a puzzle back then, and more puzzling later as I realized that it was little noted in dialogue about the group over the years. I've taken fresh looks at the work that was produced by members at that time, finding myself to have become more critical. I haven't come to any conclusions yet, but feel as though mimesis was the one principle that should have been more intellectually challenging to pursue. In direct answer to your question, I do not recall how others felt about the concept, and I do not think that most of the work even deals with it. But that begs the question as to what mimesis is and what were we trying to do with it? And how did or do we define it? A point between abstraction and realism, I think, was reached by originators of Africans, Australasians, etc., many years ago, but doing the same thing within the environment of the sixties and seventies, or even today, is still a viable endeavor. I'm not sure I fully agree with the sentiment of Spellman's quote. ("Abstraction didn't cost consciousness."[5]) I have to see it within the context of his whole assertion. There are probably some mandates required for black consciousness and probably some universally agreed upon parameters. Identification with black consciousness has always been a complicated matter for some artists, who may easily find comfort in the contemporary notion of this supposedly post racial period.[6]

Mimesis at midpoint may, quite simply, be the way that these BAM visual artists were wrestling with naming their art and also keeping that name in a state of productive suspension. Just as the AfriCobra artists made "process" a part of their visual aesthetics, the writers in the movement were thinking deeply about the process of "becoming black."

The movement's love affair with blackness has been misread as a love affair with something known and stabilized. The collective love affair with blackness was actually a collective process of falling in love with the idea that "black" could be beautiful and powerful and known more intimately than the sticky white masks. As the process ("becoming black") was performed in the poetry, drama, and visual art, the movement could not help but dramatize the next step after blackness. This drama often took the form of "after the cultural revolution, what will we have created?" Nation-building was invoked as a way of thinking about the work that needed to happen after minds were decolonized. The art of cultural revolution was tinged with the fury and joy of collective artistic movement and the melancholy of not knowing what these new collective self-images ("becoming black") would enable. Too many current performances of post-blackness treat investments in blackness as an investment in an old tired badge as opposed to an investment in an individual and collective process of putting on new clothes (one of the most lucid BAM images, in *In Our Terribleness*, of the corporeal enactment of black consciousness). The process of putting on new clothes continues as the wardrobe expands, but the "post-black" T-shirt does not seem to be tied to this process of black consciousness raising. Indeed, the prefix "post" suggests that a process has ended.

The process of black consciousness raising was transnational, and the word "black" was a unifying concept that enabled people to see the global nature of white supremacy. During the 1970s, U.S. mobilizations of the word greatly inspired a similar hailing process in the South African Black Consciousness movement. During the 1975–1976 trial, Steve Biko, the founder of Black Consciousness in South Africa, is asked to explain why black South Africans refer to themselves as "black" as opposed to "brown." As the trial puts "blackness" itself on trial, Biko and Judge Boshoff have the following exchange:

JUDGE BOSHOFF: But now why do you refer to you people as blacks? Why not brown people? I mean you people are more brown than black.
BIKO: In the same way as I think white people are more pink and yellow and pale than white.
JUDGE BOSHOFF: Quite . . . but now why do you not use the word brown then?
BIKO: No, I think really, historically, we have been defined as black people, and when we reject the term non-white and take upon ourselves the right to call ourselves what we think we are, we have got available in front of us a whole number of alternatives.

(Biko 2002, 104)

Biko claims the power of the word "black" when it is reclaimed as a strategy of self-decolonization. The word "black" is also put on trial when the post-blackness becomes the new brand that translates the 1960s and 1970s unifying concept into a twenty-first-century divisive relic that fails to acknowledge the complexity of fluid, liminal identities. We need to pause and put "post-black" on trial. If advocates can make the case that this neologism is a gesture (not any name or new brand) that signals post-1960s black movements and postnaming, we might feel hope that the embrace of this word will not continue to put "black" on trial. But even this claim, that the playful term was never supposed to settle and become an object of study or way of understanding twenty-first-century African American cultural productions, must be troubled. Between 2001 and 2012, we have moved from the use of post-black in art catalogs and literary journals to the use of post-black in the public intellectual books that hail readers outside the academy. Now "post-black" (unlike the earlier murmurs) begins to sound like "post-race" as public intellectuals such as Touré use their personal anecdotes about black exceptionalism to celebrate an Obama-inspired post-racial terror mood. Touré's title, *Who's Afraid of Post-Blackness?*, is disingenuous; "post-black" often sounds comforting compared to the tension tied to "Black." Martin Luther King Jr., in "Letter to Birmingham Jail" (1963), reminds us that tension is productive. He writes, "My citing the creation of tension as part of the work of the nonviolent-resister may sound rather shocking. But I must confess that I am not afraid of the word 'tension.' I have earnestly opposed violent tension, but there is a type of constructive, nonviolent tension which is necessary for growth" (King 2003, 87).

Constructive tension shaped the circulation of "black" during the BAM. Poems, for example, with performances of "blacker than thou" competed with poems that performed critiques of the superficial displays of blackness (the idea that black has to appear and sound a certain way). "What will blackness be" (Fred Moten's resonant question in *In the Break: the Aesthetics of the Black Radical Tradition*) is the subtext embedded in the BAM performances of the word "black."

At the beginning of his poem "Gwendolyn Brooks," Haki Madhubuti writes:

into the sixties
a word was born........BLACK
& with black came poets
& from the poet's ball points came:
black doubleblack purpleblack blueblack beenblack was
black daybeforeyesterday blackerthan ultrablack super
black blackblack yellowblack niggerblack blackwhi-te-
    man
blackthanyoueverbes ¼ black unblack coldblack clear
black my momma's blackerthanyourmomma pimpleblack
    fall
black so black we can't even see you black on black in
black by black technically black mantanblack winter
black coolblack 360degreesblack coalblack midnight
black black when it's convenient rustyblack moonblack
black starblack summerblack electronblack spaceman
black shoeshineblack jimshoeblack underwearblack ugly
black auntjimammablack, uncleben'srice black
        williebest
black blackisbeautifulblack i justdiscoveredblack negro
black unsubstanceblack.

(Lee 1971, 90)

In addition to being a unifying concept, "black," in the 1960s, was
recharged. Of course, the word before the 1960s had sometimes been
the chosen self-reference term, but the Black Power movement and the
BAM politicized the term. The Black Power movement performed the
transformation of conciliatory "Negroes" into assertive "black" people. In
our post–Black Power era, "black" may not sound the same as it did in
the 1960s, but it seems to still pose a threat. Any progressive use of "post-
black" will have to avoid the taming of the threat of "black." What are the
politics of post-blackness? I am most interested in the aesthetic dimensions of the post-black tag. How, for example, might the depth of some
post–Black Art movement literature and visual art be greatly reduced

when this art is approached only as a post-black departure from the 1960s and not as nuanced post-BAM entanglements with the threads of the 1960s and 1970s?

BLACK ARTS / POST-BLACK ARTS

Some of the texts and visual images that some will want to tag "post-black" deserve the less marketable names such as "post–Black Arts" and "black post-black." Consider, for example, what we see when we look at Percival Everett's novel *Erasure* (2001) as an extension of the BAM critique of the publishing industry and, most importantly, the BAM critique of the assumption that form is not tied to formlessness. In one of his most metanarrative passages, Everett writes: "In my writing my instinct was to defy form, but I very much sought in defying it to affirm it, an irony that was difficult enough to articulate, much less defend. But the wood, the feel of it, the smell of it, the weight of it. It was so much more real than words. The wood was so simple. Damnit, a table was a table was a table" (139). The first layer of this passage (the notion of the shape of shapelessness) is stunningly similar to the language used in a *Black World* essay on Ed Bullins's drama. In this essay, the *Black World* critic responds to a white critic's assessment of Ed Bullins's drama as "shapeless." As the white critic performs a hostility toward the experimentation in the BAM, he wonders, "What is the shape of shapelessness?" In the *Black World* essay, the "shape of shapelessness" takes on an entirely new meaning as the *Black World* critic argues that the seeming shapelessness in BAM drama actually has a shape. The belief in the shape of the shapelessness, during the BAM, explains the investment in free verse poetry and free jazz as well as the movement's counterintuitive depictions of blackness as both the shapeless process of becoming black and the actual shape (the actual identity) of the process—as Everett says, "a table was a table was a table."

Erasure is a harsh critique of the cultural industry that markets African American literature as the literature of "pafology." Everett's protagonist wants to publish a type of literature that will not cater to this marketable "pafology" and he also does not want to be a writer of racial uplift and black respectability. This dual desire is a vital part of the BAM sensibility. The short play *Malcolm: '71, or Publishing Blackness: Based Upon a Real Experience* by Ed Bullins (1971) is the type of BAM parody that, when read alongside *Erasure*, exposes the changing same of African American frustration with the publishing industry's marketing of a certain version of blackness and the BAM anticipation of the post-movement play that would ridicule the serious playfulness and productive experimentation that the movement itself represented. Bullins shapes the tension of this short play around a white woman editor's inability to understand why naming her dog after Malcolm X is deeply offensive to the African American writer she calls to ask for a submission to the "Black Culture" project she is editing. The black writer hears the dog barking, and hears her call him "Malcolm," and after receiving confirmation from the white "publishing blackness" editor that he has heard her correctly (that her dog really is named Malcolm), he simply hangs up the phone. He cannot bear to explain to her the irony of her literal reduction of Malcolm X to a domesticated pet, given her supposed expertise on the subject of blackness and her current position of as an editor of black texts.

This BAM play captures the movement's awareness of not only the power of self-naming but also the power of a dominant culture industry to distort the names mobilized during decolonizing movements. One of the best ways to fight this distortion is to refuse to accept the dominant culture industry's marketing of the "new" and to refuse to accept that twenty-first-century African American cultural productions are necessarily removed from the earlier movements of black self-determination. When frames cut frames (Black Arts / Post-Black Arts), we see prisms of what lingers (the splitting of the "black light" often depicted in the BAM). Just as we need to rethink the relation between the BAM and *Erasure* in order to see what Fred Moten calls "frames cutting frames" (2003, 109), we also see the power of the post–Black Arts frame (not the "post-black" brand) in the poem "Denigration," written by Harryette Mullen.

Mullen, in this poem, cuts the word "nigger" into sounds as she thinks about all of the other words that contain some of these cut up sounds. The full prose poem is worth citing:

Did we surprise our teachers who had niggling doubts about the picayune brains of small black children who reminded them of clean pickaninnies on a box of laundry soap? How muddy is the Mississippi compared to the third-longest river of the darkest continent? In the land of the Ibo, the Hausa, and the Yoruba, what is the price per barrel of nigrescence? Though slaves, who were wealth, survived on niggardly provisions, should inheritors of wealth fault the poor enigma for lacking a dictionary? Does the mayor demand a recount of every bullet or does city hall simply neglect the black alderman's district? If I disagree with your beliefs, do you chalk it up to my negligible powers of discrimination, supposing I'm just trifling and not worth considering? Does my niggling concern with trivial matters negate my ability to negotiate in good faith? Though Maroons, who were unruly Africans, not loose horses or lazy sailors, were called renegades in Spanish, will I turn any blacker if I renege on this deal?

(2002, 19)

The last words in this prose poem—"will I turn any blacker if I renege on this deal?"—capture the embeddedness of the "nig" sound in words that seemingly have no relation to "nigger." As Mullen plays with the sound of words such as "denigration," "niggling," "nigrescence," "neglect," and "renege," she makes her readers hear a sonic racial terror that is so terrifying, the poem suggests, precisely because it is so unintentionally embedded in the everyday affect of those who have never been called a nigger. Like Mullen, Black Arts poets were (as Baraka explains in his introduction to Larry Neal's *Black Boogaloo*) "dealing in sound." Baraka, as he explains this sound work, uses the phrase "post-literary." He writes, "Post 'literary' because we are men who write.... Literary sound like something else ... sound like it ain't sound. And sound is what we deal in ... in the real world ... sound for sounding" (i). Many of the current "post-black" assessments of BAM poetry do not understand the post-literary. These critiques often focus on the supposed lack of "literary" worth and ignore the innovations with sound. The power of the Mullen/BAM "frame-cutting-frame" is the power of rehearing the 1960s Black Power "reneging on the deal" of assimilation.

Mullen's poem "Denigration" sonically performs an African American never-ending process of counternaming. Each word that almost sounds like "nigger" grates against the word "blacker" in the final line. Mullen uses the word "blacker" in a manner that parallels the tone in one of the less known Black Arts poems, "What Color Is Lonely." In this poem, Carolyn Rodgers calls for a politicizing of loneliness itself, that extreme zone of disidentification. She writes:

Since you wrote a poem
explaining
the color of Black—
and I know that I am black
Blacker
and Blackless sometimes,
Tell me sister,
What color is lonely?

(1970, 23)

Mullen's "Denigration" is a "poem explaining the sounds of nigger" (as opposed to Rodgers's "poem / explaining / the color of Black." But both poems create room for the simultaneous identification and disidentification, the sounds of the "black / Blacker / and Blackless." Mullen seems to tell us that there is no ethical way, in the face of transnational structural antiblack racism, to revel in a state of post-denigration (subjects of antiblack racism cannot get "any blacker"). Her poem can be read, slantwise, as yet another troubling of the post-black brand. Rodgers also troubles simple expressions of post-black. Rodgers, during the BAM, anticipates the impulse to articulate the post-black, but she frames the questions in a manner quite different from the current post-black market. She moves to the inner zone, the loneliness, as opposed to the televised nonrevolution that post-black branding relies on.

The depth of that loneliness (the feeling of blacklessness and the sense that there is something more than black) suggests that the BAM led some writers to a nascent interest in "more than black" as opposed to "post-black." The "more than" impulse has a temporal dimension that differs from the linearity of the post-black brand. Rodgers, in another poem, helps us grasp the productive play with time as "nation time" was being performed. In her poem "All the Clocks" Rodgers writes:

> All the clocks
> are
> off
> or have stopped in
> the Black ghetto
> . . . .
> It occurs to me.
> The people in the (neighbor) hoods
> don't
> know
> what
> TIME
> it is . . .
>
> (in Randall 1970, 265–66)

Rodgers paints this picture of stopped clocks (due to the lack of resources in the "ghetto" neighborhoods), but the stopped time also signals that the rhetoric of nation time has not quite reached the everyday people on the street. We can imagine that James Brown's "Say it Loud, I'm Black and I'm Proud" might have resonated more in some of the streets of "stopped time" than Baraka's elongated powerful chant of "It's Nation T(eye)ime." James Brown's lyrics "I'm Black and I'm . . . " may rarely be heard with an emphasis on the "and," but the rhyme of "loud" and "proud" may make us not hear what Kevin Quashie calls the "sovereignty of quiet" (2012). The move from "I'm Black" to "and I'm" has the "more than black" texture that in the song is clearly inseparable from the full assertion of blackness.

Rodgers dramatizes the everyday experience of the "stopped time" that would make people who live in the ghetto unable to answer the resonant Black Power question "What time is it?" The only answer to this question may not be "nation time," it may be simply "time to fix the clocks in the neighborhood," but it is hard to imagine that the answer should ever be "It's Post-Black time." These words sound like a shutdown of earlier flows. The temporal flow of black aesthetics remains the "flow, layering, and rupture" that Tricia Rose uses, in *Black Noise: Rap Music and Black Culture in Contemporary America*, in her analysis of hip-hop (1994). Post-black stages rupture and forgets the flow and layering that produce the power of the ongoing rupture in the dialectic of the three energies. James Brown's "I'm Black and I'm . . . " is the black post-blackness that post-black branding erases.

Langston Hughes's *Ask Your Mama* (1961) directly dramatizes the desire to "rub off" blackness and anticipates the BAM's mobilization of blackness as a unifying concept. *Ask Your Mama* is literally on the edge of the 1960s, calling and calling (as Baraka's iconic "SOS" poem insists) for black people "to come on / in." The indelible mark of the BAM on *Ask Your Mama* is rooted in the refrain "AND THEY ASKED ME . . . / IF MY BLACKNESS, WOULD IT RUB OFF? / I SAID, ASK YOUR MAMA" (8). The poem presents people's decision to embrace their blackness as a bold refusal to be erased in a global system of racialized capitalist oppression. Hughes wrote the poem in direct response to the 1960 Newport Jazz Festival and the riot took place when young white people rioted against their difficulty in getting in the festival. As Scott Saul explains in *Freedom Is, Freedom Ain't: Jazz and the Making of the Sixties*, Hughes was in a precarious position at the festival. He was the emcee for what became "the mop-up act for the festival after it was summarily cancelled by the city council in the wake of the Saturday night riot" (2005, 131). For the "mop-up" event, Hughes wrote the lyrics to "Goodbye Newport Blues" (which was performed by Muddy Waters and Otis Spann). The lyrics include the words: "What's gonna happen to my music? / What's gonna happen to my song?" (2005, 131). Hughes started writing *Ask Your Mama* at a hotel in Newport. *Ask Your Mama* is an extension of the question "What gonna happen to my music?" On the one hand, the answer (given the diverse range of music the poem brings together) seems to be that black music mixes with everything as the categories of "blues" and "world music" become inseparable. But this anticipation of "What gonna happen to my music?" leads Hughes to something much more complex than a "we are the world" sensibility. Universal sounds make him hear the notes that are not *specifically* black but *still* black. His anticipation of the poetics of the BAM lies in this sounding out of the layers that create deep political, aesthetic, and pleasurable investments in blackness.

The pleasure of being black was a core part of the cultural revolution staged during the Black Power movement. Reading Black Arts texts, we often fail to see the power of the pleasure factor. The humor cannot be separated, at times, from the rage. And in the post–Black Power land-scape, as the price of the ticket for many admissions into nuanced, open (post-Black) identities becomes the tacit agreement that the black consciousness raising of the 1960s was silly, violent, and ineffective, people created a parody of the Black Power / Black Arts movement. The use of humor in the movement itself is lost as people laugh at the movement. Hughes, in *Ask Your Mama*, seems to anticipate that the power of black rage humor would be reduced to twitches and not recognized as winks.[7] *Ask Your Mama* is a sustained wink. Each time Hughes uses the refrain "AND THEY ASKED ME . . . / IF MY BLACKNESS, WOULD IT RUB OFF?," the words "ASK YOUR MAMA" have the gestural effect of a wink that asks other kindred spirits to remember that we should not continue to explain who we are (that too many of the inquiries themselves have been deeply offensive). Too many of the framing questions have made blackness into a problem that must be "rubbed off."

As opposed to the post-black brand's direct positing of a "before" and an "after," Hughes's anticipation of the BAM in *Ask Your Mama* makes blackness into a "mood," not an object that can be rubbed off. In the eleventh mood of *Ask Your Mama*, Hughes directly calls for the expression of black rage when he writes,

IN THE NEGROES OF THE QUARTERS
PRESSURE OF THE BLOOD IS SLIGHTLY HIGHER
IN THE QUARTER OF THE NEGROES
WHERE BLACK SHADOWS MOVE LIKE SHADOWS

CUT FROM SHADOWS CUT FROM SHADE
IN THE QUARTER OF THE NEGROES
SUDDENLY CATCHING FIRE
FROM THE WING TIP OF A MATCH TIP
ON THE BREATH OF ORNETTE COLEMAN.

(77)

These words dramatize the full anticipation of the BAM. The title of the central Black Arts anthology, "Black Fire," is on the "tip" of Hughes's tongue. The free jazz of Ornette Coleman speaks to many of the poets of the BAM as they search for the word and sound interplay that Hughes creates in *Ask Your Mama*. Hughes titles this eleventh mood "Jazztet Muted." As he dreams about black resistance "suddenly catching fire," he throws a flame on the more "muted" resistance in *Fire!!* (1926), the Harlem Renaissance publication that he produced with Wallace Thurman, Zora Neale Hurston, Aaron Douglas, and others. Although we lack full certainty that Hughes wrote the explosive poetic foreword to *Fire!!*, scholars' assumption that Hughes wrote it makes sense. The foreword begins with the following words: "*FIRE . . . flaming, burning, searing, and penetrating far beneath the superficial items of the flesh to boil the sluggish blood.*" Even during the Harlem Renaissance, as he remained under the influence of white patronage, Hughes could see that a different type of movement of black aesthetic warfare would happen, that what he calls "black shadows" (in *Ask Your Mama*) would become "Black Light" (the BAM term for the new epistemology of light and darkness that the artists were creating).

The productive force of anticipation is its difference from waiting. Anticipation is much more active than waiting. Anticipation, like invisibility (in Ralph Ellison's theorizing in *Invisible Man*), gives one a "different sense of time" (1952, 8); it makes one's present deeply tied to the future. This sense of anticipation is what the more facile versions of post-blackness lose; they flatten the mystery of what will come next. We hear the raw power of the mood of anticipation in the last words in the foreword to *Fire!*: "Fy-ah, / Fy-ah, Lawd, / Fy-ah gonna burn ma soul!"

(Thurman 1926, 1). Anticipating fire makes one sweat before the actual heat. During the Black Power and Black Arts movements, the "actual heat" was the revolution that people in the movements thought was "right around the corner." The BAM, like more militant moods of the Harlem Renaissance, was the anticipation of "fire." During the BAM, the anticipation sometimes masqueraded as post-anticipation; the black cultural revolution (the black cultural nationalism) was an experimentation with new self-images and ways of walking through the actual new world that was anticipated. The Black Arts cultural workers were not waiting for the world to change; they were anticipating change, believing that change could happen, and creating art that would, in the words of Ed Bullins, create a "sense of reality confronted" and "consciousness assaulted" (1968, 93). Given this mood of anticipation, Sun Ra's afrofuturism found an unsettled home on the jazz mobile of the Black Arts Repertory Theatre. Ra was drawn to the BAM's future-oriented engagement with the present. His resonant query—"Suppose we came not *from* Africa but *to* Africa"—explains what "Africa" symbolized in the BAM.[8] The idealization of "Africa" was rooted in afrofuturism—an anticipation of a new understanding of heritage as not where one is *from* but where one must travel (what pulls one forward and makes one believe, in spite of global antiblack oppression, in a black future).

At the beginning of *Interrogating Postfeminism: Gender and the Politics of Popular Culture* (2007), volume editors Yvonne Tasker and Diane Negra write, "Postfeminism broadly encompasses a set of assumptions, widely disseminated with popular media forms, having to do with the 'pastness' of feminism, whether that supposed pastness is merely noted, mourned, or celebrated" (2007, 1). The tone of celebration in Touré's *Who's Afraid of Post-Blackness?* is the most troubling feature of the post-black brand. In order to flesh out what is at stake in these performances of naming and unnaming, let me share an exchange I had with someone who feels that "post-black" may not be a troubling tag or brand. In the first part of the conversation, we both agreed that Thelma Golden's framing of the art in the *Freestyle* exhibit as post-black does not trouble because her full curating of the show produces post-black as a question, a frame that is not supposed to be a name. The conversation then moved to the word "post-black" itself and my interlocutor said, "Well, it might be as simple as post-slave; it's not really a problem." The comparison of "post-black" and "post-slave" is striking. Since I hear "black" in such a different register than "slave," I cannot begin to understand this comparison. I am, literally, a child of the Black Power movement. "Black" necessarily, for me, cannot sound like "slave." But this exchange shows why the post-black brand may appeal most to those who can analyze the seductiveness of the 1960s performances of black self-determination and aesthetic warfare without leaning into the power of that enchantment and the enchanted people it produced.

In *Once You Go Black: Choice, Desire, and the Black American Intellectual* (2007), Robert Reid-Pharr asserts,

> What I propose then is to disavow the aloof posture toward black nationalist thought, personnel, and practice that I believe ultimately leads us to political and theoretical dead ends. Specifically, I want to make sense of the odd slippage in my own thinking, and that of many Americans, that allows us to understand Black American nationalism as quintessentially performative (and thus almost painfully ineffectual) but nonetheless terribly captivating, incredibly compelling, remarkably seductive." (125)

The BAM's seductive performances of becoming black makes us break out of the binary of problematic investments in *being* versus the subversive flow of *becoming*. Being black and becoming black were fused in the movement. When becoming does not sound liminal, it sounds like a self-fulfilling prophecy. Fred Moten's question remains, "What will blackness be?" And we might hear the liminality and the self-fulfilling circle (the hailing will become the *matter*; black begets black). As the power of (black) enchantment continues, Claire Colebrook's focus on becomings that attach to other becomings may be one way to understand the black post-blackness. Colebrook writes, "Here, becoming does not realize and actualize itself, does not flourish into presence, but bears a capacity to annihilate itself, to refuse its ownness" (2011, 31). But the vital point here is that the refusal of the "ownness" and the lack of a "flourishing into presence" were only achieved, in the 1960s black consciousness raising, through the *collective becoming*, the collective movement. The "flourishing into presence" was a collective performance. The post-black brand, in contrast, relies on a fetishism of individuality and the dead end of exceptionalism.

Amiri Baraka, in the short story "Heathen Technology at the End of the Twentieth Century," in *Tales of the Out & the Gone* (2007), refuses to accept this "dead end." In this science fiction story, Baraka imagines a certain apocalypse that includes the "dis/imaging" of people, a type of mind control that makes people disappear by stealing and collecting their image making (158). The first-person narrator is a witness linked to other survivors who resist the mind control by listening, "eight times a day," to John Coltrane's jazz, and looking, "eight times a day," at Aaron Douglas's images (ibid.). This counterhypnotism harkens back to BAM images of black collective resistance to dominant image making. The short story's call for continued belief in collective resistance emerges most clearly when the narrator asks his apocalypse-era listeners to "remember" and then realizes that "remembering" is no longer possible in the era of the "brain switch" but nonetheless continues to remember the power of "bound metaphor" (ibid.). This bound metaphor is described in the following manner: "If the metaphors of a heavy group were rendered collective and focused on whatever, energy and power could be produced" (ibid.). This language captures Baraka's recognition that the power of the BAM's mobilization of blackness as a unifying concept was the power of people realizing that blackness was such a productive collective metaphor.

NOTES

1.   Faulkner states, "Remember Quentin was not trying to put time into perspective. He was trying to escape from time into the past. He was trying to escape back into a time when all this which I hate was not. He failed,

and so he committed suicide. There was only one more step left to him. He couldn't be alive and escape back before when his sister was pure. And so he had to commit suicide. That was all that remained for him. Dilsey accepted the past, and she didn't waste herself trying to discard it or get away from it. She simply accepted it and said, 'All right. So it is. Let's go on. Let's go forward.' That time was—was in its perspective, I think, for the both of them, but—but one of them hated 'now' and wanted to return to 'was,' which you can't do because what was, is. There's actually no such thing as "was." As we said any man is the victim of—not only victim, but the sum of his past. He never escapes from it. Quentin wanted to escape back into it." (Transcript of audio recording, "Writing and Literature Classes, tape 1," May 2, 1958, *Faulkner at Virginia*, http://faulkner.lib.virginia.edu/display /wfaudio26_1.)

2. Ellison writes, "Invisibility, let me explain, gives one a slightly different sense of time, you're never quite on the beat. Sometimes you're ahead and sometimes behind. Instead of the swift and imperceptible flowing of time, you are aware of its nodes, those points where time stands still or from which it leaps ahead" (1952, 8).

3. As Darby English analyzes the compartmentalization of African American art as "black representational space," he argues that African American aesthetics are often reduced, through the dynamics of the American color line, to expressions of race and culture. When we do not assume that we are looking at a black aesthetic but rather a more open realm of aesthetics produced by African Americans, what do we begin to see? English explores this question in *How to See a Work of Art in Total Darkness*.

4. In the catalog for the 2001 Studio Museum's *Freestyle* exhibit, Golden explains that, as soon as the visual artist Ligon said "post-black," she "knew exactly" what he meant.

5. A. B. Spellman, in one of his Black Arts manifestos, "Big Bushy Afros," writes, "Abstraction did not cost consciousness," as he considers the burden of meaning placed on the more abstract art produced during this movement (Spellman 1998, 53).

6. Transcription of interview conducted by Margo Natalie Crawford, March 2012.

7. Jackson 2005, 33; Jackson, drawing upon Clifford Geertz, reminds us that the winks are very different from the twitches.

8. Author interview with Kalamu ya Salaam, July 11, 2013, Tulane University. Salaam explained that Sun Ra delivered this speculation during many of his performances.

REFERENCES

Baraka, Amiri. 2007. *Tales of the Out & the Gone*. New York: Akashic Books.

Bessire, Mark H. C., ed. 2002. *William Pope L.: The Friendliest Black Artist in America*. Cambridge, MA: MIT University Press.

Biko, Steve. 2002. *I Write What I Like: Selected Writings*. Ed. Aelred Stubbs. Chicago: University of Chicago Press.

Bullins, Ed. 1968. "A Short Statement on Street Theatre," *TDR: The Drama Review* 12, no. 4 (Summer): 93.

Colebrook, Claire. 2011. "Queer Aesthetics," in *Queer Times, Queer Becomings*, ed. Mikko Tuhkanen. Albany: State University of New York Press.

Crawford, Margo Natalie. 2013. Unpublished interview with Kalamu ya Salaam, July 11, Tulane University.

Ellison, Ralph. 1952. *Invisible Man*. New York: Random House.

English, Darby. 2010. *How to See a Work of Art in Total Darkness*. Cambridge, MA: MIT Press.

Everett, Percival. 2001. *Erasure*. Hanover, NH: University Press of New England.

Golden, Thelma. 2001. *Freestyle*. New York: Studio Museum of Harlem.

Hughes, Langston. 2009. *Ask Your Mama: 12 Moods for Jazz*. 1961. Reprint, New York: Art Farm West.

Jackson, John L., Jr. 2005. *Real Black: Adventures in Racial Sincerity*. Chicago: University of Chicago Press.

King, Martin Luther, Jr. 2003. *I Have a Dream: Writings and Speeches That Changed the World*. New York: Harper One.

King, Woodie, ed. 1972. *Black Spirits: A Festival of New Black Poets in America*. New York: Vintage.

Lee, Don L. (Haki Madhubuti). 1971. *Directionscore: Selected and New Poems*. Detroit: Broadside Press.

Moten, Fred. 2003. *In The Break: The Aesthetics of the Black Radical Tradition*. Minneapolis: University of Minnesota Press.

Mullen, Harryette. 2002. *Sleeping with the Dictionary*. Berkeley: University of California Press.

Neal, Larry. 1969. *Black Boogaloo: Notes on Black Liberation*. San Francisco: Journal of Black Poetry Press.

Quashie, Kevin. 2012. *The Sovereignty of Quiet: Beyond Resistance in Black Culture*. New Brunswick, NJ: Rutgers University Press.

Randall, Dudley, ed. 1970. *The Black Poets*. New York: Bantam Books.

Reid-Pharr, Robert. 2007. *Once You Go Black: Choice, Desire, and the Black American Intellectual*. New York: New York University Press.

Rodgers, Carolyn. 1970. *Songs of a Blackbird*. Chicago: Third World Press.

Rose, Tricia. 1994. *Black Noise: Rap Music and Black Culture in Contemporary America*. Middletown, CT: Wesleyan University Press.

Rustin, Bayard. 1989. "Blacks? African Americans? What's in a Name?" *New York Times*, February 1, A25.

Saul, Scott. 2005. *Freedom Is, Freedom Ain't: Jazz and the Making of the Sixties*. Cambridge, MA: Harvard University Press.

Spellman, A. B. 1998. "Big Bushy Afros," *International Review of African American Art* 15, no. 1: 53.

Tasker, Yvonne, and Diane Negra, eds. 2007. *Interrogating Post-Feminism: Gender and the Politics of Popular Culture*. Durham, NC: Duke University Press.

Thurman, Wallace, ed. 1926. *Fire!! A Quarterly Devoted to the Younger Negro Artists* 1, no. 1.

2

Black Literary Writers
and Post-Blackness

STEPHANIE LI

In *Who's Afraid of Post-Blackness: What It Means to be Black Now* (2011), cultural critic Touré declares that we are living in a new age of racial identity. He characterizes post-blackness as encompassing individualist representations of what it means to be black. In his formulation, supported by dozens of interviews with leading black artists and critics, blackness has no boundary, no responsibility to positive or politically minded depictions. He explains, "We are in a post-Black era where the number of ways of being Black is infinite. Where the possibilities for an authentic Black identity are boundless" (20). Touré seems to describe the fulfillment of Stuart Hall's declaration concerning "the end of the innocent notion of the essential black subject" which involves "the recognition of the extraordinary diversity of subjective positions, social experiences and cultural identities which compose the category 'black'" (1995, 224–25). However, writing over two decades before Touré, Hall concludes that such multivalent representations of blackness demand "a recognition that the central issues of race always appear historically in articulation" (225). This awareness of history and its relationship to black identity is notably lacking in Touré's totalizing claims. With its emphasis on individualist expressions of racial identity, post-blackness threatens to become a dangerous abdication of history. This is especially apparent when considering post-blackness in relation to literature, an area that Touré conspicuously neglects. Black literature can never be post-black because the signifyin(g) language of black narrative affirms history, even as texts may alter or transform that history, through intertextual exchange. The tradition of African American literary expression refuses the unmooring of racial identity that Touré celebrates by encoding what Toni Morrison terms an ancestral presence into its very language.

In the first chapter of *Who's Afraid of Post-Blackness*, Touré loosely categorizes the 105 people he interviewed for his book. The list includes politicians, visual artists, musicians, academics, and writers. This latter category is composed of journalists, social critics, and political commentators but, notably, no creative writers. The novelists Tananarive Due and Colson Whitehead are listed in the "Bios" section at the end of the book, suggesting that both were interviewed.[1] However, Due is not cited in any other part of *Who's Afraid of Post-Blackness* while Whitehead has a minor quote in chapter 2 about the changing nature of "oreoness."[2] Like all of the other interviewees, neither Due nor Whitehead comment on trends in contemporary black novels nor do either of them speak to what a post-black literary aesthetic might mean. Touré offers little explanation for how he chose his interviewees, identifying them only as "prominent Black people" (12). This loose description is not applied to a host of foundational black literary writers including Toni Morrison, John Edgar Wideman, Alice Walker, Samuel R. Delaney, Walter Mosley, Charles Johnson, Jamaica Kincaid, Edwidge Danticat, Edward P. Jones, and Caryl Phillips, to name only a few.

The glaring omission of black novelists in *Who's Afraid of Post-Blackness* would seem to imply that literature is the one realm of black artistic production that has been uninfluenced by the rise of post-blackness.[3] What does this significant absence in Touré's work suggest about the nature of black language and black narrative? Although visual artist Glenn Ligon and musician Lupe Fiasco are presented as pioneering figures who challenge the conventions attributed to racial authenticity, are contemporary African American literary authors still bound by the protocols of race? Do Ligon and Fiasco suggest a troublesome exception to Touré's otherwise sweeping claims? In short, what does post-blackness mean for black creative writers?

Recent novels by Jesmyn Ward, Ishmael Reed, Toni Morrison, and many of the authors previously mentioned are not easily classified as post-black because they return to concerns specific to the black community. In Ward's acceptance speech for the 2011 National Book Award, which she received for *Salvage the Bones*, a novel set in New Orleans immediately before Hurricane Katrina landed, she stated, "I wanted to write about the experiences of the poor and the black and the rural people of the South" (quoted in Italie 2011). Ward echoes concerns about racialized representation and marginalization that are centuries old. Similarly, Reed's most recent novel, *Juice!* (2011), and Morrison's *Home* (2012) are deeply entrenched in the kind of racial realism that has historically been associated with African American literature. Gene Andrew Jarrett identifies racial realism as reflecting the "long history in which authors have sought to re-create a lived or living world according to prevailing ideologies of race or racial difference" (2007, 8). Beginning in the post-Reconstruction period and spanning through the Black Arts movement, racial realism has demanded socially and politically minded texts that advance the interests and well-being of black people. Consistent with many of these aims, *Juice!*, *Home*, and other contemporary African American novels depict black protagonists confronting racial tensions and long-standing power hierarchies based on color and class. These novels trouble Touré's breathless declaration of a new post-black era by largely conforming to previous narrative and thematic models. Do African American literary writers maintain a more narrow understanding of black authenticity? Are literary texts somehow exempt from Touré's characterization of post-blackness?

In responding to these questions, it is imperative to note that the expansive nature of post-blackness poses critical problems to the notion of a coherent racialized identity and consequently to the development of a recognizable literary tradition. In his review of Touré's book, Randall Kennedy warns against the uncritical inclusivity of post-blackness, which threatens to empty racialized identity of any meaningful distinction or political force: "To the extent that Touré wants to perpetuate black communities but eschew policing, he seeks a sociological impossibility. The erection of boundaries and the enforcement of stigmatization, including the threat of expulsion, are inescapable, albeit dangerous, aspects of any collective enterprise." Kennedy argues that "some folks," like Supreme Court Justice Clarence Thomas, "ought to have their racial credentials lifted," though he also makes room for "different grades of blackness" (2011).

"Different grades of blackness" is an apt description of what the African American literary canon has long showcased. Henry Louis Gates Jr. reminds us that that "there is no black voice; only voices, diverse and mutable." He explains, "There's no hidden continuity or coherence among them. History makes them like beads on a string: there's no necessary resemblance; but then again, no possible separation" (1990, 46–47). This movement across various forms of blackness highlights a rejection of racialized singularity that is hardly unique to a supposed post-black age. Paul Laurence Dunbar, Zora Neale Hurston, George Schuyler, and many others demonstrate that black writers have been challenging the meaning of racial authenticity for centuries. The multivalent nature of blackness evident in countless African American literary texts demonstrates the historical oversights of Touré's thesis. However, despite such diversity, these wide-ranging manifestations of racial identity still emerge from the kind of coherent foundation that Kennedy demands of blackness

In understanding a literary tradition, we must bear in mind the formal qualities that shape language and narrative. There is a crucial gap here between individuals who are black and literature that is black. Morrison has usefully elaborated on this distinction: "I don't regard Black literature as simply books written *by* Black people, or simply literature written *about* Black people, or simply as literature that uses a certain mode of language in which you just sort of drop *g*'s. There is something very special and very identifiable about it and it is my struggle to *find* that elusive but identifiable style in the books. My joy is when I think that I have approached it; my misery is when I think I can't get there" (2003, 2288; emphasis original). Morrison's observations suggest the provocative conclusion that she may not always write black literature since she admits that she sometimes struggles to achieve that "very special and very identifiable" quality. Blackness is not automatically bestowed on her writing. Unlike Touré, who seeks to include and celebrate every personal permutation of blackness in his book, Morrison presents blackness as a deliberate and difficult achievement. Moving from the person to the page, blackness necessarily becomes a chosen struggle, an inheritance that must be embraced rather than simply assumed. Morrison emphasizes the "elusive but identifiable style" at the base of the African American literary tradition, but what is this "very special" quality and how does it manifest in black novels?

Touré is primarily concerned with individuals and the identity labels that adhere to specific people. However, a literary tradition is composed not of individual authors but of texts that use and manipulate language in specific ways. These texts also engage with a discrete selection of other works which they reference and revise. Responding to her own question— "What makes a work 'black'?"—Morrison has stated, "The most valuable point of entry into the question of cultural (or racial) distinction, the one most fraught, is its language—its unpoliced, seditious, confrontational, manipulative, inventive, disruptive, masked, and unmasking language" (1988). The gap that Morrison identifies between an individual's blackness and a text's blackness lies in language. What, then, is the language specific to blackness? And how does a language so deeply rooted to a vernacular tradition translate onto the page? Geneva Smitherman, John Russell Rickford, and other scholars of linguistics have done much to delineate the contours of Ebonics, or African American Vernacular English (AAVE). Smitherman defines Ebonics as "a set of communication patterns and practices resulting from Africans' appropriation and transformation of a foreign tongue during the African Holocaust" (2000, 19). However, many of the key texts of the African American literary canon do not specifically engage with the grammar and syntax Rickford and others have insightfully analyzed.[4] Although scholars continue to debate whether AAVE is better described as a language or a dialect, it bears reminding that Morrison's prose, like that of other African American writers, is written in familiar, standard English.[5] What, then, makes their language black?

In *The Signifying Monkey: A Theory of African-American Literary Criticism* (1988), Gates states, "The black tradition is double-voiced," and affirms, "Whatever is black about black American literature is to be found in this identifiable black Signifyin(g) difference." Signifyin(g) is repetition with a difference, a difference encoded through intertextual relationships. For example, Gates identifies work by Ralph Ellison and Ishmael Reed as "double-voiced in the sense that their literary antecedents are both white and black novels, but also modes of figuration lifted from the black vernacular tradition" (1988, xxiii). The language of Ellison and Reed signifies on multiple levels, seeking to incorporate a broad range of allusions that affirm and expand the primacy of the black literary tradition. In *Invisible Man* (1952), Ellison unites Dostoevsky and black vernacular folk culture through language that signifies: language that performs plurality and resistance. Black language, the "elusive but identifiable" quality Morrison describes, is language that signifies within and beyond the black literary tradition. Black literature is premised upon this dynamic exchange that enlivens an ever-evolving legacy. Consequently, the notion of post-black literature presents an impossibility: texts that are effectively unbound to literary history.

The signifyin(g) black difference exists as a chain of meaning, not simply as the use of AAVE or even double-voiced language in a specific novel. The black language that Morrison crafts is language that responds to a particular set of texts, slave narratives as well as Greek tragedy, blues performances as well as the King James Bible. This does not mean that Sophocles and First Corinthians constitute black literature; instead, Morrison invests these texts with a black difference, a difference that resides in the signifyin(g) chain of the black literary canon. This is both a strategy of inclusion and exclusion, of celebration and resistance. Most importantly, for the purposes of understanding the fundamental problem of Touré's conception of post-blackness, signifyin(g) is about encoding history. Signifyin(g) simultaneously gestures to the past and changes meaning to fit the present. For signifyin(g) to repeat with a difference, there must be something to repeat, a prior experience, a prior relationship to language and narrative. Touré's notion of post-blackness severs this vital connection to history. He asserts that "there is no such thing" (2011, 4) as black authenticity, but this claim dangerously unmoors blackness from the stories and past experiences that have come to define it.

Post-blackness is a notion that simply cannot be applied to literature because narratives are fundamentally concerned with historical experience even when texts purport to tell us about the future. Literary traditions emerge from a web of intertextual meaning; texts gain coherence by responding to the past and becoming part of a legacy that exceeds any single performance. To sever that tie, that crucial mooring, is to cease to be part of the black literary tradition or, in fact, any literary tradition. In "Rootedness: The Ancestor as Foundation," her most direct discussion of what constitutes the "blackness" of black literature, Morrison highlights the presence of an ancestor in understanding textual blackness. She explains, "There is always an elder there. And these ancestors are not just parents, they are sort of timeless people whose relationships to the characters are benevolent, instructive, and protective, and they provide a certain kind of wisdom" (2003, 2289). The ancestor may be understood as the personification of the black signifyin(g) difference, a presence that reflects familial legacy and historical continuity. Touré's notion of post-blackness effectively banishes the ancestor and, therefore, the grounded core of being necessary for historical meaning and relevance. In his conception, the ancestor becomes a false guardian of authenticity, a danger to the fully liberated self. It is especially telling that Touré opens his book with a description of him skydiving; in free fall, he is at last rid of all racialized pressures and influences but also of all connection to history and community.

In highlighting the primacy of the ancestor to the African American literary tradition, it is important to note that this figure is not static but has evolved in key ways even in Morrison's own oeuvre. These dynamic explorations do not point to a new post-black age but instead allow us to understand black culture and experience in new ways. I conclude with a reading of Morrison's most recent artistic creation, *Desdemona*, which highlights the fallacy of post-black literature even as it reaches toward new representations of blackness, representations that are always historically informed. The multimedia collaboration with theater and opera director Peter Sellars and the Malian singer-songwriter Rokia Traoré reflects Morrison's continued interest in the possibilities of ancestral meaning and influence. The innovative production, which is part play, part concert, opened in Vienna in May 2011 before showing in Berkeley and New York. In the script, Morrison imagines an ancestral figure for the murdered wife of Shakespeare's Othello. Staged as a dialogue and musical exchange between Desdemona and various characters, most prominently with her childhood nursemaid, the performance represents Morrison's first application of an ancestral figure to a white character. In the production notes, Sellars reminds audience members that in act 4 of Shakespeare's play, Desdemona sings the "Willow Song." During the final hours of her life, Desdemona describes how she learned the song from a servant named Barbary. In Elizabethan England, "Barbary" was a synonym for "Africa." Sellars explains that the collaboration is premised upon the notion that "courageous, loving, independent-minded Desdemona was raised by an African woman, growing up with African stories and learning African songs" (2011). Morrison's script and Traoré's music enact a blues performance that finds both commonality and difference in the relationship between Desdemona and her black nursemaid, named Sa'ran, or "joy," in the production. Their shared lamentation is transformed into a meditative exploration of enslavement, grief, and cross-racial love.

Touré might label *Desdemona* post-black because it focuses upon an unusual protagonist for black literature and in so doing clearly departs from the expectations of racial realism. However, whereas the post-black impulse jettisons history, Morrison seeks to restore a black signifyin(g) difference to a key literary figure. Her Desdemona is not so much post-black as pre-black, reminding audiences of the silent but potent influence the white woman's black nursemaid had on the original play's entire development. The new production signifies on Shakespeare's *Othello* by foregrounding black difference and making an ancestral presence primary to the love between Desdemona and Othello. Morrison's script links Desdemona's childhood relationship to Sa'ran to the reason she was first attracted to her black husband. Othello explains in the opening act of Shakespeare's play that his wife became enamored with the stories he told her, stories of his travels and battles, of being sold into slavery and the wonders, both human and natural, he witnessed. He states, "if I had a friend that loved her, I should but teach him how to tell my story, And that would woo her" (1993, 41). Othello's statement would seem to deemphasize the role his race played in their courtship because it suggests that his storytelling, not his blackness, was the primary cause of her love. However, Morrison newly racializes Othello's narrative by implying that Desdemona first developed a love of story through the black nurse of her youth. In this way Morrison draws an important connection between Desdemona's love for Othello and her love for Sa'ran. Desdemona's attraction to Othello reflects her childhood affection for her nurse as well as her intimate relationship to the African tradition of oral storytelling. Rather than offering an individualist image of blackness, Morrison reenvisions history with a signifyin(g) black difference.

Morrison describes the exciting tales that Othello told his future wife—of his capture by Syrians, his escape from slavery, his encounter with mysterious but compassionate creatures, and even how he and Iago rape an old woman while a young boy watched. Othello recounts these stories in the afterlife following Desdemona's repeated introduction, "And this is what he told" (2012, 31). Her prefatory comment, recited like an incantation, emphasizes the effect these stories have on her rather than on the stories themselves. Audience members understand how she came to love her husband even if she could not always forgive him for his exploits. The account of Othello's disturbing rape suggests that Desdemona was fully aware of her husband's violent impulses as well as the unsettling influence Iago held over him. She was no unwitting girl, mesmerized by Othello's dark power as her father, Brabantio, claims in Shakespeare's play.[6] Instead, her love derives from the complex portrait of the man that emerges through these seductive stories.

In the play's ambiguous afterlife, Desdemona recounts her courtship and marriage to Sa'ran. Played by Traoré, Sa'ran sings in a variety of languages, including her native Bambara, while accompanied by a band of traditional string players and singers. Morrison's emphasis on the relationship between Desdemona and Sa'ran further unsettles the patriarchal dynamics of the original play in which the former functions largely as an object of exchange between dueling men. Before Brabantio and Othello, Shakespeare's Desdemona explains "her divided duty": the "life and education" (41) she owes her father and the absolute loyalty she must now give her husband. However, Morrison's Desdemona finds a third way, fulfilling her loyalty neither to father nor husband but to the woman whose life provides a striking reflection of her own. By presenting Desdemona primarily in dialogue with Sa'ran, Morrison suggests that the more fundamental bond involves the two women. Much like her novels *Sula* (1974) and *Love* (2003), which emphasize the power of female friendship over heterosexual union, *Desdemona* challenges and even undermines the passion between Othello and Desdemona. Their love originates in the relationship between Desdemona and Sa'ran as if the former seeks her husband only as a surrogate for her lost nursemaid. Desdemona falls in love with Othello because of his stories, not his physical appearance, and in this contemporary production, she unites with Sa'ran, not her husband.

Desdemona describes Sa'ran as "more alive than anyone I knew and more loving. She tended me as though she were my birth mother" (18). However, when the two speak, Sa'ran is hostile and accusatory toward her former ward. She criticizes Desdemona for not even knowing her real name but instead calling her "Barbary," which "is the geography of the foreigner, the savage." (45). Sa'ran further rebukes Desdemona, stating, "So you don't know me. Have never known me" (46). Desdemona suggests that they are alike because while Sa'ran died of a broken heart, she was slain by Othello. In Shakespeare's play, Desdemona recounts how Barbary "was in love, and he she loved proved mad / And did forsake her. She had a song of willow, / An old thing 'twas, but it expressed her fortune, / And she died singing it" (1993, 213). Like Sa'ran, Desdemona dies at the hands of her mad lover, moments before she sings the "Willow Song." This continuity between the two women marks a tragic death unbound by differences of race. As Desdemona's ancestor, Sa'ran anticipates the white woman's fate. Following their first exchange, Sa'ran begins to sing the Willow Song from the original play.

> The poor soul sat sighing by a sycamore tree,
> Sing all a green willow.
> Her hand on her bosom, her head on her knee,
> Sing willow, willow, willow.
> The fresh streams ran by her, and murmur'd her moans;
> Sing willow, willow, willow;
> Her salt tears fell from her and soften'd the stones;
> Sing willow, willow, willow—
>
> (47)

Sa'ran abruptly stops her singing and reminds Desdemona that ultimately she was a servant, a woman with "no rank in your world." Desdemona responds by emphasizing their shared experience as women, "Sa'ran. We are women. I had no more control over my life than you had. My prison was unlike yours but it was prison still" (48). Sa'ran concedes that Desdemona never abused her, unlike the man she loved. This admission suggests the beginning of a new understanding between the two women. They recognize that though they have been oppressed and hurt in different ways, they are not adversaries and can in fact be allies. Sa'ran then announces that she will "no more" sing "willow," offering a new song, a choral poem written by Morrison.[7]

> Someone leans near
> And sees the salt my eyes have shed.
> I wait, longing to hear
> Words of reason, love or play
> To lash or lull me toward the hollow day.

Silence kneads my fear
Of crumbled star-ash sifting down
Clouding the rooms here, here.
I shore up my heart to run. To stay.
But no sign or design marks the narrow way.
Then on my skin a sudden breath caresses
The salt my eyes have shed.
And I hear a call—clear, so clear:
'You will never die again.'
What bliss to know
I will never die again.

Desdemona concludes, "We will never die again," merging her voice with that of her black ancestor.

By replacing the "Willow Song" with her own choral poem, Morrison moves away from one woman's solitary lamentation to a song about union and transcendence. While the "poor soul" of the "Willow Song" has no one to console her, the speaker of "Someone leans near" is aware of a presence who caresses her skin and affirms that death has no hold over her. Morrison's poem also signifies on the image of the "salt tears" in the "Willow Song," offering a new perspective on grief and its aftermath. In the first song, the "salt tears fell from her and soften'd the stones." The only influence the tears have is on the natural world as they remain invisible to others. By contrast, in Morrison's poem, "the salt my eyes have shed" is observed by another. The woman's cries in the "Willow Song" are mimicked by the "fresh streams" that "murmur'd her moans," again affirming nature as the only audience for her lamentation. This solitary sadness is transformed in Morrison's work, becoming a site of empathy and transcendence. "Someone leans near" changes the line, "You will never die again," first written with quotation marks, to "I will never die again." This shift highlights how the grief in Morrison's poem is not static but evolves, taking solace from others. The sorrow of the "Willow Song" is replaced by the promise of healing and the comfort of understanding.

Both the "Willow Song" and "Someone leans near" resonate with the most fundamental qualities of a blues performance. Houston Baker understands the blues as a matrix foundational to African American literary history. He explains, "When personae, protagonists, autobiographical narrators, or literary critics successfully negotiate an obdurate 'economics of slavery' and achieve a resonant, improvisational, expressive dignity," they "provide cogent examples of the blues matrix at work" (2000, 238). Importantly, both Desdemona and Sa'ran have experiences of enslavement that underscore their blues performance. Despite vast differences in culture and historical time period, the "Willow Song" and "Someone leans near" voice "the feeling of the blues," which Ralph Ellison described "as close as Americans can come to expressing the spirit of tragedy" (1995, 140). He further explained the paradox of pathos captured by the blues:

The blues is an impulse to keep the painful details and episodes of a brutal experience alive in one's aching consciousness, to finger its jagged grain, and to transcend it, not by the consolation of philosophy but by squeezing from it a near-tragic, near-comic lyricism. As a form, the blues is an autobiographical chronicle of personal catastrophe expressed lyrically. (78–79)

In arguing that the "Willow Song" operates as a blues performance, it is important to recognize the temporal displacement that the new production effects. In Shakespeare's play, Desdemona sings the "Willow Song" before her tragedy comes to its awful conclusion. The "personal catastrophe" that Ellison places at the center of the blues has not yet occurred. Consequently, the "Willow Song" only becomes an evocation of the blues in the afterlife envisioned by "Desdemona." The title character and Sa'ran sing fully aware of the "painful details" in their "aching consciousness," and thus their song emblematizes Ellison's characterization of the blues, this "art of ambiguity, an assertion of the irrepressibly human over all circumstance" (246).

Although she joins her ancestor in the afterlife, Desdemona does not become black. Racial identity is not so fluid or malleable as to become meaningless. Instead she remains the white Venetian woman Shakespeare originally imagined. However, in returning to the woman whose fate mirrors her own, Desdemona has discovered traces of blackness in her own whiteness, the source of her love for Othello as well as the tragedy she shares with Sa'ran. Desdemona embraces the black ancestor who has guided her life, and together they voice their signifyin(g) song. There is no individualist representation of blackness here, but instead one deeply guided by history and culture.

NOTES

1. In his book, Touré references a few black novelists, including Morrison, Ralph Ellison, James Baldwin, Zora Neale Hurston, and Zadie Smith but only as points of inspiration, not to offer a sustained consideration of what post-blackness means to literary writers.

2. Whitehead is quoted as saying, "What was called oreoness ten to twenty years ago is being who you are and being comfortable doing what you want and not caring about what other people think. Being called an oreo was stupid then and it's stupid now. People are just more aware that those categories are dumb. If you're an authentic person, true to who you are and how you're wired, then like what you like, whether it's Led Zeppelin or 'Happy Days'" (55–56).

3. Although my focus here is on black novelists, it is notable that Touré similarly neglects black poets in his book. Elizabeth Alexander and Saul Williams were interviewed but neither comments on the state of contemporary black poetry or what post-blackness might mean to their creative work.

4. On vocabulary, pronunciation and grammar, see chapters 6 and 7 in Rickford's *Spoken Soul: The Story of Black English* (New York: Wiley, 2000).

5. On this point, Smitherman writes, "The question of whether Ebonics . . . is a language or a dialect is not one that can be definitively answered by linguistics. Ultimately, this is a political, not a linguistic, question" (2000, 13).

6. Brabantio says of his daughter: "She is aused, stol'n from me, and corrupted / By spells and medicines bought of mountebanks; / For nature so

prepost'rously to err— / Being not deficient, blind, or lame of sense— / Sans witchcraft could not" (33).

7. "Someone leans near" originally appeared in slightly altered form in Morrison's 2002 book of poems, *Five Poems*, a book that remains largely unknown because only 425 copies were produced by Peter Koch Printers, and it lacks an International Standard Book Number.

REFERENCES

Baker, Houston A., Jr. 2000. "Belief, Theory and Blues: Notes for a Post-Structuralist Criticism of Afro-American Literature." In *African American Literary Theory: A Reader*, ed. Winston Napier, 224–41. New York: New York University Press.

Ellison, Ralph. 1995. *Shadow and Act*. New York: Vintage International.

Gates, Henry Louis, Jr. 1988. *The Signifying Monkey: A Theory of African-American Literary Criticism*. New York: Oxford University Press.

——. 1990. "Talking Black." In *The State of the Language*, eds. Christopher Ricks and Leonard Michaels, 42–50. Berkeley: University of California Press.

Hall, Stuart. 1995. "New Ethnicities." *The Post-Colonial Studies Reader*. Eds. Bill Ashcroft, Gareth Griffiths and Helen Tiffin. London: Routledge. 223–27.

Italie, Hillel. 2011. "Book Awards Honor the 99 Percent." *Salon*, November 7. http://www.salon.com/2011/11/17/book_awards_honor_the_99_percent/

Jarrett, Gene Andrew. 2007. *Deans and Truants: Race and Realism in African American Literature*. Philadelphia: University of Pennsylvania Press.

Kennedy, Randall. 2011. "The Fallacy of Touré's Post-Blackness Theory." *The Root*, August 11. http://www.theroot.com/articles/culture/2011/08/whos_afraid_of_postblackness_tours_postblackness_theory.html.

Morrison, Toni. 1988. "Unspeakable Things Unspoken: The Afro-American Presence in American Literature." The Tanner Lectures on Human Values, delivered at the University of Michigan, October 7. http://tannerlectures.utah.edu/_documents/a-to-z/m/morrison90.pdf.

——. 2003. "Rootedness: The Ancestor as Foundation." In *The Norton Anthology of African-American Literature*, 2nd ed., eds. Henry Louis Gates Jr. and Nellie Y. McKay. New York: W. W. Norton.

——. 2012. *Desdemona*. London: Oberon Books.

Rickford, John Russell. 2000. *Spoken Soul: The Story of Black English*. New York: Wiley.

Sellars, Peter. 2011. "Program Notes Desdemona." http://www.calperfs.berkeley. edu/learn/program_notes/2011/pn_desdemona.pdf.

Shakespeare, William. 1993. *The Tragedy of Othello, the Moor of Venice*. The New Folger Library Shakespeare. New York: Washington Square Press.

Smitherman, Geneva. 2000. *Talkin That Talk: Language, Culture, and Education in African America*. New York: Routledge.

Touré. 2011. *Who's Afraid of Post-Blackness? What It Means to Be Black Now*. New York: Free Press.

3

African Diasporic Blackness Out of Line

Trouble for "Post-Black"
~~African~~ *Americanism*

GREG THOMAS

I've had trouble all my days.
> —Chester Himes, *The Real Cool Killers* (1959)

If trouble was money, I swear I'd be a millionaire / If worries was dollar bills, I'd buy the whole world and have money to spare.
> —The Blues (n.d.)

I realize I'm saying some things that you think can get me in trouble, but ... I was born in trouble.
    I don't even care about trouble. I'm interested in one thing alone, and that's freedom—by any means necessary.
    So I'll bring you now the country's number one freedom-fighting woman ... "
> —Malcolm X, "At the Audubon" (1964)

PRELUDE

"B-l-a-c-k / n-u-s-s."
    First on an eclectic 1971 album of the same name, and later on his double-disc *Does Your House Have Lions?* (1993) collection, Rahsaan

Roland Kirk gave us "Blacknuss" in some rambunctious jazz before the official advent of hip-hop, the Negrophobe's current musical nightmare of choice. He commences this song with words spoken over Cissy Houston's otherworldly singing in the background: "Now we gathered here on the universe at this time, this particular time, to listen to the 36 black notes on the piano." There are thirty-six black notes and fifty-two white notes, which will for once not take center stage, perhaps for the first time in his or any other artistic career. "We don't mean to eliminate nothing," Kirk reassures, as he insists upon rearranging our universe of music and our universe of meaning at this particular time and in this particular manner.

He will embody, theorize, and resound what we have come to call Blackness, or "Blacknuss." Prefiguring a remarkable scene from Haile Gerima's film *Ashes and Embers* (1983), Kirk's mash-up of churchy instrumentation, chants, exclamation, and intonation lead to an explosive relish of food—"soul food." He shouts it all out: "blackberries! / that good chicken! / them old biscuits! / that smothered steak! / them sweet potatoes!" For five minutes and thirteen seconds, "Blacknuss" is recoded as sustenance, pleasure, and epistemology too: "Blacknuss" feeds us; "Blacknuss" pleases; "Blacknuss" gives us keys to the cosmos. The multi-instrumentalist instructs us in the end to "get down in it," "jump on up and down in it," and, finally: "Don't let it *goooo*!" "Hallelujah," he closes, in tune with the Sweet Inspiration's "*Yeeahhh!*"

"*B-l-a-c-k / n-u-s-s*," it's spelled out—three times in succession, for a thrice-repeated refrain, clearly to make the spirit come: "*B-l-a-c-k / n-u-s-s . . . B-l-a-c-k / n-u-s-s*." And almost inaudibly, punctuating this choral call is another climactic statement: "Blacknuss, oh yes!" or "Blacknuss, okay" or it could be "Blacknuss or death!"[1] How is it possible to "post" the Black in such "Blacknuss," on or off the record, in any event? What kind of music does "post-Blackness" make? Who or what in the world does it feed, please, and sustain?

INTRODUCTION

Some of us might wonder why society today is hooked on "posting" things, perhaps most of all those things that it has never fully understood, such as "modernity," "colonialism," and "Blackness." Once, I thought a possible mode of intervention here could be to "post" something that is not supposed to be "posted" at all, either in the academic or pop intellectual marketplace, like "COINTELPRO"—the infamous FBI counterintelligence program of the U.S. federal government—to propose sincerely yet sardonically that we live or suffer in a "post-COINTELPRO" epoch, a historical thrust of the most vicious counterrevolution, a raging period of counterinsurgent repression in general and backlash against Black or Pan-African revolution in particular, an epoch whose local and global violence for white Western imperialism is political, economic, and cultural as well as military without a doubt. But, if much needed in some form, this formulation would hardly be commodified in North America and would continue to ensconce something else.

The rhetoric of the "post" so fashionably in play recycles a very political and provincial approach to history. This "post" always smacks of synchronic monoculturalism, the old and false universalism of Europe, and its diachronic evolutionism. The "post" is never meant for "some"; it's supposed to be for "all." It is never a questionable desire; it is a supposedly unquestionable reality. It is class elite-led yet presented as a supposed cure for the masses. Anyone or any place that does not fall in love and in line with these "posts" is represented as "backward," "savage," or "barbarian," more or less. The halo and spoils of "History" will never be on their side, theoretically or not so theoretically as a matter of fact.

Yet we need pose just a few questions here to crumble the subterfuge's house of cards: "Why this 'post' and not that one? Why these and not those?" The faddism of "posting" does not lend itself to certain questions. The commercial notion of post-Blackness imitates white intellectualism in too many ways to count and fails to imagine what should be an immediate, logical correlate or prerequisite, even on its own spurious ideological terms: "post-whiteness." If, as alleged, Blackness is going or gone, outdated or obviated, where is the whiteness that is ravaging the planet and scripting Blackness's much-desired, much-ballyhooed demise? One can delve further into the black hole of "post-Black" discursive posturing. Where is "post-Americanism" (indeed, "post-amerikanism" or "post-amerikkkanism"), if post-

Blackness does not successfully eradicate for us Malcolm X's Black radical critique of both whiteness and Americanism? Or does legitimizing post-Blackness mean that some of us don't speak so critically anymore? Where is "post–African Americanism" as well? Could "post-bourgeois African Americanism" then make any kind of sense? How quickly it becomes clear that "post-Blackness" is a subterfuge subtended by whiteness, Americanism, and the elite "African Americanism" that it ventriloquizes, making some "posts" desirable or thinkable and others so undesirable and unthinkable, so unquestionable in the current scheme of things.

OUT OF LINE: (AFRICAN DIASPORIC) BLACKNESS VERSUS ("POST-BLACK") AFRICAN AMERICANISM

Although "post-Blackness" may be examined and exposed from a number of angles, it remains to be examined in light of a resurgent, counterinsurgent "African Americanism" among the Black middle-class elite inside and outside U.S. academia. Beyond a propagation of self-abolition, "post-Blackness" must be more than "non-Black." It must actually be something *in lieu of* Black; and "African Americanism" provides this supposed escape hatch in a five-centuries-long context of Western European racism and imperialism, at least in the mentality of the propagators of abolition or self-abolition as a new mode of neocolonial assimilationism. In other words, an unexamined politics of "African Americanism" lay at the bottom of "post-Blackness" as its matrix or launching pad in the wake of whiteness's destruction of the most recent watershed Black liberation movements in North America of the 1960s and 1970s.

The language of "African American" *could* signify in a variety of ways, but in the white-dominated public space of North America today it does not. For some, it used to signify a militancy now linked more fully with a Blackness despised. At one point in the 1990s, a brief article in *Time* magazine announced, curiously, "Black Is Back."[2] It reported on a poll which revealed to readers who did not already know better that the preferred name of most Black people in the United States was, by a large margin, *not* "African American." There was no evidence to suggest that over the

previous decade it ever had been. There was instead a predictable ignorance of the history and politics of naming, which continues till this day.
While white society was learning to avoid saying "Black," as if this one
change in speech were an act of charity that could be reparation for eons
of oppression, it was Jesse Jackson's "rainbow" liberalism that was given
credit for this sudden "emancipation." The Black press could recall poet
Gwendolyn Brooks, for example, who once wrote that she was thank-
ful that she lived to see the 1960s, or the global Black Power movement,
because otherwise she would have died a "Negro fraction" (2003, 71–72).
The Black press could recall Sonia Sanchez, too, who would militate for
explicit African identification herself. Since Black was ecstatically tied to
the concept of "Black *Power*" for the likes of Brooks and Sanchez, neither
would suggest that "African" terminology should replace and erase any
"Black" terminology in its relationship to any given "American" terminology. Both "Black" and "African" expressed a radical Black politics that
the current usage of "African American" rejects. Then, Sanchez could say
"Afro-American," or "African American," and emphasize the African with
militancy. Brooks did away with the "American" altogether, calling herself
an African woman, again with militancy. Yet these speech acts are entirely
different from the rhetoric that would please *Time* or other corporate
media magazines. That specific usage of "African American" now perva-
sive in academic and popular media, nationally and internationally, has
nothing to do with any history or memory of Black militancy and should
very well call to mind Richard B. Moore's work, *The Name "Negro"—Its
Origin and Evil Use* (1960).

A "Caribbean militant from Harlem" and Barbados, Moore traced
the social origins of the name "Negro" to the "Hispano-Portuguese Slave
Trade" and noted that resistance to this slur "has never ceased among
people of African descent in this country" (1992, 33).[3] It is a misnomer
that wasn't partially adopted by some until around 1892. Since our history
does not begin in "the stinking hold of a slave ship" (33), and there is no
such place as "Negroland" (46), Moore spurns the association of ideas writ
large in the noun "Negro," which is synonymous for "natural slave" (40).
This linguistic device was deployed by "oppressors for murderous and evil

ends," and should be no less violently denounced. In 1960, Moore said that he never used this word at all, "except as a necessary quotation," and that he hoped it wouldn't be "necessary even to quote this offensive term much longer" (33). Insisting that "names can be changed" out of necessity, he upheld "Afro-American" as a more appropriate designation for those in this country, comparing it to "Afrocubano" and "Afrobrasileiro" and citing its core attention to "land, history, and culture" (67) in a distinctly Pan-African vein.

The name "Afro-American" is hence said to proclaim "our past continental heritage and our present national status" (68). Still, our present "national" location or status begins to raise problems for Moore long before the matter is thought to be solved in theory. He observes that some Caribbeans have been "infected" with the word "Negro" while in the United States and were "taking the disease" back home with them and spreading it. The virus causing this disease, according to Moore, should be called "americanensis" (50). This "Negrified" condition has the influence of "dollars" behind it, but it must be thwarted nonetheless. It is targeted for combat, however, in the Caribbean only. So, as extraordinary as Moore's praxis is in resistance to the name "Negro," Black resistance to the geopolitical terms of white oppression—or the national rhetoric of "America" itself—is never here envisioned for the Black subjects most immediately colonized by the U.S. settler-colonial regime.

A more comprehensive analysis of the racial name game can be found in the oratory of Malcolm X. He can be heard loud and clear in Brooks and Sanchez, who recognized his influence explicitly. His own disdain for the word "Negro" was notorious. When he used it, he almost always spat it in quotation marks—"The so-called Negro"—before explaining exactly why we were "so called." In "Some Reflections on 'Negro History Week' and the Role of Black People in History" (1965), he said the term could only signify a heinous crime of "Western Civilization" (1990b, 322). This belief would be reiterated by Walter Rodney in *The Groundings with My Brothers* (1969): "We are the only group in the world who deny ourselves, preferring to be known as 'Negroes' rather than Africans" (1996, 35). As Malcolm continued to affirm "Blackness" in a manner that would make the "Black Power" movement possible, his use of the label "Afro-American" in his Organization of Afro-American Unity (OAAU) made more of a historical splash more than did Moore, who can be heard in Malcolm nonetheless. Years later, Betty Shabazz would recount that Malcolm had preferred the term "*African*-American" rather than "*Afro*-American" for the OAAU, which was patterned to the letter after the new Organization of African Unity (OAU) on the continent, but he thought there might be too much backlash against it at the time. He used it in official speaking capacity anyway. For, while Moore felt "African American" was "too long" and didn't "sound right," Malcolm's point was to promote Pan-African radicalism against the white nationalism of the "U.S.A." empire state; and, legendarily, *he* would do so in the name of the Black masses who spent time in "the field" rather than "the master's house."

Unlike academicians who casually reinscribe anthropological imperialism locally as sociological imperialism, "nationwide," Malcolm dissected and rejected "America" as an ideological construct that merely poses as the country of a "common culture" of an immigrant "melting pot." In "The Ballot or the Bullet" (1964), he fired famously: "I'm not going to sit at your table and watch you eat, with nothing on my plate, and call myself a diner. Sitting at the table doesn't make you a diner. Being here in America doesn't make you an American. . . . No, I'm not an American. I'm one of the 22 million Black people who are the victims of Americanism. One of 22 million Black people who are the victims of democracy, nothing but disguised hypocrisy" (1990a, 26). These lines were once pictured on the back cover of the old Pathfinder edition of *Malcolm X Speaks*. Today they have been erased and replaced on the book jacket of the current Grove Press edition of the collection, much like Malcolm's Pan-African militancy has been erased from the prevailing usage of the term "African American" in the hegemonic mainstream of the United States.

Malcolm's radical demystification: the white nation-statism of "America" is part and parcel of his bold denunciation of the *mis*-leadership class of the "N/negro" or "B/black" elite. He made serious use of the term "Negro" when, as in "Message to the Grassroots," he identified himself as a "field Negro" in opposition to the "house Negroes" and the "Big Six" of the Civil Rights establishment (1990a, 10–16). A mere week before his murder on February 21, 1965, Malcolm attacked neocolonialism and its elites in "Not Just an American Problem, But a World Problem" (1965). "Call it benevolent colonialism," he said: "Philanthropic imperialism. Humanitarianism backed up by dollarism. Tokenism" (1992, 160). He renewed his assault on "Uncle Tom" "Negro leaders" as he aimed to *decolonize* Black struggles worldwide. He blasted "Toms" so much that, anticipating a lawsuit, he started saying "Uncle Roy, Uncle Whitney, and Uncle A. Philip" instead (97). He knew that the deployment of "tokens," or the strategic positioning of "a handful of hand-picked Negroes," was yet "another foul trick" designed to keep us "going around in circles for another thousand years" (169).

His critical analysis produced a class analysis that could explode on the other side of the Atlantic Ocean. Malcolm's admiration of the "Mau Mau," and their liquidation of "Uncle Tom Africans," is famous for some and infamous for others. Recall further his furious condemnations of Moise Tshombe in the Congo. He could, besides, denounce the neocolonial hypocrisy behind support for Léopold Senghor in Senegal and campaigns against Kwame Nkrumah in Ghana. His "Appeal to African Heads of State" (1964), the eight-page memorandum he submitted to the "African Summit," or second meeting of the OAU, entailed this perspective as well. It ended with a special insistence due to Gamal Abdel Nasser's unmindful celebration of the Civil Rights Act of 1964: "'No one knows the master better than his servant.' We have been servants in America for over 300 years. We have a thorough, inside knowledge of this man who calls himself Uncle Sam. Therefore, you must heed our warning: Don't escape from European colonialism only to become more enslaved by deceitful, 'friendly' American dollarism" (X 1990a, 77). This is how Malcolm aimed to take back the category of "Blackness" from the Black "middle-class" for the Black majority on either side of the Atlantic Ocean.

His goal was to redirect the U.S. civil rights platform and convert it into a global human rights program that could be put to use for an antiracist struggle that is an anticolonialist or anti-imperialist as well as an anti-elitist and anticapitalist struggle. So in "Not Just an American Problem," he insisted that when we make reference to the "Afro-American," we should be speaking of "that large number of people in the Western hemisphere, from the southernmost tip of South America to the northernmost tip of North America, all of whom have a common heritage and have a common origin when you go back into the history of [our] people" (X 1992, 145). Who but Malcolm X would supply us with a double demystification of "America"—"America" as a white racist ideological construct of settler-colonial nationalism on the one hand and, on the other hand, "America" as a hemispheric or continental unit bonding all African victims of the former, inside and out, historically?

Working out of Brazil, Abdias do Nascimento warned against the appropriation of the Americas for the "United States of America" exclusively (1995, 97). This is a pan-American perspective of a diaspora. Jack Forbes, author of *Columbus and Other Cannibals* (1992) and *Black Africans and Native Americans: Color, Race, and Caste in the Evolution of Red-Black Peoples* (1988), employs the term "African American" to stress the bodily coalition of Blacks or Africans and the "First Peoples" of the land. The name "American" cannot fail to index the indigenous population subject to genocidal erasure by white Western imperialism with any legitimacy in discussions of racism and anti-racism. The matter at hand was made all the more visible by Nancy Morejón in "The Invisible Afro-America," a verbal text spoken from the Cuban region of the Caribbean that was without a doubt an explicit part of Malcolm's conception of "African American."[4] Critically, one of his crucial demystifications of "America" can explain why the other demystification never caught on with permanence under U.S. "Americanism" in particular. If "African American" should in principle describe African diaspora, and "Red-Black" *maroonage*, at all points across the Americas, it does not in practice for North America as a rule because "America" is, more than anything else, an ideological phantasm of "white supremacy" with a highly restrictive scope of racial and geographical-territorial reference.

Thus, the U.S. Black "bourgeoisie" may adopt the rhetoric of "African Americans" in an anti-Black and now "post-Black" fashion and remain faithful to the white bourgeoisie's U.S. colonial nationalism. They can do so under the guise of "ethnicity" rather than Pan-Africanism or diaspora and can refuse to query the politics of this "ethnicity" of settler imperialist social science. They reproduce the official state doctrine of the "melting pot," which makes space for "Irish Americans" and "Italian Americans," among others, to become pseudo-generic "Americans" in the grand finale. As a result, they "forget" that this "common culture" of "Americanism" is a white culture of anti-Black racism, and they "forget" that while colonial anthropology defines "*true* culture" as *really* white, colonial or neo-colonial sociology defines "*real* ethnicity" as *truly* white as well. This is why Daniel Moynihan and Nathan Glazer (1965) could describe "Negro Americans" as the only group in "America" that has "no culture to protect." That blind old dogma still bears the mark of Robert Park, whose "race-relations" theory was conceived to guarantee the dominance of European culture in the space captured as the "U.S.A." Nevertheless, this elite "African Americanism" seeks to join this Aryanist history of Occidentalism and leave Blackness or the despised Black masses behind.

For as much as this "lumpen-bourgeois" elite strives to be "post-Black," the masses remain *most Black* in racist logical hierarchy of white capitalist empire. The "post-Black" posture is not only an illusion, moreover. It is an illusion that promotes the illusion of "post-Blackness" for *some* while accentuating the B/blackest B/blackness of *others*, which is to say, the B/blackest of the Black masses or "The Wretched of the Earth." The "post-Black" delusion and illusion of the elite indeed B/blackens these masses of Black folk with this rhetorical sleight of hand, out of "lumpen-bourgeois" self-interest.

To some extent, Geneva Smitherman synopsizes this process "socio-linguistically" in her study of the "creole" origins of "U.S. Ebonics" as an "anti-language," so to speak. Her *Talkin That Talk: Language, Culture, and Education in African America* (2000) includes a chapter titled "From African to African American," which chronicles a history of naming that climaxes for many in the media persona of Jesse Jackson. She first notes how, before Jackson, Ramona Edelin of the National Urban Coalition proposed the shift from "Black" to "African American," which Jackson would publicize countrywide (41). She then recalls that the prior shift from "Negro" to "Black," at bottom, "signaled an ideological shift, a repudiation of whiteness and the rejection of assimilation." She deduces what may be easily "forgotten" or effaced in the main: "It was a profoundly classic case of the semantic inversion characteristic of Black English Vernacular speakers. Bad was truly turned on its head and made good as the celebration of 'Black'—Black Culture, Black skin color, the Black Experience—became a rallying cry for unity, empowerment and self-definition" (47–48).

But why is reconceptualizing "the identity of the African in North America" thought to require that "Black" be replaced by "African American" in due course? Smitherman writes that the "new semantic constructs an identity of unified global struggle against race domination, linking Africans in North America with Continental Africans and with other Diasporic African groups" (49), and that "for African Americans the issue is identity through *Nommo*," the well-known African "belief in the power of the word" (54). However, she ultimately concludes that "*African American*" brings "the 'Black' race into semantic line" with "other ethnolinguistic traditions" which denote "land of origin," as in "Polish Americans, Italian Americans, Hispanic Americans, German Americans, Asian Americans" and the like (56). It must be noticed how U.S. "Americanism" hegemonizes and reappropriates the African yet again in spite of an alleged or declared Pan-African cultural or political project.

If the ideological shift to "Black" signified a rejection of assimilation and its "Coloracracy," an attempt "to purify Negroes of idealization of white skin, white ideas, and white values" (48), there is no good reason why Black-African "ethnolinguistics" should be "brought into line," as it were, under a white settler nationalist umbrella. There is no reason for this identity of ours to be subsumed under any such "American" politics— when these "American" politics are those framed by and for the U.S. colonial state. But this is precisely what happens when Smitherman's *Black Talk: Words and Phrases from the Hood to the Amen Corner* (1994) also posits a basic linear progression from "'African' to 'Colored' to 'negro' to 'Negro' (with the capital) to 'Black' to 'African American,' with side trips to 'AfroAmerican,' 'AfriAmerican,' 'AfraAmerican,' and 'Afrikan'" (10).

Its beneficiaries—despite their routine exploitation of Blackness, for "Black Talk" and so on—quickly and swiftly cast it aside as "unevolved," an obstruction to the assimilation of the dominant Americanism, *"out of line."* In another chapter of *Talkin That Talk*, "'A New Way of Talkin', or Language, Social Change, and Political Theory," Smitherman confesses: "I had never given thought to referring to the US as 'America' until a comrade in Chicago linguistics called it to my attention. Even as I critiqued 'America' for its participation in the repression of the people of Nicaragua and elsewhere in the 'Americas,' I was unconsciously reinforcing US cultural chauvinism and its regressive ideology." She is consequently if belatedly able to question "the traditional model of race relations in the U.S.," the very model of race hegemony that uses "melting pot Americanism" to contain its Black African threat of subversion (2000, 106–7). It is this very anglophone and anglophile model of *blanqueamiento* that reduces the referential range of the "Ebonics" to "U.S. Ebonics" alone. Robert L. Williams (1975) and his colleagues coined the term in the 1970s as

a superordinate term, covering all the African-European language mixtures developed in various African-European language contact situations throughout the world—e.g., Haitian Creole, a West African-French language mixture; the Dutch Creole spoken in Suriname; the English-based Creole spoken in Jamaica; West African Pidgin English; the West African-English mixture spoken in the US—all would be dimensions (varieties or dialects) of Ebonics, not of any European language. (29)

Oddly, if Smitherman never mentions Malcolm in her preoccupation with Edelin and Jackson, her "womanist linguistics" (2000, 56) does claim a passing class analysis that could link her diasporic moment to his words along with the work of Sterling Stuckey. At one point, *Talkin That Talk* highlights "class and generational conflicts about language" (328) while specifying the morpho-syntax, phonology, and rhetorical and semantic styles of its vernacular (137); and it proposes to consider "U.S. Ebonics" as a "class sociolect" that a "progressive" Black "bourgeoisie" could adopt in a mission of "class suicide" (108). No such suicide has been reported, needless to say. The Pan-African conception of "Ebonics" has been subject to the same co-optation and distortion that mangles Malcolm X's Pan-African deployment of the term "African American" for the global Black masses. What's more, most of Smitherman's sociolinguistic field has moved on from "Ebonics" of any sort to the language of "African American English," "African American Language," "African American Vernacular English" as "African American" has been "brought in line" and moved further away from Black radical or international conceptions of "Blacknuss" as well as "African Americans."

Earlier Stuckey, in *Slave Culture: Nationalist Theory and the Foundations of Black America* (1987), reviewed this "names controversy" and remarked how conservative members of the "colored elite" strove to remove the word "African" from all modes of Black self-identification as early as 1835 (203). Many "free Blacks" preferred to present themselves as "Americans of African descent" and not, like the Black majority, "African" plain and simple (207). As Stuckey argues, "much of African culture was unknown even among the most loyal sons [and daughters] of Africa in the North" (244). Furthermore, "Black leaders" bound by white influence knew enough to hold "themselves aloof culturally" from those masses who were supposedly "born" to be "led" (232). There was another factor still energizing the elite's problematic relationship to Africa or substantial rather than superficial African identification: "With the establishment of the ['American'] Colonization Society, growing numbers of blacks avoided use of the term *African*, opting for a safer appellation, *colored*, because to continue to refer to oneself as African might encourage colonizationists to believe one wanted to be shipped *back* to Africa" (202). So, quiet as it's kept, what Carter G. Woodson's *The Mis-Education of the Negro* (1933) deftly dubs "pro-slavery deportationism" (99) played a crucial role in the perhaps surprisingly recent shift away from "African" in the linguistic practice of Black self-identification in the United States. Stuckey concludes "Identity and Ideology: The Names Controversy" by stating that the "American" in the term "Afro-American" seriously overstates its case; and that only "under threat, real or imagined" did most of our ancestors cease referring to themselves simply as "Africans" or "free Africans" in the late nineteenth or early twentieth century (1987, 274).

For *Slave Culture*'s tradition of resistance and rebellion, "Afro-American" would coexist with color designations such as "Black" and refer "people of African ancestry in the Americas to the land, history and culture of their forebears, while recognizing their presence as an unassimilated people" (243). These days, ironically, "African American" would seek to exclude or repress color designation such as "Black" and, by means of an ever problematic and now "post-Black" elite, place the African under erasure—like "Americans of African descent"—by referring people of African ancestry to U.S. settler nationalism for an agenda of neocolonial bourgeois assimilation in the twenty-first century of Western Christian time.

Toni Cade Bambara wrote to reverse a certain sail in "Deep Sight and Rescue Missions" (1996), long after criticizing—let alone condemning—assimilation's agenda was thinkable in white and "Black" elite-dominated public spheres. She changes language, too, with her neglected references to "Amero-Africans" (1996, 147, 178) and "Amero-Europeans" (155). No less neglected is her radical reconceptualization of "citizenship," or pseudo-citizenship, as "a bribe contract." In other words, "we'll grant you citizenship, and in return you drop your cultural baggage and become 'American,' meaning defend the status quo despite your collective and individual self interest" (153).

Regard, to recap, Cyril Briggs of the old African Blood Brotherhood and its militant "New Negro"-era publication, *The Crusader*. At the end of his life, he wrote what reads like mean a reiteration of *Malcolm X Speaks* in "American Neo-Colonialism" (1966–67), a four-part essay for *The Liberator* magazine. He urged us to resist the shackles of a "spurious patriotism" to a "white power structure" that has "historically violated" our people with no concern for "justice" at all (1966a, 15). It is to "many of our middle-class elements" that Briggs directs his critical scorn specifically, as they "tend to support" the "putrid racist 'American Way of Life'" at the beck and call of their rulers (16). He invokes the trials of Robert F. Williams—the radical activist and author of *Negroes with Guns* (1998) who was expelled from the

NAACP before his revolutionary trek to Cuba, China, and Tanzania—
to illustrate "how highly negro middle class elements rate loyalty to the
white power structure above the interests of the Afro-American masses"
(17). This treachery is that of "Black Anglo-Saxonism" (17). Briggs is compelled to craft a genealogy of Europe's so-called social contract, nullified
over and again in the case of "negro patriots." He traces "modern nation-
state patriotism" to "Feudal Age loyalties" after "the fall of Roman Empire."
The development of "nation-state loyalty" is rooted in a situation where
standing outside any "social contract" was the European "serf," whose situation or standing was itself far superior to the "American slave's" in North or
South or Central America and the Caribbean (1966b, 14–15). Such patriotism without the pretense of "justice" bears a pathetic resemblance to "the
loyalty of a hound dog to his master" (1966c, 14). It is the white national
middle classes of Europe, Briggs continues, who would design world wars
of destruction and colonial conquest and perversely "superimpose imperial patriotism upon local patriotism" (1966b, 16). They also trained and
train "those middle-class elements who presume to speak for the Afro-
Americans" while acting like "the Handkerchief Heads of American Slavery." Back in the era of the New Negro Movement, or the so-called Harlem
Renaissance before that movement's expropriation by white and "negro"
middle-class forces of Americanism, Briggs wrote a requiem for the October 1919 issue of *The Crusader*: "The Old Negro and his futile methods
must go. After . . . years of him and his methods the Race still suffers from
lynching, disenfranchisement, Jim Crowism, segregation and a hundred
other ills. His abject crawling and pleading have availed the Cause nothing.
He has sold his life and his people for vapid promises tinged with traitor
gold. His race is done. Let him go. . . . For the Old Leader, *Requiescat in
Pace!*" (quoted in Vincent 1973, 64). What has gone for the old "negro" has
been resurrected today—under "American Neo-Colonialism"—for the
"post-Black" and anti-Black "African American," those new-old "negroes,"
who "in their compulsive desire to be accepted by [the white ruling] class
and permitted a crummy share of its loot," have "time and again given pri-
ority to its interests above the interests of the Afro-American" of the Pan-
African Black masses worldwide (Briggs 1967, 15).[5]

CONCLUSION

Everything that they present as "American" [at home and abroad]—
music, speech, gesture, style—is immediately identifiable, certainly
to a Black spectator, as Black.

—Toni Cade Bambara, "Deep Sight and Rescue Missions" (1993)

A people without a collective consciousness that transcends national
boundaries—freaks, Afro-Amerikkkans, Negroes, even Amerik-
kkans, without the sense of a larger community than their own
group—can have no effect on history. Ultimately they will simply
be eliminated from the scene."

—George L. Jackson, *Blood in My Eye* (1972)

It should surprise no one that the rhetorical phenom of "post-Blackness"
does not coincide with or even begin to imagine a "post-whiteness," a
"post-Americanism," a "post-Occidentalism," or a "post-bourgeois" politics. It could not and would not locally or globally in its regimatic provin-
cialism. The bad performance-phantasm of "post-Blackness" reflects no
reality but a desire for a reality where both desire and reality are upheld by
a white American politics of Occidentalism or Western bourgeois modes
of cultural, political, economic, and psychological domination on planet
Earth. Both academic and kitsch "theorists" of post-Blackness continue to
"get down in" such whiteness. It's their slavery and "post-slavery" or neo-
slavery tradition. They strain to "jump on up and down in it." They don't
want to "let it go." They act as if only whiteness can really feed them and
please them and endow them with knowledge in a world where Blackness
is posited as limitation and liability—at best.

By contrast, James Baldwin said to whiteness, "as long as you're going
to be white, I'm going to be Black," in *James Baldwin: The Price of the
Ticket* (1989). He is one of a long line of sirens placed on mute by new-
millennial "post-racial" and "post-Black" illusionists. But Blackness cannot
be reduced to a mere side effect of whiteness. The Blackness of Blackness
came to transvaluate the blackness of whiteness and to "anthropologize"
whiteness for the sake of Blackness itself in the struggle for Blackness and
an Africa unsullied by the whiteness of slavery, colonialism, segregation

or apartheid, and empire. Even Wole Soyinka, "tigritude's" wounded critic of some schools of Negritude, could remind us that cosmological formulations of B/blackness predate the European invasion of continental Africa:

> The Yoruba peoples, whose culture is not conditioned by any historic phenomena like malformations of the manifest racism of the European world, refer to themselves (and to others with whom they experience an affinity of being, including their descendants wherever they are) as *enia dudu*, the black peoples. Other languages in African have similar expressions. For the Ga it is *meedidzii*, for the Hausa, *baiki mutane*.... Our societies have recognized this particularist reality of our ethnic consciousness, one that has not, in our history, bred racism.   (1989, 16)

This is one more reason why Blackness and African identification go hand in hand in resistance to "white supremacy," past and present and future. And this is why Rahsaan Roland Kirk would immerse himself in the black notes of the piano to rearticulate Blackness as a cosmological site of articulation and self-determination as opposed to a degraded and disposable object locked in the cosmological articulation of white racist domination.

Too few recall what Frantz Fanon wrote in *L'An V de la Révolution algérienne* (1959), or *Studies in a Dying Colonialism* (1965): "It is the white man who creates the negro. But it is the Negro who creates Negritude" (47). This *nègre* of Negritude was the "nigger" of Négro-African or "Black-African" history and culture. It is the Negro of Aimé Césaire's *Cahier d'un retour au mon pays natal* (1939), or *Notebook of a Return to My Native Land* (1956). It is not the negroism of *Uncle Tom's Cabin*, or "Topsy." It does not divorce Africa from Blackness to "post" Blackness via an "African Americanism" in which Africa signifies a European or European-American telos; a falling away from Africa, strictly, for anglophilia; a running away not from slavery itself but from antislavery and Pan-Africanism instead. As "post-Blackness" embeds itself anew in "Obamamania," moreover, quite predictably—in the midst of U.S imperial war crimes, drones, "disaster capitalism," a pandemic of Black bodies murdered by police officers with impunity "every 28 hours,"[6] and international "prison indus-trial complexes," etc.—another quotation from Fanon comes to mind from *Pour la révolution africaine* (1964) or *Toward the African Revolution*: "It has become truly intolerable and unacceptable for Africans to hold a post in the government that dominates them. Every colonized person who today accepts a governmental post must know clearly that he will sooner or later be called up to sponsor a police of repression, of massacres, of collective murders in one of the regions of 'the . . . Empire'" (1988, 118). That this manic madness is pretext and cause for celebration for the "Afri-can Americanism" of a "post-Black" elite speaks volumes and volumes.

Finally, reflecting on the social movements of the 1960s and 1970s, Sylvia Wynter explains "why Black Studies could not be allowed to exist as Black Studies," in lieu of "Ethnic Studies," or a shadow imitation of "Ethno-Class [i.e., Western bourgeois] Man" (2006, 122). Black Studies in its "original thrust" was a brief and partial emancipation from "our pres-ent order of truth and aesthetics" and "our present mainstream aesthetics and order of knowledge" (153). Soon enough, the various Black Power–age movements for Black Arts and Black Aesthetics as well as Black Stud-ies are "reterritorialized." They are "wiped out" or "sanitized" of their her-esies and reincorporated back into "the Liberal-universalist mainstream" or "the ostensible universalism of Euro-American-centered scholarship" (114, 163). Black Studies is defused and reformed on "multiculturalist terms" so as "to re-verify the very thesis of Liberalism universalism against which the challenges of [it] had been directed in the first place" (109). It was subverted to become simply another "sub-version" of something else in the West; another subordinate version of the order of knowledge once confronted and renounced: "no longer a Black utopian alternative mode of thought but, rather, an Ethnic sub-text of the Ideologies of *Man*'s Word—that is, as *African-American* Studies" (158).

It is a U.S. nationalist rendering of the name "African American," after all, that facilitates a wide range of reactionary politics that are not "post-Black" but anti-Black. Half a century ago, Richard Moore asked, "Who has not noticed how often some . . . citizens of European origin hesitate to use the term 'colored,' when they wish to be friendly and do not wish to insult or give offense?" (1992, 71). Who could not notice how that "color" has morphed into Black, more insultingly, offensively, and preposterously? For the once "negro" and now "African American" elite as well, Blackness is trouble itself. It is ontologically "out of line." It must be repressed or "brought in line" by the elite agenda of class assimilation or "African Americanism." And this line-towing is made synonymous with "History" (or "evolution") itself. Alioune Diop of *Présence Africaine* once redefined "History with a capital 'H'" as "a one-sided interpretation of the world emanating from the West alone" (1956, 9). Besides Negrophobia, there seems to be a kind of "Blackophobia" upon us. The white imperial Americanism of the elite reduces the "African" in a formerly Pan-African conception of "African Americans" to a receding occasion for melting pot Europeanization in Anglo–North America, whereas African diasporic Blackness remains identified at the level of the Black masses with Black militancy and Black movements as well as Black Africa at large, globally and internationally. If we don't trouble the waters of this twisted conception, it'll just be more trouble for those of us who are already represented as trouble incarnate. If we do not work for a people with "a collective consciousness that transcends national boundaries"—toward a "post-whiteness," "post-Americanism," and a "post-bourgeois" politics, by whatever name—while refusing to collude in "African Americanism," we risk zombification and, to quote George L. Jackson, effective "elimination from the scene" (1994, 185).

NOTES

1. Significantly, this song-performance defies simple transcription.
2. I ran into this article quite casually a long time ago and did not retain or recall the precise reference.
3. For more on Moore and this formulation, see Turner and Turner (1992).
4. Morejón's lecture is cited by Carole Boyce Davies in Davies (1994, 7).
5. The genealogical or etymological work of this preceding section actually began as a conference presentation and prospective contribution to a book collection that became Jean M. Rahier and Percy C. Hintzen's *Problematiz-*

ing Blackness: Self-Ethnography by Black Immigrants to the United States (New York: Routledge, 2003). Sound familiar? But it could find no conceptual or political-intellectual place in the publication, for which it could only be a "counter-troubling" force in the context of basically problematic conceptualizations like "ethnography," "(Black) immigrants" and "the United States."

6. See the Malcolm X Grassroots Movement (MXGM) report: http://mxgm .org/we-charge-genocide-again-new-curriculum-on-every-28-hours-report/

REFERENCES

Bambara, Toni Cade. 1996. *Deep Sightings and Rescue Missions: Fiction, Essays, and Conversations*. New York: Pantheon.

Briggs, Cyril V. 1966a. "America Neo-Colonialism: First of Four Articles." *Liberator*, October, 14–17.

——. 1966b. "America Neo-Colonialism: Second of Four Articles." *Liberator*, November, 14–16.

——. 1966c. "America Neo-Colonialism: Third of Four Articles." *Liberator*, December, 14–15.

——. 1967. "America Neo-Colonialism: Fourth of Four Articles." *Liberator*, January, 15–17.

Brooks, Gwendolyn. 2003. *Conversations with Gwendolyn Brooks*. Ed. Gloria Wade-Gayles. Jackson: University Press of Mississippi.

Davies, Carole Boyce. *Migrations of the Subject: Black Women, Writing and Identity*. New York: Routledge, 1994.

Diop, Alioune. 1956. "Opening Address to the First International Congress of Negro Writers and Artists." *Presence Africaine* 8, no. 10 (June–November): 9–18.

Fanon, Frantz. 1965. *Studies in a Dying Colonialism*. New York: Grove Press.

——. 1988. *Toward the African Revolution*. New York: Grove Press.

Forbes, Jack D. 1988. *Black Africans and Native Americans: Color, Race, and Caste in the Evolution of Red-Black Peoples*. New York: Blackwell.

Jackson, George. 1994. *Blood in My Eye*. Reprint, New York: Random House. First published 1972.

James Baldwin: The Price of the Ticket. 1989. Dir. Karen Thorsen. San Francisco: California Newsreel.

Kirk, Rahsaan Roland. 1971. *Blacknuss*. Atlantic Records.

Moore, Richard B. 1992. *The Name "Negro"—Its Origin and Evil Use*. Reprint, Baltimore: Black Classic Press. First published 1960.

Moynihan, Daniel P., and Nathan Glazer. 1965. *The Negro Family: The Case for National Action*. Washington, DC: U.S. Department of Labor.

Nascimento, Abdias do. 1995. "The African Experience in Brazil." In *African Presence in the Americas*, eds. Carlos Moore, Tanya R. Sanders, and Shawna Moore, 97–117. Trenton, NJ: Africa New World Press.

Rodney, Walter. (1969) 1996. *The Groundings with My Brothers*. London: Bogle-L'Ouverture Publications. Reprint, Chicago: Research Associates School Time Publications.

Smitherman, Geneva. 1994. *Black Talk: Words and Phrases from the Hood to the Amen Corner*. Boston: Houghton Mifflin.

——. 2000. *Talkin That Talk: Language, Culture, and Education in African America*. London: Routledge.

Soyinka, Wole. 1989. "The African World and the Ethnocultural Debate." In *African Culture: The Rhythms of Unity*, eds. Molefi Kete Asante and Kariamu Welsh Asante, 13–38. Trenton, NJ: African World Press.

Stuckey, Sterling. 1987. *Slave Culture: Nationalist Theory and the Foundations of Black America*. Oxford: Oxford University Press.

Turner, W. Burghardt, and Joyce Moore Turner, eds. *Richard B. Moore, Caribbean Militant in Harlem: Collected Writings 1920–1972*. Bloomington: Indiana University Press, 1992.

Vincent, Theodore G., ed. 1973. *Voices of a Black Nation: Political Journalism in the Harlem Renaissance*. Trenton, NJ: African World Press.

Williams, Robert L. 1975. *Ebonics: The True Language of Black Folks*. St. Louis: Institute of Black Studies.

Woodson, Carter G. 1993. *The Mis-Education of the Negro*. Trenton, NJ: Africa New World Press.

Wynter, Sylvia. 2006. "On How We Mistook the Map for the Territory and Re-Imprisoned Ourselves in Our Unbearable Wrongness of Being, of *Désêtre*: Black Studies Toward the Human Project." In *Not Only the Master's Tools: African-American Studies in Theory and Practice*, eds. Lewis R. Gordon and Jane Anna Gordon, 107–69. Boulder, CO: Paradigm.

X, Malcolm. 1990a. *Malcolm X Speaks: Selected Speeches and Statements*. New York: Grove Weidenfield.

——. 1990b. "Some Reflections on 'Negro History Week' and the Role of Black People in History." *Malcolm X: The Man and His Times*. Ed. John Henrik Clarke, 321–32. Trenton, NJ: Africa New World Press.

——. 1992. *February 1965: The Final Speeches*. New York: Pathfinder Press.

4

Fear of a Performative Planet

Troubling the Concept of "Post-Blackness"

RONE SHAVERS

WHAT IS "BLACKNESS"?

Touré's *Who's Afraid of Post-Blackness?* argues that racism is very much alive today and that African Americans are still subjected to racist acts and activities, but such an issue pales in comparison to his claim that Black people need to stop performing race and simply *be* who or whatever they choose to be. On its face such a noble premise is harmless, yet for reasons I will attempt to make altogether clear in the few brief pages that I have, I will show that his call to transcend racial performativity is somewhat misguided. Ultimately, his calls for the abandonment of performing Blackness do little to combat racism and in fact, in some ways, unconsciously promote it through the negation of acts of racial solidarity and cultural specificity.

That said, Touré is nonetheless absolutely correct in identifying white supremacist thinking (and, by extension, both white privilege and white guilt) as one of the main obstacles to racial equality, and he goes to great pains to explain how and why white supremacy impedes true racial equality. For that reason he should be commended. However, where my opinion differs from his is that acting or defining oneself as "post-Black" does nothing to actually undermine the systems that engender white supremacy. In fact, it does quite the opposite, as it tacitly asserts that there *are* specific ways to be Black—a belief that is fundamental to racialist and supremacist and essentialist thinking of any sort. Thus, Touré's representation of post-Blackness represents an interesting bit of interesting circular logic and magical thinking: If, as Touré posits when quoting Henry Louis Gates Jr., "there are 40 million ways to be Black" (5), then why insist that in order for Blacks to rise, we must abandon every single one of those 40 million ways of being? Furthermore, why write a book insisting that since there is no longer any real or true notion of Blackness, what Blacks therefore need to do is abandon Blackness altogether?

There is actually a very old and damaging conflation of terms here. Despite his claims to the contrary, Touré conflates "Black" (a racial identity) with "Blackness" (a specific set of cultural and social tropes that mark and define an ethnic or racial identity). What I point out here is that "Black" is a racial marker. It implies the presence of a significant amount of melanin in one's skin, to name but the most obvious physical example, and is a biological categorization and solely a biological one. That said, "Blackness" is something totally different. It implies—although it often relies upon physical markers—a shared set of historical, social, and cultural mores. As a concept, then, Blackness is a sociocultural marker indicating that one acts in culturally specific ways. And these acts, these performances of Blackness, are thus the ways in which one reaffirms one's ethnicity to others. In other words, what Blackness is, is a socially constructed category, an *affect*, and like most affects, one must perform it to a viewer or interlocutor in order to confirm one's racial or ethnic affiliation.[1]

For Touré, this having to perform one's ethnicity is a source of great angst because to sky dive or scuba dive is somehow not considered sufficiently "Black"—that is to say, it conveys none of the racial solidarity that performing acts of Blackness usually hold and therefore represents a stifling limitation for what Black people can achieve. Thus, the idea that Touré seeks to deconstruct in his work is the belief that in order to be "authentically" Black, one must first subscribe to and affect preconceived notions of Blackness. Touré is not the first to observe this dilemma, however, as the dichotomy between performing a Black (or otherwise race-based) identity and what it means to be Black (or for that matter, what it means to belong to any specific race or ethnicity) has been explored by many scholars of late and has even spawned its own academic discipline: performance studies.[2] But whereas most performance studies scholars merely highlight the tension between having to affect or perform a generally accepted marker of cultural identity and what having a racial identity actually means, Touré goes one step beyond and attempts to present a solution he believes will alleviate the tensions between racial categorization, racial performance, and race relations once and for all.

That solution is post-Blackness, and in his estimation, post-Blackness frees Black individuals from the burden of performing race and grants them leeway to sidestep and outright ignore the historical, political, and material conundrums present when one discusses what it means to be Black in contemporary society. In short, post-Blackness does away with racial anxieties and questions of racial authenticity because post-Blackness posits that any act a Black person does is automatically (or should be) an act of Blackness simply because a Black person does it. If only there were so simple a solution. I argue that post-Blackness negates performances of Blackness altogether because it substitutes a racial categorization (Black) for a sociocultural one (Blackness), and by doing so evacuates both terms of their unique history, purpose, and meaning.

FEAR OF A PERFORMATIVE PLANET

The performance of Black identity is a generally agreed-upon premise, but generally agreed-upon by *whom*? I'm afraid that this is where Touré misses the mark, for while Blackness and signs of Blackness are, yes, often sanctioned and accepted by those within Black culture, a large number of historians, literary critics, and scholars of all stripes will be the first to mention that many of these performative markers of Blackness did not originate within the culture and instead were imposed upon it. To state things another way, the oversexed Negro, the hyperviolent criminal, the loyal and devoted friend willing to commit a senseless act of self-sacrifice, the nearly magical sidekick with an unblemished sense of ethics who allows a white protagonist to realize his or her self-worth—these were and are all aspects of Black identity that were imposed upon the African American community during the era of Reconstruction; thus, what Touré fails to realize, and what recent research suggests, is that the contemporary performance of a racial identity is often committed with a definite amount of campy self-awareness, with more than a little tongue in cheek. Simply put, many of the performative aspects of Blackness are not to be taken literally because Blacks are and have always been aware of the limitations of these social performances and thus enact them only for self-preservation, to mask, or to achieve some other, material gain.

Racial performances of Blackness are another aspect of what scholar Henry Louis Gates Jr.—he of the "40 million ways" fame—would refer to as "signifying." That is, racial performances both mask and reveal at the same time and present two very different messages, depending on the person receiving them. Interracially (or better still, interculturally), performing Blackness makes no attempt to disrupt an interlocutor's deeply held, socially constructed beliefs. In that respect, the performance denotes instead of connotes because, historically (and in certain contexts even today, such as when dealing with overly aggressive police), not denoting an "acceptable" Blackness—that is, not conforming to a socially prescribed role—would likely get one jailed, killed, or subjected to some form of malicious act. Intraracially (or intraculturally), performing Blackness serves as a form of jest, an ironic way of enacting a role that its actors can drop as soon as it suits them. The performance connotes instead of denotes because the racial performance relies upon an already-agreed-upon ironic stance. The role being played is one that is already known to the parties involved, and one plays it to point out the role's socially prescribed limitations and, by doing so, to make light of it. What Touré has failed to see or understand, then, what he has accidentally done, is to take verbal statements that an action isn't Black, or accusations of "you ain't Black" (96), far, far too literally. He could not properly decode the performative codes of Blackness and has mistaken connotation for denotation, confusing signifyin' for an actual sign, and the result is his view that we should all move beyond racially performative codes altogether.

If solely for that reason, I'd like to return to the question I asked a very packed paragraph ago: Culturally sanctioned by *whom*? That is to say that if the roots of racial oppression lie in white supremacist thought, then the abandonment of "performing race" does little if next to nothing to alter or impact white supremacist ideology, since rather than untangle the skein of Black performative codes, the very idea of "post-Black" reinforces them. For one thing, the "post-" implies that there was once or is a stabilizing essence of Blackness, something that can be clearly defined and qualified, and thus we have to move past it in order to progress. Little could be further from the truth. Historically, Black identity has been defined in opposition to white identity. And, alas, the inclusion of a "post-," especially in this delicate, tenuous moment in race relations, when a significant amount of people are finally beginning to acknowledge that race may very well just be solely skin deep, undermines the biological concept of race (and—if you must be put at ease—again, I mean just the presence of melanin and ascribe nothing more to it than that) because it leaves all manner of racist, racial, and racialist assumptions intact. It simultaneously insists that there is an essentializing aspect to Black racial identity that can be culled from the ether but conveniently discarded at any moment's fanciful whim.

All that is to say that although Touré's book is subtitled "What It Means to Be Black Now," it contains a great omission. That is, its focus is on the few luminaries who, in his opinion, have managed to transcend a common or stereotypically Black identity but whose claim or adherence to Blackness still remains unquestionable. However, it's easy to call oneself post-Black when one earns a six-figure salary or has a position of prominence in one's respective field. While Touré interviews exactly 105 successful artists, scholars, and public intellectuals in his book, it is nonetheless safe to say that his sample size is too small. A true estimation of what it means, or would mean, to be post-Black would have to include laypersons, the everyday individuals who constitute the majority of the Black community, because they more than others would be able to provide necessary insight into the *everyday* realities of race as it is lived now—especially since, unlike their successful counterparts, anonymous Blacks are in many ways as much trapped by race as they are aware of it. That is, it's not enough to gather household names, individuals who command respect because they are recognized as unique elites; for a full assessment of his concept, it is necessary that, when arguing what a community needs, one include more than a community's most elite members.

Additionally, Touré's work ignores the many contemporary movements that, rather than attempting to reject or transcend a race-based identity through the negation of racial performance as a socially relevant act, instead absorb and accept the realities of race—and, on occasion, acknowledge and even highlight the ironies and contradictions of racial performances—as much as they seek to present new methods of affecting and illustrating Blackness in the twenty-first century. One need only look at several of these burgeoning contemporary movements to get a better example of my point. The rise and popularity of Afro-Futurism, Afro-Punk, and the social prominence of the "Black geek," to name just a few new phenomena, may seem as if they are perfect examples of a post-Black aesthetic, but in truth they're quite the opposite.[3] In some respects, the "post-Black" fantasy that Touré envisions—one in which race and racial matters take equal credence with other aesthetic, social, and material concerns, without one's racial authenticity ever being called into doubt—is already here; it's just that no one has had to abolish, diminish, or subvert their racial identity in order to achieve it.

THE FUTURE OF BLACKNESS IS PRESENT

For simplicity's sake, one need only focus on the Afro-Futurism movement. A common and generally agreed-upon definition of Afro-Futurism is that it's a literary, visual, and cultural movement that includes elements of magic realism, non-Occidental (meaning not white or Western) religions, and speculative fiction to not only address the present-day issues of Black people but also to revise and critique the highly racist and racialized statements of the past. In other words, Afro-Futurism is Black interest(s) in science fiction, science-fiction culture, and its tropes, writ large. Its main concern isn't so much in future and fantastic societies but rather in using fantastic elements as a way to address contemporary problems without seeming overly polemical or didactic. To describe the movement in terms of its literary output, one need only think of some of its most famous practitioners and forebears, such as Samuel Delany, Octavia Butler, and Ishmael Reed. In their novels, each author devotes special attention to the variegated modalities of identity, such as—and most important, for the purposes of my argument—race, gender, and sexuality.[4] These authors also show how each of these modalities affects the other in order to show how identity is a multifaceted thing, where no one aspect is dominant but all equally important within the context of race and racial performativity. Such a view runs counter to Touré's in that it highlights how Blackness (and race in general) isn't something to police, decry, or merely move beyond because to do such a thing, again, leaves the racialist system of white supremacist thought in place, for white supremacist thinking is the historical default position of many of our supposedly race-neutral environments.

Afro-Futurism as a movement emphasizes race in science fiction because for too long future and fantastic societies are portrayed as ones in which race does not matter; problems between the races become magically superseded or elided due to other larger social, cultural, or technological concerns. There are notable exceptions—Ray Bradbury and Isaac Asimov spring immediately to mind—but it is as if authors of the genre treat the topic of American race relations as something ephemeral. Yet Afro-Futurists, by including and paying attention to racial difference in their work, illustrate that, yes, race does matter. The inclusion of non-Occidental religions, histories, cultures, and concerns, for example, is deliberate, underscoring the fact that even supposedly race-neutral societies tacitly acknowledge the supremacy and, ultimately, the alleged "rightness" (and here's where the system, the ideology of white supremacist thinking comes into play) of Occidental thought, history, and technological innovation—one need only glance at science fiction's lack of cultural and ethnic specificity to see my point. In many contemporary sci-fi novels, race and ethnicity are reduced to a few superficial, skin-deep sociocultural aspects. Blacks are the same as whites, in that they are completely Westernized and exhibit almost no Black or African-influenced names, beliefs, or traditions, and specific Asian cultures, with their own individual rivalries and unique practices, become "flattened" into a homogeneous, pan-Asian mess. Therefore Afro-Futurists highlight how race is an issue because whiteness (read, white culture) is always assumed to be the default position, and anything that strays from this very policed boundary, or, to state things in a more sophisticated way, any text that does not reinforce Western philosophy and culture as its dominant and correct ideological position must therefore be seen or placed in the realm of "other" (read, "alien"), somehow discursive and counter to the norm.

In brief then, race matters, because Afro-Futurists highlight the ways in which race *does* matter, how it differentiates and collectivizes. To illustrate how "white" quickly comes to represent "native," they show how mere mentions of race carry unconscious cultural messages. And anything, anyone, or any culture outside of such a nebulous racial category gets shunted into other(worldly) "alien" territory.

So because attention is given to race in these works—many times pointedly so, to label or define these works as "post-Black" would be a misconception. On the contrary, the attention given to racial identity and the problems that arise out of racialist thinking is precisely what makes Afro-Futurist works such *decidedly* Black texts. The attention they devote to race—how it's lived and perceived now as a way to portray how Black identity can be maintained and strengthened in the future—is what makes Afro-Futurist work and Afro-Futurist texts so exciting to study. The past fifteen years have seen an explosion of new, young science-fiction authors of color, and, equally as important, a new generation of scholars of color has emerged to place these lively authors' work in an important critical and theoretical context so that what could easily be dismissed as marginal becomes major when viewed through the lens of race, aesthetics, and academic cultural studies debates.

BACK TO BLACKNESS

To paraphrase noted author and critic Samuel R. Delany, "Racism is a system," and that is precisely what post-Blackness fails to take into account. Racism is a system, meaning that it is an all-encompassing way of looking and categorizing the world. Simply put, racism is an ideology, and post-Blackness cannot stop and will not abate racism in any way.[5] In some respects, it will only serve to reify it because. despite whatever benefits may arise from a sloughing off of prescribed modes of acting (i.e., racial performances), the actor of this racial performance (or lack thereof) will still be identified as racially Black and therefore subject to an interlocutor's racist worldview. That is to say, identifying as post-Black and discarding all the affects of Blackness will not stop Blacks from being racially profiled, disenfranchised at the voting booth, followed home and shot for walking alone in a gated community while wearing a hoodie, or suffering histrionic denials of their faith and national citizenship because they happen to be president of the United States. It matters not whether one subscribes to a pre-, post-, or ür-Black idea of Blackness; the fact that one possesses the biological markers for Black will engender racist assumptions, however casual, naïve, or downright hostile. Delany identifies this quite succinctly when he describes racism as a systematic way of viewing the world.

Furthermore, Blackness and the performance of Black identity has always been contested; by way of example, I only need mention that, were this not the case, we would not have had the highly contested struggle between Booker T. Washington and W. E. B. Du Bois over the direction that Black culture should take in the early twentieth century (or, for that matter, the battles between Du Bois and the younger "New Negroes" he initially helped to foster just decades later); neither would we have been witness to the competing and sometimes contradictory responses to overt racism embodied in the figures of Martin Luther King Jr. and Malcolm X; nor would we have seen something like the rise of Black Feminism and Womanism in the 1970s as a counter to the gender biases inherent within Black Nationalism, for all of these philosophies attempted to (re) define not only what Black identity and Blackness is and was but also what Blackness could be.

In the spirit of graciousness, then, I will say that Touré's book attempts to do the same, but what his premise lacks is a cogent understanding that the multiple definitions and redefinitions of Black identity—begun decades before, during, and immediately after the Civil Rights era—all worked. Touré can only arrive at a post-Black identity because he creates a straw man argument against a macho Black Nationalist identity, something that was being contested and dismantled even as it was being built. What we see in his book's pages, then, is an attempt to arrive at a viable definition of Black identity without a clear understanding of the *history* of Black identity as something, to quote the scholar Paul Gilroy, that has always been a "changing same": one wherein what it means to *be* Black remains constant while what it means to *act* Black differs according to one's audience.[6]

Finally, I'd like to return to the claim that lies at the heart of Touré's work, his explication of "what it means to be Black now." Genres such as Afro-Futurism and Afro-Punk and the explosion of people and characters who are sometimes called "Black geeks" into mainstream culture (think of Donald Glover's character of Troy in the television show *Community*, for example), help to highlight the fact that the performative aspects of Blackness are changing, adapting to new times and technological access. But whereas Touré sees these shifts as evidence that we are moving away from a monolithic definition of Blackness, I posit that there never was any such monolithic notion, for if there are indeed 40 million ways to be Black, then why insist and argue against the false belief that Blackness was once defined by a singular, inviolate definition—the Black Nationalist stance that Touré alludes to—when it has never been true?

Throughout history, the specific affectations necessary to prove one's Blackness have always changed, and they are changing yet again. Touré is correct in his belief that we are seeing categorical definitions of Blackness expand, but that's because the accomplishments of the Civil Rights era have ushered in an age of new Black tropes. Black people—or better still, the post–Civil Rights era of young Black people who are now coming into their own—continue to address the needs and concerns of African Americans in new and novel ways, using tools and methods that would have been both impossible and unthinkable under Jim Crow laws. Yet, because of the racialized ideology that engenders white supremacist thinking, coupled with the fact that forms of overt racism are no longer socially or scientifically acceptable, racism has changed from an overt to an often covert and unconscious form, and thus how one addresses racist and racialist thought has had to change too. While there are unfortunately too many racist acts still going on in America, the fact that Blacks are now interjecting racial and racialized concerns into supposedly race-neutral environments, all to highlight, as Delany so rightfully notes, how systems of racialized thinking work, helps illustrate the point that what it means to be Black now is what it means to address covert racism and the racialized ideology that supports it. It means, as the Afro-Futurism movement attests, that the struggle for equality still continues, but the field of battle has changed.

Thus, while Touré's heart may be in the right place, the solution he posits for highlighting and addressing racial inequality falls woefully short. Post-Blackness is akin to using conventional means to fight an asymmetrical war; it simply does not, cannot, and will not work because it leaves all the underlying structures of racialist ideology intact. A better approach, then, is to ground oneself in history, historical facts, and cultural evidence with a clear eye toward the past, present, and future. A better approach, then, may be to illustrate what being Black is all about by injecting aspects of Blackness and ethnicity into circles where it's conveniently ignored or least expected, like Afro-Futurists do, so that covert and inadvertently racist acts will be brought completely into light. And once that happens, when we ask, "What does it mean to be Black now?" it will again be necessary to respond with a wink and a nod, a sign and a signal, and a simultaneously connotative and denotative phrase because it is what it is, and it is as it always was, and that's part of the changing same.

NOTES

1. I use "affect" in a neutral, nonpejorative sense simply to convey that performing Blackness is a (self-)conscious action that can be taken positively or negatively, for reasons I will soon explain.

2. Several young scholars in the field who are doing intriguing work are E. Patrick Johnson, Kristie A. Ford, and Vershawn Ashanti Young.

3. In fact, they undermine the entire post-Black concept in their very names. In each instance, an emphasis is placed on racial identity; the word "Afro" or "Black" takes a dominant position in its description, to remind the interlocutor that their categorizations do indeed tackle racial concerns, as much as these concerns exist in a web of other specialized or secondary interests.

4. Although that is not to say that these authors are ideal in every respect. For example, gender is a fraught concept in Ishmael Reed, and the full ramifications of socioeconomic class as something that affects a person's relation to the world tends to be dismissed or diminished in Butler's work. Delany, unfortunately, is too infatuated with characters who exist on the margins of any given society to ever present anything that can be read as a manner of resisting or overcoming hegemony. Then again, in fairness, as a literary critic, I don't read novels for solutions to contemporary problems but only as a means to identify how authors address them and to see what they think those problems are.

5. Solely as an aside, Black Nationalism, or the belief that Blacks are somehow inherently superior to whites, is as much a racist ideology as white supremacy. To be fair, let's call racism for what it is.

6. I'd like to be totally clear on this point. I say "history" because so little attention has been paid to the texts, individuals, and events that Touré claims define how we arrived at and how we determine precisely what Blackness is, and instead we are treated to personal reflections, recollections, anecdotes, and quotes from various prominent figures cobbled together with little or no context.

5

E-Raced

#Touré, Twitter, and Trayvon

RICHÉ RICHARDSON

We're clearly not in a post-racial America. We're in a post–Trayvon Martin America.

—Rachel Noerdlinger[1]

In the wake of the stalking and tragic shooting death of the seventeen-year-old teen Trayvon Martin in Sanford, Florida, on February 26, 2012, widespread public outcry at the national level unfolded over the failure of police to arrest his assailant, George Zimmerman, a man who was eventually revealed by the media to be of both white and Latino ancestry. This tragic incident catalyzed demonstrations, vigils, and public dialogues across the nation and was widely discussed in the media in contexts from television to the Internet. In the ensuing weeks, it was shocking that the African American critic Touré joked about the incident on the Internet on the Twitter social network, remarking, "New slang! You're Zimmerman-ning Me = You're killing me."[2] Here the implication is that the surname of Zimmerman could stand in as a euphemism for the kind of vigilante shooting assault that Martin had experienced at Zimmerman's hands. This comment in the wake of the teen's death also seemed to make light of black mortality rates at a time when black deaths due to gun violence had reached epidemic proportions in cities such as Chicago. To be fair, it is important to acknowledge that Touré has made valuable and insightful critical social commentary on the case in the national media and also offered thoughtful commentary during the nationally televised trial of George Zimmerman in the summer of 2013. Even so, it is nevertheless important to reflect critically on the implications of Touré's early response to the case emphasizing humor, which seemed quite insensitive and inappropriate. I want to suggest that this infamous Twitter post about Trayvon Martin's shooting is centrally steeped in Touré's investments in the discourses of post-blackness.

In this essay an analysis of Touré's Twitter commentary is a useful lens for thinking about the racial discourse on the Trayvon Martin case and further understanding how social media impacted it. We can also draw on this scenario to ponder ways in which discourses of post-blackness (along with an emerging post-whiteness) have been confronted and reconsolidated yet also radically unsettled through the Trayvon Martin case. That Trayvon Martin's tragic death widely mobilized and unified black communities once it gained national attention in the media made it a site that challenged, threatened, and even radically unsettled the prevailing ideologies of the post-racial and post-blackness that have proliferated in the new millennium, particularly in the wake of the election of Barack Obama as the nation's first black president. Touré's initial humorous reaction that seemed to go decidedly against the grain of black thought, reflection, and reaction concerning Trayvon Martin might be interpreted as a willful application of some of the arguments that he makes in his book-length treatise titled *Who's Afraid of Post-Blackness: What It Means to Be Black Now* (2011). My training and investments in fields from literary studies to cultural studies has provided me with critical apparatuses and inclinations for thinking through, recognizing, and closely analyzing various kinds of texts, including something like a Twitter post, to meditate on their larger meanings and implications.

For the efforts to politicize the Zimmerman case and to relate it to race, reactionaries have tended to blame Rev. Al Sharpton, host of the MSNBC show *Politics Nation*, and attorney Benjamin Crump, from the Parks & Crump LLC firm based in Tallahassee, Florida, and retained by Martin's parents, Sybrina Fulton and Tracy Martin. Such narratives are far too reductive and obscure the political agency in black grassroots communities as well as their capacity to initiate and sustain activist movements. The fact that Zimmerman murdered Martin but was not being held accountable by law enforcement was intolerable and unacceptable to many, including numerous blacks in the United States and around the world. In the early years of the new millennium, Martin's murder and the failure to arrest the perpetrator hearkened back to infamous cases during the era of segregation, such as the 1955 case involving Chicago, Illinois, youth Emmett Till, who allegedly whistled at Carolyn Bryant. Till was brutally murdered by Bryant's husband, Roy, and his accomplice, J. W. Milam, in Money, Mississippi, and the two men were later vindicated for the murder by an all-white jury. Moreover, the failure of the police to arrest Zimmerman for what was widely perceived to be the stalking and murdering of a black teenage boy, who was still classifiable as a child, dramatized the expendability of the black body and its accessibility to violence in public spaces along with its lack of protection under the law, which was being rationalized on the basis of Florida's controversial Stand Your Ground Law, passed in 2005. The Zimmerman case profoundly resonated with black parents throughout the nation by exponentially heightening their concerns about the safety of their own children, particularly given the prominence of Martin's parents in the media in the weeks after their teen's murder and in the wake of several public pleas made in the media by Martin's tearful mother and father for Zimmerman's arrest. The Zimmerman case has garnered widespread concern because it has threatened to set a problematic precedent in authorizing and legally sanctioning vigilante strategies of profiling, policing, controlling, and annihilating the black body. It is unsettling because it has threatened to recast and revive anachronistic social customs that hearken back to the antebellum era, when black people needed passes to travel on the streets, when even freedom was a volatile status, and when "slave codes" regulated every aspect of behavior and public comportment, only to be replaced by "black codes" in the late nineteenth century, and eventually by Jim Crow laws that remained solidly entrenched at least until *Brown v. Board of Education* in 1954. This has been the kind of case that has made some people feel as if we are moving back in time, not forward. When we consider the state-sanctioned police violence against Amadou Diallo, Sean Bell, and Oscar Grant, the authorization of regular citizens such as Zimmerman to enact vigilante violence on the black body, as demonstrated in the cases of Trayvon Martin, Jordan Davis, and Darius Simmons, further sanctions and rationalizes violence against the black body and attests to the precariousness and expendability of black life. At the same time, it reinforces behavior that threatens Americans in general, along with democracy itself.

Yet the impulse to link Martin and Emmett Till becomes more complicated when we consider the arguments in Imani Perry's compelling 2011 study titled *More Beautiful and More Terrible: The Embrace and Transcendence of Racial Inequality in the United States*, which argues for a recognition and analysis of inequality as a practice in this nation and points out that "a mid-twentieth century framework for understanding race and racism handicaps our comprehension and action in the twenty-first century. Our experience of racial injustice has a derivative, but distinct, zeitgeist" (2). The critical frameworks that Perry provides in this study, including her work on persisting and exceptional forms of surveillance for blacks, are also valuable for analyzing why the relevance of race was denied by the defense during the trial, and for exploring reasons and rationales about why Zimmerman was so obsessed with following Martin around at the Retreat at Twin Lakes apartments in the first place, on the stormy night that he killed him.

In the infamous sound bite that he delivered about Martin on Twitter in the spring of 2012, Touré's failure to name him—notwithstanding the subjectivity that Touré accords Zimmerman, and Touré's juxtaposition of Martin and Zimmerman through a metaphorical mathematical equation that is inherently imbalanced—perversely anticipates and parallels the defense team's strategies of pathologizing, disembodying, and desubjectifying Martin throughout the Zimmerman trial in the summer of 2013, *State of Florida v. George Zimmerman* with Debra Nelson as the presiding judge. The trial denied Martin a sense of selfhood and unsettled and confused the very meaning of self-defense in the sense that the controversial legalized precept in Florida of "Stand Your Ground" and principles of self-defense implicitly seemed to be wholly divorced from Martin as entitlements and prerogatives yet were ascribed to Zimmerman. Martin's actions—whatever they may have been in the case that he had felt threatened after being accosted by Zimmerman and had made a preemptive effort to subdue his perceived attacker, an adult man and total stranger—did not seem to be legible, classifiable, or admissible as a form of self-defense or within the definition of "stand your ground." At bottom, in compromising the very notions of his personhood and humanity, the case frustrated notions of being and what it means to be a self, obscuring the reality that Martin was a self. In this sense, it constituted Martin prior to his death as a nonbeing, beckoning an existentialist framing that seems equally relevant to think its complicated racial politics. It recalls Ralph Ellison's model of invisibility and, even more specifically, invites us to recollect the famous opening scene in the 1952 novel *Invisible Man* under the street light involving the nameless protagonist who is willfully unseen by the white man that bumps into him. "Nothingness" seems to be the ascribed lot of the black masculine within this case's formulation.

The defense reduced this case to the issue of self-defense based on the tacit presumption that only Zimmerman had the right to self-defense that night, and that Martin had no rights at all. It made the principle of self-defense reducible to possessing and firing a weapon. The legitimacy of hand-to-hand combat did not seem to be a factor in defining this prerogative but simply situates Martin as an aggressor who had threatened and assaulted Zimmerman (i.e., "You're going to die tonight"). Indeed, the defense's argument that Martin, while unarmed, had used the sidewalk concrete as a weapon against Zimmerman, whose head Martin allegedly banged against the cement, as bizarre as the argument sounded to some trial viewers, fell within the limits of plausibility and was persuasive for some given the outcome in the jury room. For many, the defense's logic seemed absolutely absurd, considering Zimmerman's stalking of Martin, his initiation of the encounter with Martin in the first place, and his flagrant defiance of the 911 police dispatcher's orders not to follow the teen. If nothing else, the case seemed to be about race and racial profiling regardless of how vehemently the defense team—attorneys Mark O'Mara and Don West—denied the relevance of race. To be sure, blackness was the main factor that preconditioned and preordained the denial of Martin as a subject in this case, and that precluded a narrative of selfhood in relation to him. More to the point, blackness was the primary factor that led Zimmerman to profile Martin, to stalk him, and, in all likelihood, even to kill him.

Touré's perverse Tweet equally anticipates the ways in which the defense attempted to rationalize and defend Zimmerman's actions by disclosing information in the media about Martin's Twitter and Facebook social networking accounts in an effort to portray him as a teen who used drugs such as marijuana, who was obsessed with fighting, who had tattoos and wore the kinds of gold tooth fronts popular with gangsta rappers, who had stolen jewelry, and who was fascinated with guns. Such efforts to pathologize him attempted to counter, undermine, and invalidate the salient photographic images of Martin circulating in the media that depicted him as a friendly, athletic boy who had engaged in activities such as football, skiing, and horseback riding and who loved children. Moreover, the negative publicity aimed to vindicate his assailant by attempting to unsettle scripts that portrayed Martin as an innocent teen who had been racially profiled, stalked, and accosted by Zimmerman while walking back from 7-Eleven on the rainy Sunday evening to the apartment of his father's fiancée at the Retreat at Twin Lakes after purchasing Skittles and iced tea. Such narratives accorded with portrayals of black masculinity as pathological and criminal. It is quite significant that a major weapon in the effort of Zimmerman's defense to attempt to portray Martin as a violent teen was to subpoena his Twitter account as "evidence," an account that had been deleted after his death at the request of his family. While Martin's social networking accounts were ruled to be inadmissible as evidence within the trial proceedings, it is sobering that their content was insistently interpreted literally in the defense's effort to malign him in the media, and seemed to emerge as a subtext nevertheless. The surveillance of information from Martin's Facebook and Twitter social networking accounts, along with his cell phone text messages, was pivotal in the effort to pathologize and criminalize him and to vindicate Zimmerman in the court of public opinion, and to some extent it inflected the court proceedings during Zimmerman's trial for the murder. The extent to which Martin's posts may have been performative, imaginative, and illusory and grounded in aspects of black vernacularity was not at all a consideration as they were publicly disclosed and disseminated.

In light of public outcry in social media, Touré quickly recanted his tasteless comment. His mocking and trivializing of the voice of Martin in the content of the Twitter post also seemed improper when considering evidence collected by voice enhancement analysts on the part of the prosecution suggesting that Martin, not Zimmerman, had been the one recorded screaming on 911 tapes recorded by neighbors. Touré's abuse of social media in making this remark, which immediately went viral and began a "trending" pattern, also seems particularly ironic when considering that the Internet, from the circulation of news stories about the case on Facebook to the "Justice for Trayvon Martin" petition at Change. org that reached 2.2 million signatures and numerous blog commentaries, was playing the most influential role in enlightening the public about the Trayvon Martin case. The petition, which went viral, was identified at the fastest-growing one ever in the history of Change.org (Fox 2012). An average of one thousand people were signing the Change.org petition every minute, but the momentum of the petition measurably slowed precisely when reactionaries attempted to portray Martin as a "thug" who had initiated the attack on Zimmerman, going so far as to falsely identify a photo on Twitter of a tattooed black male youth wearing gold tooth fronts as Martin. Even as social media from Facebook to Twitter was a primary instrument in building literacies about this case, it also played a decisive role in the effort to criminalize Martin, which contradicts the ideals associated with these media that have heralded their potential to unsettle conventional race and gender inscriptions on the body, and also raises important issues related to First Amendment rights and privacy. Yet, perhaps more profoundly than any other measure in our time, the Trayvon Martin case has underscored the continuing legibility of racial inscriptions on black body in the United States.

In her groundbreaking study *Digital Diaspora: A Race for Cyberspace*, Anna Everett pinpoints 1995 (incidentally, the year that Martin was born) as the moment that the Internet shifted from being a realm dominated primarily by elite white men to one that engaged a critical mass of African Americans in its audience, a shift that she links to Yahoo's introduction of a specific search engine for "Afrocentric" content (10). However, Everett goes on to suggest that the politics related to the Internet have reinforced patterns of domination that parallel colonialism and imperialism and limited the potential for its true democratization. According to her, "No sooner had the centripetal forces of technological innovation produced newer, democratizing models of mass media diversity such as cable, satellite, Internet, wireless and other wide-ranging digital communications systems, than the older media concern set in motion a centrifugal counter-model of mass media monopolizing and reconsolidation, better known as convergence" (32–33). She goes on to point out that "many believed the centralized nature and transnational reach of these new media industries signaled a new age of participatory democracy and by extension progressive social equity and creative cultural rejuvenation. It seemed that finally new multimedia forms might function to serve and promote the diverse communicative needs of a changing, multicultural world" (33). At its inception, the vast realm of cyberspace was routinely idealized for its potential to move beyond the conventional emphasis on the corporeality of the body in human interactions to deemphasize variables of identity such as race, class, gender, nationality, and sexuality, in turn yielding a virtual global society more democratic and relatively free of oppressions such as racism, classism, sexism, homophobia, and xenophobia that define reality in the social world. It portended a time when the mind/body dimorphism enshrined within conventional Western philosophy, along with the tacit linkage of disembodiment and rationality to white masculine individualism as a prerogative and the concomitant association of hyperembodiment and subjection with blackness, would meet one of its best challenges since the Enlightenment, the period when this ideology was fully consolidated. Indeed, such early idealizations of the Internet were inflected by ideological notions of the post-racial and post-blackness, and arguably helped to set the stage in the late 1990s for their increasing popularization in the national context in the new millennium of the twenty-first century.

While Martin was born into a world in which the Internet had already been invented and at a time when its uses in the African American context had increased exponentially, it is significant that the Internet's perverse uses and abuses in the wake of his death in the effort to criminalize him have thrown into relief the Internet's conservation of conventional racial politics and hierarchies. Indeed, this tragedy revealed and dramatized the Internet's status as one of the most publically accessible forums for race-baiting and disseminating notions of antiblackness.

In some cases, Zimmerman's supporters and defenders Photoshopped photographs that attempted to criminalize Martin and portray him as a "thug." Notably, Zimmerman's younger brother, Robert Zimmerman Jr., used Twitter in an effort to pathologize Martin in the weeks before the trial when he juxtaposed a photograph of Martin flipping a middle finger with an image of De'Marquise Elkins, a black teen in Georgia accused of . shooting a toddler to death in the attempted robbery of the baby's mother on their morning walk. The caption read, "A picture speaks a thousand words" (Yates 2013). Eerily, the voyeuristic effort to excavate and expose Internet archives related to Martin in the wake of his death mirrored, extended, and paralleled Zimmerman's stalking and racial profiling of the teen on the fateful night of his death.

In an odd way, then, whether it was his intention or not, Touré's offensive post about Martin in the weeks after his murder heralded and anticipated this perverse economy of Internet slander on Twitter and various other social networking forums as well as in the blogosphere that attempted to caricature and ridicule Martin. It is noteworthy, too, that the phone records of Martin's friend, the African American teen Rachel Jeantel, the last person who talked to him on the phone, were similarly probed during the trial proceedings in the attempt to discredit Martin and label him as the aggressor with Zimmerman. In the process, she was pathologized on the basis of factors such as race, gender, class, and nationality. It is also significant that after her testimony at the trial, the Internet emerged as a salient medium in disseminating the reductive and unfair scripts that portrayed her as inarticulate and uneducated and that linked her to the "angry black woman" stereotype for her assertive and witty responses when being cross-examined by the defense attorney Don West while she gave her testimony and served as a witness for the prosecution team led by Bernie de la Rionda.

Touré's Twitter comments were not only entirely irreverent but also seemed to indicate a profound if unintentional affective indifference to the loss of Martin that might be expected of young white Southern racists haunting the contemporary blogosphere more so than a young black male intellectual, who should ideally know better.[3] Touré used his salient voice in the public sphere recklessly and insensitively by attempting to insert comic relief into an incident that was obviously in no way funny. Touré's infamous joke about the case on Twitter seemed to be animated by a discourse of colorblindness. When closely read, the logic of his comments, however brief, seems to suggest that a psychosis in Zimmerman implicitly mocked here, more than anything related to race, led to the death of Martin. The framing of the comment marginalizes and dismisses the racial subtexts of the case or, at best, implies them—and Zimmerman—to be a joke. Notably, Martin's violent death, because of factors such as his age and the Southern location, has also been widely compared to the murder and lynching of Emmett Till in Mississippi in 1955, a case that launched the modern Civil Rights Movement. Yet the central premise of Touré's critique that attempts to downplay the continuing relevance of civil rights legacies in contemporary black life to promote the premise of post-blackness also further explains how and why Touré may have been invested in lampooning the case rather than acknowledging its deeper racial implications in a context such as social media. This is another reason that analyzing this episode on Twitter is crucially important.

Twitter has increasingly emerged as a social networking forum for public figures, from celebrities and athletes to academic scholars, including public intellectuals, to circulate information and express ideas. The site's policy of limiting the posts of its members to 140 characters makes it an ideal forum for circulating shorter statements and sound bites to a large audience, depending on one's following. Moreover, Twitter's relatively open and public access gives its posts the potential to go viral immediately and to draw in a broad audience. To date, Touré has more than 130,000 followers on Twitter and has made nearly 100,000 Tweets, or posts, to the site. These conditions and his salience in the media as a correspondent on the MSNBC network made it almost a certainty that this controversial post about Martin would garner substantial public attention. Predictably, the backlash was immediate.

The brevity of his statement does not lessen its weight or minimize its problematic resonances, linguistic or otherwise. A closer reading and analysis of his Twitter statement will underscore some of its deeper implications. In invoking the word "Zimmermanning" as a verb, Touré links Zimmerman's surname to a chain of other action words such as "zinging," "zapping," and "zipping." The statement makes the fact and act of Martin's death look like a form of animated combat and annihilation that one might find in cartoons or comic books primarily geared toward the imaginary of adolescent boys. Its phrasing, too, portended the narratives that emerged during the trial of Martin as some kind of bionic boy who supposedly, by the defense's account, performed a litany of actions in record time, such as jumping out of bushes to accost Zimmerman, banging Zimmerman's head against the concrete sidewalk, attempting to take his weapon that had been concealed, and telling Zimmerman that "you got me" when Zimmerman fired the shot into his heart. If the trial rendered Martin as invisible, at these levels it was also steeped in a narrative of his hyperembodiment that accorded with essentialist scripts relating the black masculine body to athleticism, brutality, violence, and hypersexuality and that have remained embedded in the American consciousness since antebellum slavery.

Touré's gross simplification of Martin's death to the opportunity to coin a new slang word trivializes this horrific tragedy and seemingly fails to grasp the gravity or significance of the widespread public response to the loss of the teen or to demonstrate measurable concern. It is provocative at one level that Touré's Twitter post makes Zimmerman's name a synonym for the act of killing, which accords with the broad belief in the nation among some, including predominately in black communities, that he murdered Martin. Here, of course, Touré's intentions may have been well-meaning, and one of his aims could well have been to satirize the expendability of black life when lost at the hands of both white perpetrators such as Zimmerman and other blacks. If so, then it is regrettable that the message is entirely lost in translation.

On Twitter, Touré basically renders Martin's death in a sense that echoes the classic performative utterance and scripts it as a speech act. The invocation of discourses related to performativity and, by extension, performance is by no means accidental or even coincidental (Parker and Sedgwick 1995). That is to say, in light of Touré's emphasis on humor as a lens through which to discuss Martin's death, I want to suggest that it is useful to frame his statement about Martin on Twitter as a social media forum in relation to Touré's discussion of the freedom and autonomy that comedians such as Dave Chappelle have long claimed to address race in comedy as a medium without the obligation to focus on black uplift or to represent blackness in a reverential way (Touré 2011, 57). I do not want to get too speculative, but it is provocative to hypothesize that Touré's Twitter statement reflects to some degree an imagined if momentary, temporary, and provisional solidarity with artists, figures that he fundamentally links to an impetus for truth-telling and subversion in black communities in his treatise on post-blackness.[4]

In the third chapter of *Who's Afraid of Post-Blackness*, titled "The Rise and Fall of a Post-Black King," Touré discusses Dave Chappelle's acclaimed comedy show, "Chappelle's Show": "Artists must work with dangerous truths the way scientists who don protective gear work with dangerous chemicals. But my truth is not necessarily yours. To demand that artists conform to a sort of group-think is to reduce them to being propagandists and to put chains on the collective imagination" (58). It has been widely rumored that Chappelle famously walked away from a lucrative $50 million contract with the Comedy Central network because the network's executives mocked him and propagated stereotypes of black masculinity such as cross-dressing, which they encouraged him to do as a comedian. While Touré applauds Chappelle's edgy comedy routines and the comedian's seeming refusal to toe the conventional racial party lines, he argues that:

> Chappelle's comic mouth has written checks that his body is afraid to cash. And the abundance of whites at the party that is his edgy cultural production makes him wonder if he's gone from brilliant cultural commentator to a culture-damaging sellout. Telling abrasive jokes about your family when it's just family in the room can feel cathartic but telling them to a massive audience of outsiders is treason. The freedom of the post-Black era has scared him to death. So he picks up the gauntlet he threw down at the beginning of the show and he runs. (74)

I find it intriguing to draw on these passages from Touré's book because if we insert Touré into this scenario as an artist/actor and use it as a backdrop to reflect on his Twitter post, then we can plausibly read the post as an indicator of his willingness to go that extra mile that even a great artist like Chappelle fails to walk, in flouting racial prohibitions in black communities and daring to speak his mind and be a provocateur and dissident when it comes to racial matters. In other words, precisely because the collective responses to it suggest the notion of a cohesiveness in black communities that is so abhorrent, and even threatening, within post-blackness, the issues related to Trayvon Martin were actually an ideal and irresistible site for Touré to draw on to attempt to edify this platform.

Critical and theoretical dialogues in poststructuralism that emerged during the 1980s were pivotal in underscoring race as being a social construct rather than a biological fact. These debates unsettled racialist scientific epistemologies.[5] The title of this essay in part alludes to Diana Fuss's famous chapter in *Essentially Speaking*, "'Race' under Erasure: Poststructuralist Afro-American Literary Theory," that appeared during the height of this poststructuralist movement related to race in the 1980s (1989,

73–96). The title also registers the tacit post-racial ideals associated with the Internet, including features such as electronic mail or email, during its earliest years, along with the post-blackness epistemology that Touré's propagation has helped to take to viral proportions through forums such as Twitter in the contemporary era.

Touré's polemic on post-blackness obscures the critical enterprise of deconstructing race and the attendant debates associated with it that spanned fields from literature to philosophy (Appiah 1992; Outlaw 1996). His methodology of drawing on the personal alongside interviews of public figures in developing his platform on post-blackness and his outreach to a popular audience are fascinating when comparing the association of deconstructionist debates related to race with high theory and its primarily academic audience. Yet his arguments lack the energy, acumen, and depth of the earlier poststructuralist debates on race that animated African American literary theory and criticism. Touré's arguments that construct racial identification as an individual choice, preference, and prerogative fall short and seem empty, shortsighted, and banal to the extent that they are grounded in an ahistorical outlook that fails to consider the legalized forms of racial classification that emerged in the colonial era during slavery and that have been salient in shaping notions of American subjectivity, which has been largely premised on a purist narrative of whiteness and on maintaining systemic and hierarchical racial distinctions. Moreover, his arguments are also premised on a view of white subjectivity as deracialized and normative. His implication that race is primarily an obsession of black America in the contemporary era obscures this long history that has made and that continues to make the politics of race inescapable on the American landscape, as so many facets of the trial of George Zimmerman for the murder of Trayvon Martin threw into relief.[6] Legibility and identification as a black racial subject is not as simple as making an individual choice to be (or not to be) primarily associated with this designation, as his argument seems to suggest.

Since the publication of her first novel, *The Bluest Eye*, in 1970, Toni Morrison has consistently engaged the problem of race in the United States. From her 1983 short story "Recitatif" to her 1998 novel *Paradise*,

Morrison has demonstrated an investment in meditations about race and has engaged in experiments in her writing to deconstruct and unsettle prevailing ideologies and stereotypes related to it. I find her approaches of reading and reflecting on race to be more compelling, convincing, and plausible than the discourse on post-blackness precisely because she acknowledges the long history of race as problematic in the United States and also frames its impact in relation to a critique of the race and gender ideals that have been established within Western culture. Morrison consistently offers more compelling and grounded reflections on unsettling race and moving beyond it than we have witnessed on the current critical scene that has been invested in advancing the concept of post-blackness/post-racialism. Indeed, the critique related to race that Morrison offers in her signal work of literary criticism, *Playing in the Dark: Whiteness and the Literary Imagination*, underscores the inescapability of what she elaborates as the "Africanist" presence in canonical texts of American literature, whether or not they figure and embody black characters within their narrative economies (1992).

The Trayvon Martin case is further relevant for thinking discourses on race when weighing how Zimmerman was translated into a "white" man, even within black grassroots activist discourses, notwithstanding his Latino ancestry. The reactionary endorsements of Zimmerman have accorded him a symbolic white masculine status in spite of his complex ethnic background, and, ironically enough, they herald a "post-whiteness" for the future that has the potential to be as ideologically abusive and shortsighted as notions of post-blackness have been in the contemporary era. This whitened script of Zimmerman has profound implications for the nation's discourses on Latinos, immigration, racial profiling, and strategies of racial classification when considering the conventional pattern in the United States of absorbing previously ethnically marked and marginalized subjects (i.e., Irish, Italian, Jewish) and redefining them as white to exponentially expand the demography of this conventionally dominant category.

Touré's problematic scripting of Martin in the wake of the teen's murder ironically mirrored and recast the propagandistic strategies of representing Martin that were evident among reactionaries in the media. As the movement in support of Martin crystallized, Touré's comments portended the intensification of the barrage of narratives in the mainstream media that would increasingly elide the teen boy's subject position and accord legibility and rights in this respect primarily to George Zimmerman. Touré's engagement of the Trayvon Martin case in the infamous Twitter post that made a joke of the boy's death underscores the potential abuses and profound limitations of ideologies of post-blackness in the contemporary era. At the trial, it was sobering that both the defense team and prosecution seemed invested in repressing and denying the relevance of race to the trial, along with the role that it played in his murder. While these arguments likely reflected the impact of the ideology of colorblindness on the legal system in the United States during the post–civil rights era, they must also be recognized as an outgrowth of the rhetoric of postracial and post-blackness that has been popularized in recent years. Such evasive tactics obscured how much race mattered.

NOTES

1.   Noerdlinger made this statement on *The Melissa Harris-Perry Show* on August 11, 2013.

2.   This post by Touré can be accessed at the Twitter site through the following link: https://twitter.com/Toure/status/181766239255937025.

3.   But mentioning Martin would also be unlikely for some racial reactionaries in this day and time when considering Tara McPherson's compelling observation that young white men who identity as neo-Confederates on the Internet do not frame or reference blacks as part of their imagined community at all. See McPherson (2000, 117–32).

4.   Michael Eric Dyson's authorship of the preface to Touré's volume is intriguing when considering Dyson's rhetorical emphasis in media interviews on the importance of achieving a society that is "post-racism" rather than "post-racial."

5.   See, for example, Omi and Winant (1991), Fuss (1989), Gates (1992), Appiah (1996), and West (1993).

6.   It is ironic and yet not at all surprising that a voice such as Touré's has emerged as a pied piper of sorts related to notions of post-blackness in our time. His insistence that a new generation has emerged with new post–civil rights values reflects a clear "urban bias" within this discourse, which fails to

consider the continuing significance of civil rights legacies in light of factors beyond race, such as region, for example.

REFERENCES

Appiah, Anthony, ed. 1992. "The Uncompleted Argument: DuBois and the Illusion of Race." In *"Race," Writing and Difference*, ed. Henry Louis Gates Jr., 21–37. Chicago: University of Chicago Press.

——. 1996. *Identities*. Chicago: University of Chicago Press.

Everett, Anna. 2009. *Digital Diaspora: A Race for Cyberspace*. Albany: State University of New York Press.

Fox, Zoe. 2012. "Trayvon Martin Petition Is Fastest-Growing in Change.org History." Mashable, March 28. http://mashable.com/2012/03/28/trayvon-martin-petition-change-org/.

Fuss, Diana. 1989. *Essentially Speaking: Feminism, Nature, and Difference*. New York: Routledge.

Gates, Henry Louis, ed. 1992. *"Race," Writing, and Difference*. Chicago: University of Chicago Press.

McPherson, Tara. 2000. "I'll Take My Stand in Dixie-Net: White Guys, the South, and Cyberspace." In *Race in Cyberspace*, eds. Beth E. Kolko, Lisa Nakamura, and Gilbert B. Rodman, 117–32. New York: Routledge.

Morrison, Toni. 1992. *Playing in the Dark: Whiteness and the Literary Imagination*. Cambridge, MA: Harvard University Press.

Omi, Michael, and Charles Winant. 1991. *Racial Formation in the United States from the 1960s to the 1990s*. New York: Routledge.

Outlaw, Lucius. 1996. *On Race and Philosophy*. New York: Routledge.

Parker, Andrew, and Eve Kosofsky Sedgwick, eds. 1995. *Performativity and Performance*. New York: Routledge.

Perry, Imani. 2011. *More Beautiful and More Terrible: The Embrace and Transcendence of Racial Inequality in the United States*. New York: New York University Press.

Touré. 2011. *Who's Afraid of Post-Blackness? What It Means to Be Black Now*. New York: Free Press.

West, Cornel. 1993. *Race Matters*. Boston: Beacon Press.

Yates, Clinton. 2013. "Robert Zimmerman's Ugly, Dangerous Tweets." *Washington Post*, March 26. http://www.washingtonpost.com/blogs/therootdc/post/robert-zimmermans-ugly-dangerous-tweets/2013/03/26/3cd24baa-96 1c-11e2-894a-b984cbdff2e6_blog.html.

6

Post-Blackness
and All of the
Black Americas

HEATHER D. RUSSELL

On February 10, 2012, my home institution, Florida International University's African & African Diaspora Studies (AADS) was privileged to host Touré speaking on "Post-Blackness in Contemporary America," a talk drawn from his successful recently published book, *Who's Afraid of Post-Blackness: What It Means to Be Black Now* (2011). Touré's central thesis of his book and lecture—held in the heart of North Miami, the veritable hub of transnational black identities-in-motion—that there are "forty million ways to be black" seemed fitting for the audience, comprising African descended peoples from Haiti, Jamaica, Brazil, Puerto Rico, Trinidad, the United States, and other countries (ibid., 1). I was then working as the graduate program director for AADS, and the current program director

and I agreed that it would be an excellent experience for two of our graduate students to serve as respondents to Touré's presentation and book.
Jheanelle, who hails from Jamaica and is studying the phenomenon of
return migration to the island, especially logistical and psychological barriers thwarting smooth reintegration of Jamaican professionals who have
studied abroad, was one of the chosen participants. Framing her intervention around the diversity of black populations within the United States,
Jheanelle queried Touré in terms of how his thesis would play out among
Afro-Caribbean populations here, and the degree to which their ideas of
"authentic blackness" might signify differently. She further pressed him
to consider how such an elaboration might relevantly and interestingly
complicate his central hypothesis regarding post-black performativity.

Touré's response, ostensibly, was to say that he had generally interviewed African Americans, dismissively (and wrongly) adding that Caribbean people of African descent weren't necessarily "down with the Black
thing" in the same way because they lack cultural understanding about
and interest in the black experience in America. Seated beside me and
just as irritated by his comments was another scholar of Afro-Caribbean
descent; we are both fortunate to have been trained at Berkeley and Rutgers by scholars standing at the vanguard of African American studies,
and whose scholarly commitment and concerns we take very seriously and
carry forward in our courses on African American literature, the Harlem
Renaissance, black citizenships, and narratives of enslavement and resistance. In other words, our research, teaching, and service agendas conceive African American and Caribbean history/culture/issues together as
part of an overall commitment to African diaspora studies. Additionally,
Touré's response simplified the complexities of the very history to which
he referred. African Americans and Afro-Caribbeans form an integral
part of and not so easily delinked involvement in that history, whether we
are talking about the seventeenth-century settlement of South Carolina
by Barbadian planters and the enslaved Africans they transported (known
today as the Barbados-Carolina connection), the cultural anthropology
of Floridian Zora Neale Hurston in the 1930s in Haiti and Jamaica, or the
direct influence of the Black Power movement in the United States on

Black Power and anticolonial movements throughout the global South during the 1960s and 1970s.

While it would be disingenuous to suggest that African American and Afro-Caribbean populations in the United States and outside of it are always co-extensive, seamlessly and synergistically interfacing with each other, particularly since the incumbencies of geography, genealogy, and generational belonging complicate identity matters, Touré's response nevertheless did give me pause. Admittedly, the tremendous efforts of the Congressional Black Caucus (CBC) to address the 2004 ousting of Haiti's first democratically elected president, Jean-Bertrand Aristide (which was supported by the United States government) and, in the aftermath of the earthquake, to actively agitate for Haitian debt forgiveness, along with the CBC's efforts to promote Caribbean immigration reform, suggest some political awareness and will regarding critical Caribbean regional matters. Still, Touré's comments caused me to reflect: To what degree are the experiences of Afro-Caribbeans still living in the Caribbean, and those who reside in the United States with remaining close ties to the region, seen as something outside of the key interests and concerns of the U.S. black majority population despite the fact that U.S.-based Afro-Caribbeans align (as they historically and politically have done) with their African American brothers and sisters? I am thinking here of Marcus Garvey, Claude McKay, Shirley Chisholm, Kwame Ture, Audre Lorde, Barbara Christian, and even Eric Holder (some of whom were born in the Caribbean; all of whom claim Caribbean parentage).

Having migrated from complicated racialized spaces marked by rigid colonial legacies and neocolonial realities, the expectation is often for Afro-Caribbeans to pass for African Americans; and if they don't, because they too possess their own historical and politico-cultural legacies to which they lay claim, Caribbean people are often accused of being culturally condescending, elitist, or, as Touré claims, "out of touch" with the history of black experience in this country. The question becomes, what ultimately counts as black experience? And, too, whose black experience gets to count? In other words, how might restrictive and confining conceptualizations of black experience as bounded by geography and culture limit the quality of the creative engagement we might productively engender?

In the foregoing then, I attempt to tease out the following: What happens to race in the absence of transnational global discourses of blackness? Or rather, what are the implications of defining post-blackness solely from, and in, the global North? What might "post-blackness" look like (if such were even possible) enacted from, and in, the global South? Might theorizing neo-blackness as opposed to post-blackness (as with neocolonialism) overtly and centrally foreground long-standing, infinitely complicated, hierarchized structures of engagement that surround race, color, and economy while at the same time acknowledging the "modern" contingencies of how blackness is performed both in the global South *and* in the global North, oftentimes (referring to the former) in ways that fall under the radar of prevailing notions of who counts as black?

TOURING WITH TOURÉ

The transnational entailments of race, nation, and power were very much at play when in 1997, under President Bill Clinton (the so-called first black president[1]), the United States pushed the World Trade Organization (WTO) to pass legislation to remove preferential tariffs on banana exports from African-Caribbean-Pacific (ACP) countries to Europe, markets protected as a reparative mechanism for hundreds of years of slavery and colonial exploitation. Bowing under pressure from multilateral corporations such as Chiquita and Dole, which had donated generously to both the Democratic and Republican parties, the Clinton-led complaint effectively destroyed the banana production base of predominantly black Caribbean countries like Dominica, St. Vincent, Grenada, and Jamaica, whose exports constituted only 7 percent of the European market but whose reliance upon banana production for foreign exchange earnings and employment comprised huge portions of their economies. In St. Lucia, for example, one-third of the entire island's population prior to the adverse WTO ruling relied upon bananas for employment (Sheller 2003, 102). After a long and protracted negotiation during the recent "Banana

Wars," the WTO ruled that the European Union's trade deal with the ACP "violated global trade rules and that the US was allowed to impose $191.4 million in sanctions" (ibid., 101). The result of this position, along with other ensuing trade conflicts fomented by and masked under the deceptively progressive discourses of "free trade" and globalization, has been the collapse of the Caribbean agricultural economy (Ahmed 2001). As Mimi Sheller points out in *Consuming the Caribbean*, "While bananas may seem a frivolous luxury to some, they are for many a livelihood" (2003, 101).

The response to this assault on the economic infrastructure of black working-class farming communities in the Caribbean was ostensibly silence from the black majority in the United States. Being "out of touch," it seems, travels trans/nationally. But it is Touré who reminds his readers in *Who's Afraid of Post-Blackness* that, according to him, "Black Americans are quintessentially Americans" (2011, 196), without problematizing the cultural and economic imperialism that America has meted out throughout the global South. While I am not suggesting that Touré and his views stand in for African Americans in toto, I am suggesting that the cultural elisions and simplifications that his perspectives raise reflect what I see as an increasing unproductively balkanized racial landscape in both the academy and in public discourse. In fact, Touré (perhaps unthinkingly) demonstrates that he did not heed the admonitions of the committed and brilliant scholar of Africa and African diaspora theory, Robert Farris Thompson, whose reticence about Touré's "post-Black" thesis are documented in the concluding section of *Who's Afraid*, entitled "Outtakes."

In this final section of the book, Touré includes a series of loosely connected vignettes that "couldn't be shoe-horned into the text but still demanded inclusion" (203). Thompson, in two emails, insistently proclaims the diversity of black people, pointing to the *longue duree* "and therefore never post" of black culture emblematized by "the flows from the great griots, babalawos, iyalorisha, bangudi dya muntu, jazz composers, Sea Island shouters, Afro-Cuban mambo drummers, acute rap minds, inspired black writers like Toni Morrison," who "all emerge as women and men spiritually aligned" (215); he rhetorically queries: "How can you be out-of-date or 'post' when you are spiritually aligned with earth, air, fire and water? Or 125th street for that matter" (215). More significantly, in his final missive, Robert Farris Thompson argues that Touré's "post-Black" thesis (of which he remains highly suspicious) "ideally should be tested against what is happening among *all of the Black Americas*, not just ahem, the imperial USA" (216, emphasis mine). And while, anecdotally, Touré does not distinguish between post-black performance of some of his book's subjects who hail from the Caribbean and those from the United States, his revelations vis-à-vis his trip throughout Africa are troubling and reflect the kind of American ethnocentricity (with which Thompson is clearly discomfited) that perpetually interpellates black Africa and the black Americas as either premodern or as sites of pleasure to be touristically consumed by passengers disembarking their cruise ships.

"I have been to Africa—Ghana, Senegal, Cote d'Ivoire, Morocco," Touré tells us, "and marveled at its beauty. . . . I saw the remnants of *the beginnings of Black culture*" (195, emphasis mine). Here Touré employs the classic discourse of exoticization. Africa is beautiful, "epiphanous"— evoking, even—but primitive. Africa is a space where culture has "remnants," "beginnings" that can only be made modern and thus sophisticatedly "post-black," once transported across the Atlantic. As Achille Mbembe in *On the Postcolony* suggestively argues, "Africa as an idea, a concept, has historically served, and continues to serve as a polemical argument for the West's desperate desire to assert its difference from the rest of the world . . . and Africa, because it was and remains that fissure between what the West is, what it thinks it signifies, it's not simply *part of* imaginary significations, it is *one* of those significations" (2001, 2).

In other words, when Touré describes African villagers' "blunt" designation of him as foreigner, uttering the appellative "Toubab!" from their "small one-room apartments made from packed clay—places where in many ways people lived the same way they did one hundred years ago," what Touré really means is, look at how civilized and sophisticated we luckily rescued (from premodernity) Western African Americans are in comparison (2011, 196). Thus, his post-blackness is confirmed by and codified within the conventional privileged Western epistemological discourse of "progress" emanating from the global North. Here, Africa *is* "imaginary signification," what Mbembe describes as "'that something invented' that, paradoxically becomes necessary because 'that something' plays a key role, both in the world the West constitutes for itself and in the West's apologetic concerns and exclusionary and brutal practices towards others" (2001, 2). It seems to me that once we begin to apprehend blackness in terms that challenge rather than reify Africa as imaginary signification, what opens up is a kind of neo- rather than post-blackness that excavates the ways in which race, power, and privilege operate trans/nationally throughout Africa and the black Americas.

While Touré rightly asserts that African Americans' "relationship to Africa is a construct," he never ethically deconstructs the contours of his assertion.[2] In fact, Touré's argument for rejecting the mythification of Africa has little to do with the ways in which Afrocentrism fails to seriously conceive Africa as imbricated within the complicated historical, cultural, transnational incumbencies of modernity and the insidious operations of global capital; he uses by way of example instead his having experienced "*severe* moments of disconnect" on his African tour (195, emphasis mine). I was reminded of Jamaica Kincaid's brilliant treatise on the ugliness of the tourist–native encounter: "you see yourself . . . you see yourself . . . an ugly thing is what you become as a tourist" (1988, 17). Touré's expectations for his nativist "homecoming" rest upon the problematic assumption that Africa and Africans should function primarily in relation to his emotional/psychological desires for cultural belonging. Unfortunately "the natives" are uncooperative.

In fact, Touré tells us that his most "severe" moment of disconnection occurs with his epiphanic realization that he was not "one of them," catalyzed by having been "skillfully intercepted by a local hustler (there are many of them waiting for tourists)" who became his tour guide and expected meals, drinks, and gifts; he made misleading promises to take Touré to "someplace special where tourists could not go" (2011, 195). Not only is Touré's use of the term "hustler" patronizing and culturally biased, reminiscent of the oft-used appellative "thug" to describe U.S. based urban black men, but Touré concludes that his Ghanaian tour guide's "entreaties to intercontinental brotherhood were a smokescreen allowing him to treat [Touré] like an ATM" (195). Here Touré employs a banking metaphor to describe his frustrations while he touristically consumes Ghana, the place where their shared ancestors were traded for and as capital. Black bodies *were* the proverbial ATMs, inaugurating the greatest crime against humanity while simultaneously fomenting the rise of modern capitalism throughout Europe.

The economic historian of Caribbean slavery and resistance Hilary Beckles, in his paradigm-shifting work *Britain's Black Debt: Reparations for Caribbean Slavery and Native Genocide* (2013), demonstrates in graphic terms the ways in which the European banking system not only profited from the "enchainment" of enslaved Africans but also criminally benefitted from their emancipation. "John Palmer, a former governor of the Bank of England, who looked at the issue of property rights in the enslaved as indispensable to the financial culture," argued that "Emancipation without reparation to slave owners . . . would endanger the whole frame of society" (Beckles 2013, 146). The result was the collection by British slaveholders, of £20 million compensation to "the persons hitherto entitled to the services of such slaves" (148). Drawing upon the research of Nicholas Draper, Beckles reveals that £20 million, in 1838, would have constituted 40 percent of the British government's yearly expenditure, and would equate to almost £200 billion today (144). The banks at the time "received reparations money on behalf of themselves, and for acting on behalf of clients and customers" (156). According to Beckles, those banks have all been rebranded today as Barclays Bank, Lloyds, NatWest, and Royal Bank of Scotland (156–57). The fiscal implications for those involved in the crime of enslavement was exponential. As Beckles points out, the impact of the reparations money on slave owners' finances was immediate. They used funds to "pay off debts and to reduce mortgages on their plantations" and were saved from bankruptcy. "The blacks who had been the victims of the crime received nothing" (159).

Now, I am in no way suggesting complicity on Touré's part in terms of this history. What I am suggesting is that in the rush to don post-blackness, and ostensibly throw off the shackles of our respective pasts, we risk losing critical tools to not just excavate the past but to apprehend more fully the complexities of our present. The young black working-class Ghanaian brother and his "entrepreneurship" takes on a different cast, I think, when we apprehend the meanings of money, banking, and capital throughout Africa and the black Americas. As Kincaid poignantly puts it, "people like me are shy about being capitalists . . . because we, for as long as we have known you [the British] *were* capital, like bales of cotton and sacks of sugar" (1988, 37). In subsequent sections, then, I offer two examples, one pedagogical and one propositional, to suggest how thinking neo-blackness trans/nationally might open up important vistas and discursive sites that respond, at least provisionally, to Robert Farris Thompson's suggestion to "test" Touré's theory of post-blackness within the black Americas.

THE BLACK AMERICAS

I wonder how Touré's remarks at Florida International University and his post-African tour conclusions might have been refashioned had he worked to theorize post-blackness through the alembic of Stephanie Black's brilliantly, pedagogically rich documentary *Life and Debt* (2001).[3] The film documents with earnest proficiency the connections between globalization, development, and discourse as they relate to the current Jamaican nation-state and, by extension, the black Americas. It documents the dire socioeconomic and political challenges of black countries for development and emphasizes the effects of the neoliberal economic order.[4] The film is a studied investigation of the superstructure of globalization. Stephanie Black highlights the postcolonial plight in which high-interest loans from various institutions situated in the global North, such as the International Monetary Fund (IMF) and the World Bank are made to the very "independent" countries like Jamaica (which serves as her case in point), whose economies fostered the accumulation of wealth in what we now call "The First World," the very nations with controlling interests in the selfsame lending institutions. The Pandora's Box is crafted by colonialism, and, when opened by the exploited, the outcome is the darkness of debt. Having technically relinquished colonial power, neocolonial power and control are wielded via the mechanisms of economic liability and inevitable default.

Money is lent at exorbitant interest rates (and with exploitative provisos attached) to already vulnerable economies whose weakness is a consequence of the politico-historical economic exploitation endured under colonialism. As one of the Rastafarian theorists in *Life and Debt* aptly puts it, "de money come with terms and conditions, terms and conditions." These terms and conditions, these "structural adjustment programs" set as conditionalities of loan agreements send so-called independent nations throughout the black Americas into spiraling indebtedness, fostering perpetual dependence and thwarting sustainable national/ regional development. Much in the same way that African Americans and other blacks in America are targets of institutionalized economic racism in the United States, black peoples in the Caribbean continue, as Michael Manley remarks, to struggle to go "up the down escalator." [5]

Stephanie Black's film raises far more questions than it proposes solutions. But it is precisely this resistance to prescribing simplistic solutions and purposive refusal to do the work of figuring out how these globally challenging issues might be solved that is *Life and Debt's* most salient feature and provides the space for conceiving how we might effectively operationalize neo-blackness. Literately empowered, viewers—irrespective of their global positionality—are authorized to develop social justice praxis through piecing together seemingly disparate narrative strands and gleaning meaning via intersubjectively engaging the multiple voices that populate the narrative structure. Having been taken to the crossroads wherein these cross-temporal, cross-cultural narratives converge, it is we the viewers, and only we, who can determine a just course moving forward.

In this regard, then, it is instructive to consider the filmic treatment of tourists with whom Stephanie Black reveals she most "identified" precisely because, by her own admission, she (presumably like they) had been entirely unaware of how economic policies adopted by the United States and Europe have impacted developing nations like Jamaica. [6] This is a suggestive moment emblematizing the ways in which Touré might have better situated his own cultural positionality and privilege. Black reveals:

Tourists represented for me the exact naïvete or lack of information I had prior to making my first documentary in Jamaica. The tourists coming to Jamaica are seeing behind the doors of a hotel, and not really knowing what goes on beyond the doors of the hotel . . . what the policies are of the United States abroad. As an American, if my country is the strongest voting power in the IMF, then what impact is it having? What is my responsibility to explore this?

(*Buzzflash* 3)

One of the more discomfiting aspects of the film has to do with the sharp juxtaposition made between the touristic gaze and harsh politico-economic realities facing Jamaica. This unease is probably because the Caribbean in the dominant public imagination is imagined largely and primarily in terms of its paradisiacal landscape—what Mimi Sheller describes as "a perpetual Garden of Eden in which visitors can indulge all their desires and find a haven for relaxation, rejuvenation and serious abandon" (2003, 13).

In *Life and Debt*, Stephanie Black overlays and intersperses three versions of Bob Marley's popular song "One Love." The refrain of the song, "one love, one heart, let's get together and feel alright," was until recently, the theme for the Jamaica Tourist Board's North American advertising campaign. Replete within this phrase, a phrase excised from the song's more socially and politically conscious contexts, are promises of "feeling alright!" Jamaica is the site to which one escapes from daily demands of First World living. Such escapism relies upon mythologized constructions of Caribbean landscapes, not Caribbean nations. It is rare, for example, to find a local newspaper for sale at a Jamaican resort. Why expose tourists to disturbing tales of native "reality," even if they are sipping Red Stripe beer and eating fried snapper by the sea? Why remind them that they sunbathe in a country caught within the maelstrom of poverty, violence, and lack of access?

The tourist enterprise rests upon consciously masking politico-economic reality; to unveil is to foreclose the enterprise's efficaciousness. To perpetuate the masquerade, however, is to foreclose a paradigm shift regarding how the Caribbean is currently engaged. As a consequence, idyl-lic images infuse "foreign" TV screens with ads promising escape, retreat, rest, beauty, no rules, no inhibitions—the Caribbean is a place to come and simply "be." Paradoxically, the film juxtaposes the easy movement of tourists across immigration borders into Jamaica to vacation with images of hundreds of Jamaicans lined up in front of the U.S. embassy seeking visas to leave that country. Kincaid writes in *A Small Place*, and the film's voiceover addresses the audience:

> Every native would like to find a way out, every native would like a rest, every native would like a tour. But some natives—most natives in the world—cannot go anywhere. They are too poor. They are too poor to go anywhere. They are too poor to escape the reality of their lives; and they are too poor to live properly in the place where they live, which is the very place you the tourist want to go. So when the natives see you, the tourist, they envy you, they envy your ability to leave your own banality and boredom, they envy your ability to turn their banality and boredom into a source of pleasure for yourself.
>
> (1988, 18–19)

I am reminded here of Touré's Ghanaian "hustler." Even if travel is an option, if only for a holiday, the difficulty of attaining visas, of being granted permission to enter the United States or the United Kingdom (as of March 2003, Jamaican nationals could no longer enter the United Kingdom without a visa) is indescribable. Most importantly, the visual image depicting boundless lines of Jamaican visa-seekers suggests that rather than existing as a site to which to escape, Jamaica is for many a site from which to escape.

Reminiscent of Touré's casting of Africa's beauty, the mnemonic link-age of Jamaica, and by extension the Caribbean, with pastoral fantasies of escapism, with a kind of mythical and mystical enchantment, is so entrenched, so difficult to separate out as to be revelatory. In one review of *Life and Debt*, the author states: "Jamaica is so staggeringly beautiful that in *Life and Debt*, Stephanie Black's cool-headed but blistering indictment of globalization and the racist international economic policies that have shoved that country into crushing poverty, the place, its people circumvent despair to dazzle you" (Hardy 2002). What does it mean, I wonder, to be so dazzling as to circumvent despair? Another author writes, "Would Black, for all her contempt for tourists who inevitably are easy targets for satire, really want them to stop coming" (Thomas 2002)? Both reviewers miss the point.

Black's principal purpose, I think, is to demonstrate how tourists' self-referentiality precludes them from recognizing their complicity and entanglement within the matrix of political economy and history in the very nation-state they temporarily inhabit for holiday (see Kincaid 1988, 13). Touré's analysis, for instance, might have benefitted from the kind of self-reflexive recognition of privilege, power, and ignorance that *Life and Debt* arduously works to unpack. Stephanie Black's own response to the critique of the touristic gaze that the film proffers is instructive:

Well, the tourists are not the enemy in the film. The tourists are stylized—they don't speak; they're metaphors. They come to Jamaica, and they stay within the confines of the hotel. That was very comparable to me, to all of us in the United States—very often we don't have an understanding of what our policies are doing outside the country. Lack of information is a victimizing force.

(quoted in Fazio 2005)

Such victimization is all-encompassing: tourists and natives (albeit to varying degrees) are adversely affected by the ostensible masquerade.

By relegating the tourists to silent metaphors and at the same time juxtaposing their images against multiple speaking Caribbean subjects, Black's film engages in a kind of symbolic reparative gesture, for it is usually the case that the natives operate as silent metaphors within touristic practices of consumption and engagement. Such a reversal is self-consciously intended to produce, at the very least, discomfort for the gazing tourist, for whom the privileged viewer stands in. At best, viewers experience self-reflective recognition of their participation in the perpetuation of such dehumanizing practices that relegate Caribbean working-class subjects to metaphoric status in order to serve their touristic fantasies. Without self-reflexivity there can be no tangible social transformation. As a case in point, we might consider the Tom Joyner Foundation's Fantastic Voyage, which, for the past fourteen years, has cruised through the Caribbean to raise money for scholarships to historically black colleges and universities (HBCU) while participants "party with a purpose."

This year's cruise, aboard the *Carnival Conquest*, promises ports of call in the U.S. Virgin Island of St. Thomas, a private island in Nassau, Bahamas, and Grand Turk, the largest of the Turks and Caicos Islands. It was while living in Turk's Island, of course, that the enslaved Mary Prince, writing some years later in Britain in 1831, described being stripped naked and beaten with a cow-skin until "her body was raw with gashes" (2002, 268). Working in the gruesome and debilitating salt marshes for days on end, Prince exclaims, "Oh that Turk's Island was a horrible place! The people of England, I am sure, have never found out what is carried on there. Cruel horrible place!" (269). Obviously, I have no quarrel with Joyner's goal of supporting black students and HBCUs; I support his aims unequivocally. However, I do wonder about the extent to which the radio host and his supporters, who admittedly hail from "all of the black Americas," engage the Caribbean spaces they inhabit with a realizing sense of the complexities of history, culture, race, and class that are inherent to the countries they visit. More importantly, I wonder how useful and productive interrogation of the ways in which black consumers from the global North crossing into black spaces in the global South might contemporarily develop strategies for more ethical consumption.

To suggest that *Life and Debt*, Kincaid's *A Small Place*, or even my own problematization of the touristic enterprise are designed to critique the tourist industry in toto (as Kevin Thomas does earlier) is to completely miss the point and is either a rather naïve or purposely misleading proposition. Consumption is not the "enemy"; we are all consumers to varying degrees, but *how* we consume is a question of a different order. Mimi Sheller's advocacy of "ethical consumption . . . in which the connections between producer, consumer and consumed are put into play against each other" provides a useful model for beginning to interrogate these vexed and tricky domains inherent to the tourism enterprise (2003, 8). Such considerations are extremely relevant for and to black subjects privileged to cross national borders with relative ease.

For instance, since international students studying on visas usually do not qualify for financial aid in the United States, might one or two of the HBCU scholarships made possible from the Fantastic Voyage proceeds be targeted toward a black student from the Caribbean specifically, or for any student working on Caribbean development? And might there be an expanded focus on "all of the black Americas" in Joyner's daily segment of "the little known black history fact," which airs daily on his nationally syndicated radio program? Couldn't the Tom Joyner program feature an international segment that focuses on global black issues? Admittedly, once, when teaching a class on *Life and Debt* and discussing how tourists consume, one of my students tellingly asserted, "Professor Russell, when I go on vacation, I don't want to think." Touché. But, without ruining the "fun," there must be a way to create a space for recognizing how blackness signifies trans/nationally, which could foster creative engagements of ethical consumption between the cruise line industry, the media, passengers, *and* Caribbean locals and their politico-economic concerns.

In this regard, most central to *Life and Debt*'s ideological purview is the film's juxtaposition of the landscape of Jamaica, the conventional images of sea and sun and sand, with other less idyllic images that have also become dominant discourses on that country, equally resonant images that reflect civil unrest and political violence. The film's narration opens with the statement: "If you come to Jamaica as a tourist, you will surely land in Montego Bay and not in Kingston." The mythic divide between urban (Kingston) and rural (Montego Bay), ghetto and resort, is reinforced. In actuality, social turbulence in Montego Bay (the second largest city) is no different than it is in Kingston, but the success of tourist enterprise rests upon this false binary.

Additionally, development of "all-inclusive" hotels (Black's earlier point), which make it possible for tourists to consume all goods and services entirely within the gates of their resorts, have had a devastating effect on the local economy, precluding merchants from benefiting from tourists' procuring their wares. Local citizens are barred from entering these resorts without permission—unless, of course, they are workers or guests—and there is usually no public beach access on such properties. A few local craftspeople will be invited to sell their goods on one or two days a week. But because of "all-inclusive" arrangements in which visitors pay one price for hotel, transportation, meals, and so on, on their jaunts to the beach or pool (where the craftspersons are stationed), guests usually don't carry money with them. Disembarking cruise ship passengers similarly support specific locales with prearranged agreements between the cruise lines and the local establishments. Those in a better position to negotiate (i.e., business elites) are obviously better patronized.

So the structural conditions preclude viable commodity exchange. Many local marketplaces have had to close down. No thoroughfare equals no capital gains. This mechanism for controlling the flow of capital from tourism by structurally inventing blockades to local merchant participation in the economy is analogous to the phenomenon of building highways over historical African American communities in the United States, purportedly erected in the interest of "safety" and under the guise of "development." Justification for the "all-inclusive" resort structure is codified in similar terms. The consequence—the death knell is resolutely sounded to local commerce and the spirit of entrepreneurship—both of which are fundamental tenets of self-reliance and economic stability. Highways 95 and 395 built over (with no on and off ramps) the historic black city of Liberty City in South Florida in the 1960s stands as just one example of thwarting black enterprise under the guise of postindustrial development. Thousands of homes were bulldozed and tens of thousands of people were forced out or they relocated out of necessity. Naturally, capital flight soon followed. The mechanism of the marketplace in thwarting black working-class social mobility (the entertainment industry is a notable if problematic exception) is perpetually operative and acts trans/nationally across neo-black spaces. In the absence of a trans/national discourse of blackness, such shared global experiences are not only elided but strategies for solutions also become fragmented and compartmentalized and, thus, stripped of their potential efficacy.

Life and Debt opens with graphic scenes of bloody and violent turbulence in Jamaica during the 1990s, when the collapse of the financial sector led to spiraling inflation, currency devaluation, and declining investments coupled with escalating unemployment, crime, and poverty. The result: an island-wide eruption of civil chaos. The brilliance of this filmic moment, however, is in its use of the gaze to unveil the insidiousness of the globalization project. Although the gaze has conventionally been seen as inherently disempowering, Clifford Manlove has convincingly argued that "the gaze can potentially reverse hierarchy or subject/object relations" (2007). In this narrative instance, we gaze upon Jamaican citizens gazing upon the television newscast, which begins with footage of civil unrest, including the shooting death of a pregnant woman. Dread images of bloodshed, army tanks, burning tires, and brandished guns are watched on TV by onlookers whose facial affect is collectively one of horror, anguish, and uncertainty.

The newscast surrounding the violence breaks and cuts to an excerpt from a speech by Horst Köhler, then director of the IMF, in which he extols the virtues of globalization: "The issue is to make globalization work for the benefit of all." The onlookers appear doubtful as Köhler righteously continues, "There will not be a good future for the rich if there is no prospect of a better future for the pure, poor." Köhler's Freudian slip, substituting "poor" for "pure," perfectly exposes the duplicity of the neoliberal order. A Baskin Robbins advertisement appears next, with its logo and attendant promise of "one world, 31 flavors." Ice cream treats append globalization's utopic promise of a borderless diverse economy where everyone has equal and privileged choice—"31 flavors," no less. Naturally, such expanded choice is made possible only under the auspices of a liberalized economy, in which development is tied to deregulation and the "open market." That the local ice cream industry (Devon House Ice Cream, for example) has suffered tremendous financial setbacks as a consequence of Baskin Robbins's entrée into the Jamaican market is hidden beneath the allure of cosmopolitan Madison Avenue advertisement and a desire for local escape—the appeal of "foreign products" bolstered by liberalization of media via satellite technology in a society in which 88 percent of households have television.[7]

The scene shifts once again, and viewers witness reggae musician Buju Banton singing a cappella: "I and I, we wanna rule our destiny."[8] As Banton slowly traverses one of the garrison communities in Jamaica, one of the hotbeds of violent unrest, the melodious and melancholic strains of his song capture the national desire for sovereignty and at the same time decry the mammonism of the capitalist enterprise. Later, in another instantiation of Bob Marley's "One Love," the ska version, the music is overlaid atop scenes of jubilation upon the granting of Jamaican independence from Britain in 1962. Ska music was essentially created to capture the spirit, the promise, the actualization of the dream of independence.[9] In short order, scenes of jubilation, interspersed with the symbolic lowering of the blue, red, and white Union Jack and the hoisting of the black, green, and yellow Jamaican flag, are precisely accompanied by the narrator's remarks: "We were ruled over by something called a queen." Immediately the footage cuts to Queen Elizabeth's declaration of Jamaica's independence, witnessed while the phrase "we do not have a queen anymore" is narrated and the scene cuts to a shot of McDonald's golden arches. Ernest Hardy writes of this brilliant filmic moment, "The point is made, not belabored. Jamaica was delivered from the paternalistic Great Britain to the money-driven rule of the marketplace, and Jamaicans are still reeling from the blow" (2002, 2).

As Buju Banton plaintively wails for a desired destiny marked by humanity, the scene shifts to the Rastafarian Nyabinghi, "a reasoning." In this filmic instance, the Rastafarian elders read from the Bible a verse that forbids usury, hence setting us up for the moral framework from which they will interpret the current socioeconomic circumstances in which the nation finds itself. Historically, Rastafari takes as one of its central philosophies speaking with and for those who are marginalized by poverty and racism. If Rastafarian doctrine centers on critiquing black disenfranchisement, then reggae music is the vehicle through which the spirit of resistance to oppression is given public expression. That Black infuses her cinematographic montage with the spirit of resistance, signaled through working-class voices who seize the discourse around globalization and make it their own, and through the spirit of rebellion inherent to

Rastafarian doctrine and reggae music is a central feature of the ideological/epistemological thrust of the film: to present a treatment of the themes it explores, marked by inclusion, polyvocality, and multiple perspectives. Post-blackness, here, is—as Touré would have it—fluid and diverse, but it is also inclusive. The film is self-reflexive about the ways in which class position and access inform who get to speak and for whom, and, most importantly, the documentary rejects the kind of elitism that would limit analysis of realities and experiences of life in any of the black Americas, to 105 "prominent Black people" (Touré 12).

Case by case, *Life and Debt* captures in dread terms the decimation of various local industries as a consequence of free market economics. The film depicts the gradual eradication of farming industries: dairy, bananas, potatoes, poultry. Farm workers, local market producers, and industry owners articulate with precision and clarity their inability to compete with imported goods. Jamaican citizens become the social scientists fully aware of what have been the political, economic, and social implications of IMF, World Bank, Inter-American Development Bank (IDB), and WTO policies. Their polyphonous tales of victimization under the aegis of globalization debunk prevailing notions of an inarticulate lumpenproletariat unable to theorize their own condition. The working classes are savvy, articulate, and incisive, speaking on their own behalf rather than being spoken for or reduced to statistics and graphs in the academic discourse of political economy. Black's filmic representation in this instance is a radical rewriting of the propensity in postcolonial studies to give primacy to the voices of exilic academicians perched in their ivory towers, waxing poetic on the failures of the nation-state. In *Life and Debt* the nationals and not the empire speak tout court.

While I have chosen to condense my analysis of the film's treatment of the collapse of various aforementioned industries, I am compelled to pause for a minute to discuss the ways in which neo-blackness, capital, commerce, and exploitation converge in the free zones that have been established throughout the black Americas, including Haiti, the Dominican Republic, and Jamaica. The expansion of "free zone" areas in Jamaica in the 1980s was an element of the 1984 U.S. Caribbean Basin Initiative designed to provide trade benefits to Caribbean and Latin American countries to help bolster their economies. Loans were made to Jamaica by the World Bank and the Caribbean Development Bank for infrastructural development to facilitate U.S. manufacturing and provide employment opportunities. U.S.-based companies send materials for assembly in Jamaica, which are later reshipped to the United States for distribution.[10] As one free zone worker aptly remarks, "Trade and materials, they take them from abroad, dem don't buy nothing in Jamaica." Essentially, the free zone operates as a "separate entity" in that it is "free" from governmental regulations, taxation, and local controls. Naturally, there are no unions, and workers operate in "sweat shop" conditions, sewing and assembling products for companies such as Tommy Hilfiger, Mark Alexander, Brooks Brothers, and Hanes. Poignantly describing the environmental conditions, one worker remarks, "No unions, you can't talk, you watched all the time, is like you working under slavery." All products are labeled "made in the USA." Pay is pitiably low. Free zone workers speak frankly about earning thirty dollars per week or less, with additional money taken out by the Jamaican government for taxes, even though the workers are toiling in a purportedly borderless environment.

The documentary portrays the moment in which the veritable unraveling of the free zones begin. In an interview, Black discusses the paradoxical operations of private capital that inhere in scenes in which "the real Tommy Hilfiger goods [are] being manufactured in the free zone, then you had the Chinese knock-offs being dumped into the country—which is what everyone [those interviewed in this segment] is wearing—and then you had the Chinese workers being flown in to sew the real Tommy Hilfiger stuff." She continues, "It was like science fiction; you couldn't make this stuff up" (Fazio 2005, 5). Such transnational movement of capital and goods and bodies is ultimately captured in graphic scenes of abandoned free zones now defunct as a result of the movement of capital to cheaper labor markets where greater profit margins might be reaped. According to a memo shown in the film, the debt incurred by the Jamaican government to fund this project was slated to be paid off in December 2010. In the meantime, some eighteen thousand jobs migrated and, more importantly, the ideological assumptions that devalue human beings' lives subordinating fair working conditions to high profit margins have migrated along with the jobs.

Set against the strains of Bob Marley's "Work," which serves as the soundtrack framing this segment, scenes of bustling factories, frustrated workers, and the cycle of underemployment, exploitation, and unrequited work dissolve into gritty images of abandoned factories seen through hard metal gates. One laid-off worker says with deft analysis, "dem bring everything from foreign," to which another responds, "a better we do our own ting here"—the language of self-determination and self-reliance resound in their neo-black articulations. In swift succession, images of deserted buildings flash quickly to a billboard sign that reads: "Do You Need A Miracle?"—an advertisement for an upcoming religious rally to be held at the national arena. One is reminded of the title of Michelle Cliff's brilliantly searing novel on Jamaica, *No Telephone to Heaven*.

Much of *Life and Debt*'s incisive analysis of Jamaica's economic history and neoliberalism is provided by Michael Manley, the former prime minister of Jamaica. That Stephanie Black uses Manley to provide the politico-economic theory with which to ground the historical unfolding and the impact of IMF policies is of critical import. To begin with, during the 1970s Manley ran on a "grassroots" political platform of social democracy, self-sufficiency, and national development. Manley's ideological purview at that time was antithetical to the tenets of neoliberalism. By beginning with Manley and situating his leadership within the crossfire of the imperialist imperatives of U.S. and European policy makers, Black overtly challenges the dominant discourse, which holds that Jamaican independence failed to deliver on its promise because of Manley's socialist tendencies.[11]

Life and Debt captures scenes of a fiery and resistant young Michael Manley publicly proclaiming in his 1976 speech, "WE ARE NOT FOR SALE. Tell them that any time they are willing to deal with the honorable Jamaica based upon principal sovereignty, pride and dignity, then we will talk the investment of the money." Figuratively defying the proverbial auction block, Manley exposes the oxymoronic discourse of the global marketplace. Such certitude, however, dissolves in short shift to a weary and battle-scarred yet reflective and resilient sage who, in the closing scenes of his interview for the film, remarks, "And to this day, the crisis in the UN is the continuing demand of the so-called Third World for a *voice* in strategic IMF policy." As nationalistic defiance transmogrifies into reluctant capitulation, viewers watch aghast scenes of Manley signing the nation's first IMF agreement in 1977. Cries of self-reliance and refusal to pander to Western imperialism's imperatives are muted by the realities of a symbolic independence marked by a weak economic infrastructure whose fragility is exposed fully during the Organization of Petroleum Exporting Companies (OPEC) oil crisis of 1973.[12]

Manley, who would not live long enough to see *Life and Debt* debut, ends by describing his eventual signing of the IMF agreement as "one of the bitter, traumatic experiences of [his] public life." The final sequence of the film, then, closes with a haunting image highlighting an internal memo from the World Bank, which states: "These loans achieved neither growth nor poverty reduction." For many black people living in the global North, the operations of global capital under the aegis of the IMF, World Bank, WTO, IDB, and their connection to global governing bodies like the United Nations have seemingly little to do with their lives and even less to do with their immediate political concerns. That Touré concludes his treatise on post-blackness with an admonition for black people to "be like Barack" is a sad indication of the absence of intelligent analysis about the ways in which the United States and its international trade, military, and political policies continue to perpetrate literal and symbolic violence on millions of black people throughout the global South, irrespective of the amount of melanin that the "leader of the free world" possesses.

In the filmscape of *Life and Debt*, there is nothing past or post about the colonial presence in the black Americas. Its markers are transformed, transfigured, transmuted into images of golden arches set against the backdrop of a turquoise blue sky with promises of reinvestment of capital and job creation in return for tariff lifts and free market access—golden arches that are meant to signal one's arrival, a country's entrée into "first world" status, into the world of modernity, into the unfettered offices of post-black consumerism. "We have our own McDonalds," the tour guide featured in *Life and Debt* proudly announces on the tourist-filled buses en route to their resort. "There it is," she repeats, "McDonalds." McDonalds has left Jamaica now. After fighting and partially winning a long-standing court battle with Mr. McDonalds, whose restaurant of the same name served rice and peas and curry goat, plantain and brown stew chicken, the courts decided that both enterprises could coexist. No one would mistake one entity for the other. But for some inexplicable reason, Jamaicans never quite took to McDonald's, and all of their franchises have now migrated from the island. Burger King, on the other hand, is another story, for one of its most lucrative locations in its global operations is situated in the heart of Kingston's "Half-way Tree." At the time of the documentary's filming, beef producers in Jamaica were still awaiting approval from Burger King Corporation to supply meat to its local franchises.

More than ten years have passed since Stephanie Black's documentary *Life and Debt* debuted. According to a recent report in the Jamaican daily newspaper, the *Jamaica Gleaner*, between 1962, when Jamaica gained independence, and 2009, Jamaica's murder rate skyrocketed from 3.9 to 62.2 per 100,000 (Chang 2010). The nation's national airline, Air Jamaica, the plane featured in the opening and closing scenes of *Life and Debt*, was sold in 2011, a condition of a recent IMF loan. Jamaica decided to return to the IMF for the first time since its 1995 program ended—a necessity, according to the government, in the wake of the recent global economic convulsion (Silvera 2009). The current "sell" is that the IMF is a "kinder, gentler" IMF, less prescriptive, more open to dialogue, more willing to engage specificities of the nations to which it loans. Many Jamaicans remain skeptical, some are hopeful, but most are, in my humble estimation, completely disillusioned. In 2011 a national poll determined that 60 percent of Jamaicans believed their country should have remained a British colony.[13]

PERFORMING POST-BLACKNESS
FROM THE GLOBAL SOUTH

In March 2012 Prince Harry of Wales visited Jamaica on his Caribbean tour as Royal emissary to commemorate Queen Elizabeth's Diamond

Jubilee. All of the major U.S. networks carried the story, flashing images of the endearing and "down-to-earth" prince dancing with the natives while wearing bright blue shoes that closely resembled Britain's famed Clarks shoes. In fact, when Prince Harry wore Desert Clarks on a subsequent day of his visit, the blogs, Twitter, and YouTube went wild. Why? Clarks have always been extremely popular in Jamaica as a symbol of good, affordable foreign footwear with an urban edge, but they catapulted to the heights of mass consumption after Jamaican reggae dance-hall deejay Adidja "Vybz Kartel" Palmer released his major hit, "Clarks" (2010). Extolling the virtues of the British brand, according to Vybz Kartel, Clarks were so popular that "di queen fi England haffi love off yardi." In other words, even the queen would have to "love" Jamaicans (yardis) because of their visible endorsement and exponentially increasing consumption of Clarks. So widespread was the sale of Clarks in the aftermath of Kartel's song that *Clarks in Jamaica* (2012), a narrative/pictorial detailing the sales and images of Clarks since the 1920s was published. In the book, the author charts the long connection of Clarks to the "rudeboy," or "Rudie," gangster image of the 1960s that predominated black working-class urban Jamaica and was popularized by the 1972 classic film *The Harder They Come*.

As Al Fingers points out in the book, "Clarks shoes have enjoyed cult status in Jamaica for at least 60 years . . . style is everything to the sufferers" (2012, 11). The shoes' association with "rudeboys" became codified with the production and marketing of Clarks Desert Boot in the 1960s, the style donned by Prince Harry on his Caribbean tour (ibid., 44). The etymology of the term "rudeboy" lies in a series of sociohistorical determinants beginning in the 1960s when migration to and high unemployment, overcrowding, and poverty in urban Kingston created, according to historian Garth White, large numbers of young black men who became "increasingly disenchanted and alienated from a system which seemed to offer no relief from suffering" and, thus, "many of the young became *rude*" (ibid.). The term "rude" actually encodes multiple meanings: the literal one, of course, which refers to transgressing social mores whose structures must also be understood in context of the highly class-stratified nation; in Jamaican, however, "rude" is also a way to refer to something (usually food) that is very desirable and well-made, but it is also associated with the term "crude," as in raw, unpolished, and thus more "real" and authentic. Each of these meanings inheres in the term's coinage.

Cultural anthropologist Deborah Thomas further argues that rudeboy culture developed from a confluence of factors drawn from an emergent Rastafarian ideology such as "pride in blackness, the rejection of the status quo, and claims for social justice" that operated in tandem with "an antisocial temperament that was also influenced by cowboy movies imported from the United States and shown almost exclusively in working class communities" (2004, 73). So connected were Clarks to rudeboy culture that the "Rebel shoes," as they came to be called, became a marker of suspicion, placing their wearers under increased police surveillance. Fingers describes a police raid during a dance held in the 1970s in which all who were wearing Clarks were ordered by the authorities to one side of the room for ease of identification upon suspicion of criminal involvement (2012, 46). In fact, Fingers reveals that "the rudeboy/Desert Boot association became so strong that young males risked being beaten by police simply for wearing a pair" (ibid.).

The dance-hall rhythm "Clarks" was released by Kartel in 2010 after a truce had been brokered toward the end of 2009 between him and another deejay, David "Mavado" Brooks. The two had conceived and effected a "Tupac Shakur / Biggie Smalls" war, Jamaica-style. The deadly 1990s East Coast / West Coast feud between Bad Boy Records and Death Row Records and their two most famous artists had—to invoke dance-hall scholar Carolyn Cooper's phrasing—"hip-hopped across cultures and back" (2004). Vybz Kartel, who was from an area in greater Kingston that was, not ironically, nicknamed "Gaza," an unmistakable gesture homaging the oppressive conditions of the violence-laden, formally occupied, and under-siege Palestinian community, represented the West. According to Kartel, he chose the name "Gaza" "because Palestinians are serious and dem nah back down" (Dreisinger 2010, 4). However, Annie Paul, Jamaican writer/editor and founder of the influential blog "Active Voices," reminds us that the etymology of "Gaza" is no transparent matter, for, according to her, it lies in the area's former name, "Borderline," which was changed by Kartel as a result of Jamaican "culture's notorious attitude towards male homosexuals" (Paul 2009).

According to Paul, the nomenclature, "Borderline" was culturally tied to a provocative and popular stage character in Jamaican theatre called "Shebada," whose transgressive sexual performance entered into the popular cultural domain after an infamous scene in the play *Bashment Granny*. After having been questioned by the police—"Yu a man or yu a woman?"—Shebada responds, "Mi deh pon di borderline." As Paul notes, "the phrase became so popular in the context of discussions about sexuality that Vybz Kartel decided that the name of his community 'Borderline' has been irrevocably contaminated by association." Thus, Paul reveals, Kartel instead "adopted the name of the most violent place he could think of at the time—Gaza in Palestine" (ibid.).[14]

Mavado, from an area in central Kingston called "Cassava Piece" and built upon the banks of a man-made and dangerous gully, represented "the Gully side." Chanting the slogans "Gaza mi seh" or "Gully fi life," fans quickly chose sides, with the feud purportedly spilling over into dancehall sessions, inciting violence in Jamaica's overcrowded prisons, and creating serious rifts among schoolchildren in a country long renowned for deeply entrenched political tribalism and gang warfare. In fact, Dreisinger reports that, prior to the truce, "police seized R-rated Gaza-Gully buttons sold by vendors outside several schools—the pins featured explicit, Photoshopped graphics of one artist holding another's severed head, blasting off AK's" (2010, 2). In the meantime, Vybz Kartel and Mavado entered a lyrical feud, releasing songs whose incendiary titles included "Million Gunz," "Last Man Standing," "Real Killer," and "Kill Dem All and Done."

By the end of 2009 this Gully–Gaza conflict, as it came to be known, had so escalated (numerous brutal senseless murders over a few years) that then–prime minister of Jamaica Bruce Golding, along with several high-ranking ministers of government, brokered a truce between the artists with the help of the infamous Tivoli Gardens "don," Christopher "Dudus" Coke. Taken from the lionized film *The Godfather*, whose iconic gangster "don" Vito Corleone heads up the Italian American crime family, the term "don" has enjoyed increasing currency in Jamaica since the early 1980s as the appellative given to the (usually) drug lord who controls the social, cultural, political, and economic life of his respective inner-city community. The Golding-led Jamaican government had denied (for many months) an extradition request from the U.S. government, for Dudus to stand trial for drug and weapons charges. Dudus, the son of the legendary Jim Brown, the founder of the violent and powerful Shower Posse gang that dominated the drug trade in the 1980s, controlled the area politically represented by Prime Minister Golding. Jamaica's refusal to surrender Dudus became the center of an international debacle that ultimately resulted in Golding's resignation. The three-day incursion in May 2010 in the Dudus-controlled Tivoli Gardens community that followed the eventual issuance of the warrant for his arrest resulted in the deaths of seventy-three Jamaicans.

So you have a truce brokered by a sovereign prime minister and a wanted don, held at the country's national headquarters, "Jamaica House," between one deejay from a place called Gully and another from a place called Gaza, whose war of words is a commercially driven appropriation of U.S. popular cultural practices of hip-hop feuding, out of which emerges an agreement to cease using "gun lyrics" and tone down inflammatory language, which results in Vybz Kartel's pro-British commodity mega-hit "Clarks," which purports to be an innocuous celebration of the shoes, which results in an economic surge for the international company, whose shoes' long-standing historic roots are tied to the racialized incumbencies of inner-city urban blight and U.S. popular culture and whose "rudeboy" image is capitalized upon by Prince Harry as a genius public relations maneuver as he travels for the Queen's Jubilee to celebrate Jamaica's colonial heritage, during a year when the newly elected prime minister of Jamaica, the first working-class black woman to lead the country, Portia Simpson-Miller, had declared that it was time to sever official monarchical connections and that her government would not pursue reparations for slavery.

The Jamaican government has recently reversed this position and has joined with thirteen other Caribbean Community (CARICOM) heads of state from the Caribbean region in 2013 to bring a lawsuit against the

United Kingdom, France, and the Netherlands to the United Nations' International Court of Justice for their crimes against humanity committed during slavery. A CARICOM regional reparations commission headed by Professor Sir Hilary Beckles has been established.

It should be noted as well that following the commercial success of "Clarks," Kartel publicly launched his infamous skin-bleaching "Cake-soap" (2011), a product he had been testing on himself as evidenced by his increasingly lightening skin. By September of 2011, Kartel was arrested on one charge of murder and held on suspicion of another. Acquitted of the first murder, he was convicted for the second charge in March 2014. He has been sentenced to life in prison with no chance of parole until he serves thirty-five years. In the meantime, the reggae dance-hall industry continues to experience declining sales. Kartel's recently published book, *The Voice of the Jamaican Ghetto: Incarcerated but not Silenced*, features Kartel (whose nickname is also "The Teacha") donning a Malcolm X–like, spectacle-wearing pose, almost exactly replicating the cover of George Breitman's edition of *Malcolm X Speaks*. Additionally, scamming, which skyrocketed with the introduction of legal off-shore call centers and the decline of the drug trade, is Jamaica's newest emergent crime. In response to the government's clamping down on the illegal billion-dollar industry, from his jail cell, Vybz Kartel released the song, "Reparation," the lyrics of which unorthodoxly argue that scamming is a form of reparation for slavery.

Joining his voice to the current reparations discourse, Vybz Kartel's song is a quintessential example of what post-black performance might look like when enacted from the global South. He articulates the desire of "ghetto youths" to have the kind of economic access that would allow them to buy homes for their families, educate their children, and strive for the kind of success as achieved by Barack Obama. He then continues by challenging money transfer institutions like Western Union who derive huge profits from struggling immigrants and suggests that scamming provides an escape from the kind of gun violence linked to the drug trade that continues to permeate the Jamaican society. Decrying the immorality of poverty and hunger as being "more wrong" than involvement in the illegality of scamming, Kartel attempts to build a case for scamming as a kind of reparation for systemic black disenfranchisement.

Clearly, the transnational and national, racial, globalized, gendered, historical, and contemporary webs of connectivity and diffusion, the crazy juxtapositions and absurd synergies that coalesce in the Prince Harry/ Clarks/Kartel/reparations moment suggest at minimum that while a "post–civil rights" tenor may be en vogue among a small elite group of African Americans, the incumbencies of race, color, and culture continue to construct life realities for vast majorities of black people throughout the Americas. To be clear, I am in no way endorsing Kartel's proposition that the illegal activity of scamming is reparative, precisely because such acts are enacted outside of an ethico-moral base that I think is necessary for truly engaging reparations for slavery. Kartel's ingenuity, however, in deconstructing discourses of poverty and privilege, access and exclusion, violence and crime, and usurious global operations like Western Union, whose wealth is accumulated on the backs of struggling black immigrants and black working-class citizens working to live lives of decency and dignity within their nation-states, is remarkable. By way of conclusion, instead of "post-blackness," I want to invoke Deborah Thomas's notion of "modern blackness" as a more efficacious and relevant treatment of how black bodies perform and negotiate the complexities of race, history, and identity, which attends to the everyday experiences of blackness in people's material lives.

In *Modern Blackness*, Thomas argues that "everyday experiences of blackness within local and global racial hierarchies emerge as most salient in people's material and emotional lives . . . because current processes of globalization have reinscribed racial and cultural hierarchies within and between nations, communities, and regions in ways that recall the centrality of racial categorization and racism to processes of modernization, nationalism and state formation" (2004, 15). *Life and Debt* is clear attestation. At the same time, the ways in which black people navigate these realities might also be productively understood, according to Thomas, as "an ongoing negotiation of dynamic systems of power and domination at historically specific junctures" that require that we "critically and respectfully engage the complicated maneuvers people perform in order to advance their interests as individuals, families, and communities" (ibid.).

In other words, do we simply eschew Kartel and his entrepreneurial venture of selling bleaching products to black people, reading this as evidence of his (and their) internalized black self-loathing? Or, thinking in "modern" terms, as my brilliant graduate student Treviene Harris is currently arguing, could such bleaching practices in the Jamaican dance hall represent a kind of "queering" of blackness "with a view to destabilize various inequitable social structures" through enacting bodily performances of color impersonation that are "not concerned to establish a new real [i.e., actually becoming brown-skinned], but show up the un-realness of the Real" (2013, 4–5). Here is a fascinating example in which black people are powerfully playing with the meanings of color, race, and agency. Clearly, I have no quarrel with the idea that the possibilities for performing blackness are endless. However, instead of postulating a facilely glib notion of post-racial performativity in which black people can skydive, push the limits of black comedic brilliance, and be like Barack, I like Deborah Thomas's notion that we have to take blackness "seriously." To do so requires arduously deconstructing binary oppositions regarding configurations of power and place.

To this end, Michaeline Crichlow's admonition to engage in "trans/nationalizing and (re)homing the debates that surround the movement of people, commodities, capital, identities, and ideologies across territories," is a useful one for thinking about how we might conceive post-black performance or "modern blackness" in a global sense (2009, 207). Thinking in terms that conceive all of the black Americas requires that we reject false dichotomies about location, national, race, and place, replacing these instead with " 'une Pòetique de la Relation'—a cross-cultural poetics evocative of co-relational and intertwined histories" (ibid.). In other words, we are always already bound up in each other irrespective of (seemingly fixed) national borders, discourses of cultural belonging, and deeply entrenched notions of history and place. By beginning here, it seems to me that we open up the radical potential of blackness to exponentially signify ethically.

I return, finally then, to "neo-blackness." Neo-blackness is Audre Lorde's sagacious reminder: "Revolution is not a one-time event. It is becoming always vigilant for the smallest opportunity to make a genuine change" (1984, 140). Neo-blackness reminds us that past, present, and future walk simultaneously with us like haunting, daunting, im/possibility. That black struggle and resistance dance perpetually in intricate polyrhythmic lockstep. The challenges of poverty, lack of access, invisibility, visibility, antiblack violence, violence, disenfranchisement, health crises, and debt that continue to face black people trans/nationally across the spaces and places we inhabit require quality, innovative, creative address that must be conceived by all of us across the black Americas. Everything that was old is both new and old. This is what it means to be black now.

NOTES

1. Toni Morrison was the one who infamously dubbed Bill Clinton "America's first black president," in a 1998 piece she wrote for the *New Yorker*. For further discussion, see http://www.salon.com/2002/02/21/clinton_88/.

2. I mean "ethical deconstruction" in the Derridean sense, pointing to the ethical turn in Derridean deconstruction in which deconstruction and persuasive ethical consequences are vital to our thinking through of questions relating to politics and democracy. See Critchley (1999) and Luszczynsa (2011).

3. This section is a much elaborated and extensive treatment of my prior piece on *Life and Debt* (2012).

4. All references to film are to Black (2001).

5. The quote "up the down escalator" is borrowed from title of Michael Manley's book (1983).

6. "Stephanie Black Shows how the IMF Makes Developing Countries Dependent on the G-8 Nations, in her film *Life and Debt*." *BuzzFlash Interviews* (July 25, 2005), 3.

7. Technology/media data on Jamaica is available through the Commonwealth website, http://thecommonwealth.org/our-member-countries/jamaica/society.

8. Buju Banton. "Destiny." *Inner Heights*. Heartbeat, 1997.

9.   For more details on ska and its relationship to reggae, see Salewicz and Boot (2001).

10. The first free zone in Jamaica was actually established in 1976.

11. The 1970s bore witness to a mass exodus from Jamaica of the professional and intellectual classes in the form of a proverbial "brain drain" propelled by "red scare" tactics. These mostly privileged Jamaicans believed (and many still do) that "is Manley and his communism dat mash up the country."

12. The West went into an economic convulsion as a consequence of decreases in oil production and the placement of embargos on shipments of crude oil imposed by oil-producing companies protesting the backing of Israel in the Arab–Israeli war of 1973. The market price for oil instantaneously soared. The world financial system experienced, as a consequence, a series of recessions and increasing inflation, what Manley describes as a "world economic convulsion." The devaluation of the U.S. dollar as a result of the OPEC oil crisis and its residuals had an ineffable consequence on economies like Jamaica's, which were pegged to the U.S. dollar.

13. "Give Us the Queen!" *Daily Gleaner*, June 28, 2011, http://jamaica-gleaner .com/gleaner/20110628/lead/lead1.html.

14. It is important to note that inasmuch as Paul rightly locates the genesis of the changing of the community's name from Borderline to Gaza with a cultural attitude of homophobia, she also relevantly points out that the existence of characters like Shebada and the societies' engagement with transgressive sexualities demands a more nuanced analysis than is currently reflected in some international gay rights groups' "jackhammer strategies at outing and combating what is touted worldwide as Jamaican homophobia."

REFERENCES

Ahmed, Belal. 2001. "The Impact of Globalization on the Caribbean Sugar and Banana Industries." *The Society for Caribbean Studies Annual Conference Papers*, vol. 2. http://www.caricom.org/jsp/community/donor_conference _agriculture/preferences.pdf.

Beckles, Hilary. 2013. *Britain's Black Debt: Reparations for Caribbean Slavery and Native Genocide*. Kingston, Jamaica: University of the West Indies Press.

Black, Stephanie, dir. 2001. *Life and Debt*. New York: New Yorker Films.

BuzzFlash Interviews. 2005. "Stephanie Black Shows How the IMF Makes Developing Countries Dependent on the G-8 Nations, in Her Film *Life and Debt*." July 25.

Chang, Kevin O'Brien. 2010. "The Road to a Cruel Jamaica." *Jamaica Gleaner*, June 13.

Cooper, Carolyn. 2004. *Sound Clash: Jamaican Dancehall Culture at Large*. New York: Palgrave Macmillan.

Crichlow, Michaeline. 2009. *Globalization and the Post-Creole Imagination: Notes on Fleeing the Plantation*. Durham, NC: Duke University Press.

Critchley, Simon. 1999. *The Ethics of Deconstruction*. West Lafayette, IN: Purdue University Press.

Dreisinger, Baz. 2010. "Reggae's Civil War: Why Mavado and Vybz Kartel Might Be the Biggie and Tupac of Dancehall." *Village Voice*, March 2.

Fazio, Giovanni. 2005. "Documentarian Shoots from the Hip Inside Jamaica's Debtor's Prison." *Japan Times*. July 13. http://info.japantimes.co.jp/text /ff20050713a5.html.

Fingers, Al. 2012. *Clarks in Jamaica*. London: One Love Books.

Hardy, Ernest. 2002. Film Review. "Small Place, Big Hurt." *LA Weekly*, February 8.

Harris, Treviene. 2013. "Bleaching to Reach: Skin Bleaching as Re-Claiming of Identity in Jamaican Dancehall Culture." MA thesis, Florida International University.

Kincaid, Jamaica. 1988. *A Small Place*. New York: Farrar, Straus and Giroux.

Lorde, Audre. 1984. *Sister Outsider*. Freedom, CA: Crossing Press.

Luszczynsa, Ana. 2011. *The Ethics of Community: Nancy, Derrida, Morrison, and Menendez*. London: Bloomsbury Academic.

Manley, Michael. 1983. *Up the Down Escalator: Development and the International Economy—A Jamaican Case Study*. Washington, DC: Howard University Press.

Manlove, Clifford. 2007. "Visual Drive and Cinematic Narrative" *Cinema Journal* 46, no. 3 (Spring): 104.

Mbembe, Achille. 2001. *On the Postcolony*. Berkeley: University of California Press.

Paul, Annie. 2009. "Eyeless in Gaza (and Gully): 'Mi de pon di borderline.'" *Active Voice*, September 27. http://anniepaulactivevoice.blogspot.com/2009/09 /eyeless-in-gaza-mi-deh-pon-di.html.

Prince, Mary. 2002. "The History of Mary Prince, a West Indian Slave." In *Classic Slave Narratives*, ed. Henry Louis Gates Jr., 249–322. New York: Signet.

Russell, Heather D. 2012. "Life and Debt," *Transition*, no. 107: 137–49. doi:10.2979/transition.107.137.

Salewicz, Chris, and Adrian Boot. 2001. *Reggae Explosion: The Story of Jamaican Music*. London: Harry Abrams.

Sheller, Mimi. 2003. *Consuming the Caribbean*. New York: Routledge.

Silvera, Janet. 2009. "No Air Jamaica Sale, no IMF: Divestment of National Carrier Tied to Negotiations with Lending Agency." *Jamaica Gleaner*, November 20.

Touré. 2011. *Who's Afraid of Post-Blackness? What It Means to Be Black Now*. New York: Free Press.

Thomas, Deborah. 2004. *Modern Blackness: Nationalism, Globalization, and the Politics of Culture in Jamaica*. Durham, NC: Duke University Press.

Thomas, Kevin. 2002. Movie Review. "A Moving but Simplistic Take on the Perils of Globalization." *LA Times*, February 8.

7

Embodying Africa

Roots-Seekers and the Politics of Blackness

BAYO HOLSEY

In February 2012 Devin Grandison, an eleven-year-old African American boy from New York, traveled to the village of Aferie in Ghana's Western Region to receive a special recognition for his philanthropic efforts. Devin had begun sending clothes, school supplies, and library books to the village after a trip there in 2010 with a group of students. Because of these donations, the chief of the village decided to grant Devin the title of *nkosuohene*. The *nkosuohene*, or "development chief," is responsible for promoting the development of the village. A local newspaper described the day of Devin's enstoolment (or installation) as one of great festivity. Devin, who adopted the title Nana Obongu Agyeman II, was dressed in kente cloth, a material commonly worn by royalty in Ghana, and was carried in a palanquin through the streets of the town while residents cheered (Awuah 2012). The story of his enstoolment served to announce to Ghanaians his commitment to the economic development of the village, made all the more poignant because of his young age. Indeed, the existence of a foreign *nkosuohene* who can connect a given village to the global economy in new ways holds great promise for communities like Aferie. As part of the plan for his reign as *nkosuohene*, Devin announced that he planned to administer a scholarship program for students from the village so that they could continue their education.

Devin's story demonstrates the significance not only of global actors in Africa today but specifically of black diasporic ones. While some whites have become *nkosuohene*, the granting of this title to African Americans carries special meaning. Such enstoolments are accompanied by a preexisting discourse about the ancestral kinship of African Americans that has been well articulated. Indeed, in Ghana and elsewhere in West Africa, communities have promoted the notion of their connection to the African diaspora as part of tourism industries, humanitarian projects, and development schemes. Many African Americans—be they a celebrity donating money, a tourist visiting slave sites, or a child becoming chief— have traveled to West Africa in search of their ancestral roots and have welcomed the opportunity to honor their African heritage by directing their philanthropic activities toward communities on the continent.

The figure of the African American "roots-seeker" is also a ready-made media object that has, as a result, entered into public culture. Often photographed decked out in kente cloth, smiling broadly, or, alternatively, somber and sometimes in tears, his or her appearance in the press has challenged the idea that black Americans no longer care about their African ancestry. Such an argument has been made by cultural critics who posit that we now live in an age of post-blackness. If race no longer matters, then centuries-old ancestral connections certainly should not either. Here we instead find that ancestral kinship undergirds the formation of transnational black identities.

But the figure of the roots-seeker does not put to rest questions regarding the contemporary significance of race. In this individual we find a drastically different formulation of blackness from those that have previously held sway. Rather than an understanding of blackness as a shared identity that serves as the foundation of a liberatory politics, here blackness is an individual experience that becomes the basis of neoliberal development agendas. The current popularity of stories about roots-seekers turns our attention to blackness as something real, embodied, and oftentimes even imagined to be genetic, while at the same time these narratives detach blackness from radical politics. They suggest a return to a notion of biological blackness that undercuts all of the current talk of post-blackness while they represent a sharp departure from a Civil Rights/Black Power/ African decolonization notion of blackness. In doing so, they obscure the many forms of radical black politics that continue to shape the global arena in the new millennium.

A key moment in the construction of a neoliberal blackness was the 1977 airing of the television miniseries *Roots* based on Alex Haley's award-winning novel. In this essay I examine the ways in which *Roots* popularized the idea that blackness should be understood primarily in terms of an individual's relationship to Africa and at the same time encouraged private economic investments in the continent. I then demonstrate how some African governments have, in response to *Roots*, sought ways to recognize roots-seekers as part of a development strategy and, in doing so, have opened up new forms of diasporic engagement focused on individual experience. Finally, I consider the case of a millennial roots-seeker and investigate the construction of a narrative around African ancestry that challenges the idea of the politically engaged racial subject. I argue that the high degree of public attention paid to the autonomous diasporic subject/investor and to the ritual staging of his or her African kinship at the expense of greater recognition of more politicized constructions of blackness demonstrate the vicissitudes of late capitalism today.

IMAGINING AFRICA

To appreciate the significance of the *Roots* moment, one must understand the nature of diasporic encounters with Africa in the preceding era. To be sure, African Americans have had a long and deep engagement with the continent. The Civil Rights / Black Power era represents, however, an important moment in this history because of the focus on the African continent as a partner in political organizing. Indeed, the simultaneity of anticolonialism in Africa and the Civil Rights struggle in the United States led to a political moment that was pregnant with possibility. Many African Americans envisioned a black transnational sphere made up of various branches. Despite the great geographic distances that exist between some of them, as exists between the United States and Africa branches, they were still of vital importance to each other.

During this period, the black press played an important role in encouraging African Americans' interest in Africa. Black newspapers often published features on the continent to keep their audiences abreast of developments there. As a result of such media attention, many African Americans became advocates for African liberation. Throughout the sixties and seventies, for instance, some African American leaders had highlighted the similarities between racial injustices in South Africa and those in America. The timing of the Sharpeville massacre and the Greensboro sit-in led many African Americans to view white supremacy within a global context. Likewise, many African Americans supported Kwame Nkrumah's critique of neocolonialism in Ghana, and for the same reason (Meriwether 2002, 193). Showing pride in African ancestry was often part of a militant stance against U.S. racism. When African Americans fought for African freedom, they announced their solidarity with black people on the continent. To be black was to be part of a collective. Having shared goals determined the contours of the black community and the struggle to achieve those goals together was the way in which race was lived.

Though many African Americans remained engaged with Africa in the late 1970s, Alex Haley would gain the most national spotlight in this regard. The 1977 airing of the television miniseries *Roots* shaped, and continues to shape, mainstream perceptions of what it means to be a member of the African diaspora in the post–Civil Rights and Black Power eras. Through Alex Haley's presentation of his personal history and his journey toward an African diasporic identity, he provided a model of how to embrace Africa not a as group but rather as a singular raced subject, thereby shifting the key terms often associated with race from collective struggle to individual embodiment. He also encouraged a shift in emphasis from the various branches of the black transnational world to its African roots.[1]

Roots was the biggest television sensation of its time. Twenty-nine million households across the country tuned in to the first episode in January 1977. Many had read the book upon which it was based. The 1976 novel ranked number one on the *New York Times* bestseller list for eighteen weeks. Haley won a Pulitzer Prize for the book the following year. Some had read descriptions of and excerpts from the book even before it was published. In 1972, as he was working on the book, Haley published an essay in the *New Times* magazine describing how he traced his family genealogy back to the village of Juffure in the Gambia.

Whether or not viewers were already familiar with the story, that January, they watched in living color the birth of Kunta Kinte in an idyllic African village and saw him grow into a young man. The next day, they talked to their friends and coworkers about the episode. They discussed it on the bus and in the beauty parlor. And that second night, even more people sat down to watch the second episode. By the eighth night, the finale night, 100 million Americans were tuning in to watch *Roots*. Describing the phenomenon, a reporter wrote:

> Appointments were canceled and parties interrupted so that people could be in front of a television set at the designated hour each night. Young children stayed up long past their bedtimes, and morning-coffee conversations recounted the latest episode. There was an atmosphere of shared experience: everyone seemed aware not only of what had happened the night before but of events 200 years in the past. For eight days and nights, the most talked-about men in the country were a middle-aged writer named Alex Haley and his great-great-great-great-grandfather, Kunta Kinte.[2]

They would continue to discuss the show months later. They read reviews in the newspaper and saw it nominated for thirty-seven Emmy awards,

nine of which it won. College students found classes in their course cata-
logues focused on the miniseries. They understood that it said something
important about the place of black people in American society and about
contemporary race relations. But many thought, first and foremost, of that
first night and that first episode—of their introduction to Kunta Kinte
as a boy living in an African village. They noted the grace and beauty of
Cecily Tyson, who played Kunta's mother, and the order and peace of the
village. For baby boomers who were then young adults, this was a far cry
from the popular portrayals of Africa in the Tarzan films of childhoods.
This was an Africa of which they could be proud, and they readily took
it into their hearts. In this post–Civil Rights moment, African Americans found a new understanding of Africa. In contrast to an earlier era's
focus on contemporary Africa and its struggles, some chose to embrace an
imagined Africa as an ancestral homeland.

Haley's first encounter with Juffure and the inspiration for *Roots* was
a result of stories he heard growing up about an ancestor whom family
members called "the African." His African name was Kin-tay, and he had
been captured while out one day chopping wood to make a drum. The
story of his capture as well as several words in his language that he taught
his daughter were passed down through the generations to Haley. With
the help of some prominent historians, he traced the words to the Mandinka people in the Gambia. He immediately traveled there, where he
learned that there was a village named for the Kinte family. Haley had to
return to the Gambia a second time to meet with the griot of the Kinte
clan. After reciting a long lineage history that included the resettlement of
Karaiba Kunta Kinte in Juffure, the griot told Haley that one of his sons
left the village one day to chop wood and never came back. Struck by the
familiarity of this tale, he told them his grandmother's story. The people in
the village immediately embraced him as their long-lost son (Haley 1976).

For both Haley and the people of Juffure, this moment represented a
profound instance of recognition. For Haley, it also brought to mind in
vivid fashion, "as if it were mistily being projected on a screen," the historical processes of enslavement (ibid., 721). He thought of the villages that
were burned, the slavers that rounded up frightened men and women as

they ran from their homes, the coffles in which they were placed, and the long march to the coast that they were forced to endure. Recognition of the specifics of his African ancestry led therefore to profound sadness. He explains, "I just began crying as I have never cried in my life. It just seemed to me that if you really knew the ancestral history of blacks, we blacks, if you really knew the way every single one of us had come here, that no matter whatever else might later be your reaction, that you first had to weep" (Haley 1973, 19). In this way Haley centered the personal emotional effects of the experience above all else within the image of diasporic engagement.

Because of the high level of interest in his African village homeland, Haley traveled back to Juffure after the airing of the miniseries on a well-publicized trip. Traveling by a motor yacht provided by the Gambian president, he arrived with an entourage that included his two brothers, several Gambian and U.S. officials, and members of the press, including famed photographer Moneta Sleet Jr., who photographed the trip for *Ebony* magazine. Haley's trip was the cover story for the magazine's July 1977 issue, which featured a photo of Haley surrounded by the people of Juffure in a scene of joyous reunion.

And indeed it was. Haley and his entourage were greeted by "a flood of reverence." The village held a welcoming ceremony presided over by the chief during which Mandinka dancers performed in Haley's honor and women encircled him, holding up their babies, many of whom he took into his arms. In describing the scene, Hans J. Massaquoi writes, "It seemed as if Kunta Kinte himself had returned to his native African village near the banks of the Gambian River. . . . Certainly, the welcome he would have received could hardly have been more tumultuous, more emotion-packed than the one accorded his seven generations removed descendant" (1977, 31).

This was a reenactment of the moment of recognition for both Haley and the people of Juffure for television cameras. The profound sadness he felt during that first trip had turned to joy. Haley found resolution to the trauma of a memory of slavery and African origins. This tale of recognition struck a deep chord in segments of the African American community. While some media outlets were focused on the increasing doubt over the historical veracity of Haley's genealogical connection to Juffure, *Ebony* went against the grain by making the unqualified statement that the village was indeed the home of Haley's African ancestors. It described a picture of Haley holding a small child from the village as him cuddling "one of his many new-found cousins." The article also discussed Haley's reunion with Binta Kinte Fofona, the widow of the by then deceased griot who had provided the oral history that became the basis of Haley's story of Kunta Kinte's capture. It states, "Standing in the Kinte family compound surrounded by two dozen or so Kintes of all ages, the American author and African matriarch joined in a tearful embrace. At that moment, there wasn't the slightest doubt in the minds of the Kintes present that their long-lost brother and cousin Kunta had finally come home" (ibid., 33).

The language of homecoming, and the idea it captures of Haley representing the return of his enslaved ancestor, has become central to media depictions of African American travel to West Africa. The idea that an individual could go back to the African village of his or her ancestors and be welcomed as a long-lost sister or brother seemed to fascinate reporters, no doubt because it provided a different narrative about blackness from those that had been dominant for so long, many of them concerning African American involvement in anticolonial struggles on the continent. Indeed, Haley's emotional response to his visit to Juffure did not lead him to take up these causes. Instead, it formed the basis of a plan for economic investment in the continent.

According to some sources, Haley's monetary contributions to Juffure included a gift of $15,000 for the building of a mosque. But he also hoped to inspire other African Americans to give to Africa. In fact, he anticipated a large-scale diasporic development project emerging from *Roots* and its exploration of the history of slavery and the African ancestry of black Americans. In particular, he envisioned a program in which African American families would "adopt" children from anywhere in Africa and donate five hundred dollars toward their education.

The simultaneity of Haley's emotional "family reunion" and his formulation of a diasporic investment scheme is no accident. Indeed, the idea of diasporic subjectivity as individualized experience activated here fits well within a late capitalist economic framework. Under late capitalism, governmentality functions by regulating individual, autonomous actors. These individuals are responsible for their own welfare and are free to make decisions about the communities with which they want to engage. This model relieves the state of responsibility for the social welfare of its citizens. It also absolves Western governments from responsibility for the reduction of global poverty. In this context, while bettering lives, the existence of diasporic development sustains the neoliberal capitalist system that itself produces the very inequalities that development seeks to alleviate. It is, to use James Ferguson's phrase, an "anti-politics machine" (1990). Haley's plan for Africa demonstrated an acceptance of a capitalist framework rather than a challenge to it.

His plan came at a time, furthermore, when Western nations were forcing Ghana, along with other African nations, to strengthen their capitalist systems by rewarding those that did so. In response to the economic downturn in Ghana in the 1970s, the World Bank and International Monetary Fund implemented a structural adjustment program. As a precondition for aid, they called for economic austerity including decreased social services, the privatization of industries, and the devaluation of currencies. The implementation of neoliberal policies throughout Africa has meant that communities on the continent cannot rely on the state to provide for all of their needs and must therefore find ways to attract individual investors. In identifying potential investors, furthermore, they must "sell" themselves and their cultures. Jean Comaroff and John Comaroff trace this phenomenon in various communities across the globe in their book *Ethnicity, Inc.* They examine the fashioning of ethnic identities in the new millennium, arguing that "ethnicity is becoming more corporate, more commodified, more implicated than ever before in the economics of everyday life" (2009, 1).

TOURING AFRICA

Haley's formulation of diasporic engagement turned out to be a lucrative business for West African nations. His visit to the Gambia led to a tourism boom there. The Gambian minister for information and tourism had traveled to the United States for the launch of the *Roots* miniseries. This trip was followed by the travel of forty-one African Americans to the Gambia and a subsequent trip by a group of travel agents interested in promoting American tourism to the Gambia. Also in 1977, Banjul, the capital of the Gambia, and Tuskegee, Alabama, a predominately black town and home of the well-known, historically black college by the same name, became sister cities, and Tuskegee's mayor joined the list of American visitors to the Gambia. Tourism at nearby Gorée Island in Senegal took off after *Roots* as well. Gorée is home of La Maison des Esclaves, a site at which some historians claim slaves were held before they were forced onto ships to endure the Middle Passage. All told, thirty thousand Americans visited the Gambia and Senegal in 1977 and 1978 (Touray 2000).

In Ghana, the slave dungeons within Cape Coast and Elmina castles have become huge draws for diaspora tourists. Thousands travel to Ghana each year to see the dungeons and reflect on the history of the slave trade. Ghana's Ministry of Tourism launched the celebration of Emancipation Day as a way to further encourage diaspora tourists to visit the nation. Many have described the experience of participating in such events and, in particular, of viewing the slave dungeons as providing a kind of catharsis in which they move through sorrow toward pride in the strength of their ancestors and in their African ancestry, a progression similar to that described by Haley (Holsey 2008). It is a deeply personal and emotionally charged undertaking that they value highly.

West African diaspora tourism industries have developed various means to deliver an individualized experience of acceptance and belonging to diaspora tourists so that they can emulate Alex Haley. Take, for instance, the following example. During the 2007 Emancipation Day celebrations in Ghana, the Ministry of Tourism held a "healing ceremony" at Elmina Castle designed especially for members of the diaspora (see Holsey 2010). The event, which I attended, was staged as a reunification of Africa with the African diaspora. It began with great solemnity. The guests, who were primarily African American, were given strips of cloth to tie around their wrists in black and red, the colors of mourning in Ghana. As we then entered the forecourt of the castle, we were greeted by a massive structure shaped like a freestanding doorway that had been constructed especially for the event with the words "Door of Return" printed at the top. This structure was a representation of the doorway inside of the castle dungeons that slaves exited on their way to slave ships, known as the "Door of No Return." For years, tour guides have told tourists that when they, while on tours, exit through these doors and then pass through again back into the dungeons, this act represents the return of the enslaved to their homeland. These tourists are asked to imagine themselves as their own enslaved ancestors and therefore as "returnees." The freestanding Door of Return allowed us to ritually reenact this practice one by one.

After several speeches and an opening prayer, the chiefs and queen mothers in attendance were asked to come forward. They rose from their special section of the audience seating in their full regalia, including beautifully draped cloths and sumptuous gold jewelry, and entered the center of the forecourt. There they each stood at a pedestal with a basin of water and a ladle. The master of ceremonies then instructed them to pour the water over their hands in a symbolic act of purification for the past crimes of their predecessors of selling slaves. Next the diaspora tourists, hailed as "brothers and sisters from the diaspora" were asked to come forward. We rose and approached the chiefs and queen mothers. The master of ceremonies told us to pour water over our hands in order to heal us from our past victimization that took place, he suggested, at their hands. We were told then to remove the black and red strips of cloth from our wrists because we were no longer in mourning—we were healed. In this way each tourist had the opportunity to take part in the ceremony and to feel that the chiefs and queen mothers had recognized our individual loss and pain. We, like Haley, came to embody our ancestors, and, indeed, our bodies became sites of ritual work to honor their memory.

At the same time that it provided an individualized experience for roots-seekers, the Joseph Project also contained an explicit emphasis on Ghana's economic woes and the potential of diasporic investment. Speakers during the ceremony not only pointed to supposed African American success; they also argued that African Americans can use their wealth and talent to help their lost "kin" in Ghana. Indeed, during the launch, tourists were told over and over again to invest in Ghana through tourism and business ventures. In doing so, organizers identified African Americans as wealthy and successful individuals who can provide a solution for Africa's problems. A sense of community was offered in hopes that they would provide their wealth, talent, and resources in exchange. There were no fees connected to the Joseph Project launch; however, speakers encouraged visitors to donate or invest in various projects. In this way the healing ceremony was as a ritual of late capitalism.

The enstoolment of African American development chiefs, as I mention earlier, is another means by which African communities have sought to both recognize the autonomous diasporic subject in search of identity and provide a means for economic development. The position of *nkosuohene* is a relatively recent invention. In 1985 the former Asantehene, or chief of Asante, Opoku Ware II created the office and instructed all of his subchiefs to appoint men and women to occupy this position (Bob-Milliar 2009). It is given to "an accomplished individual, one with the power to mobilize the resources of the community 'both physical and human' for the advancement of such a community" (ibid., 545). Since then, the idea has spread outside of Asante and indeed throughout southern Ghana. While the *nkosuohene* position was originally intended for individuals from the communities in which they were enstooled, many chiefs began the practice of enstooling foreigners as an attempt to stream wealth from other countries to their villages through these individuals, thereby demonstrating the exigencies of late capitalism at play.

Of course, since the development of the office, many African Americans have been enstooled. While the media has tended to focus, as in the case of Alex Haley, on the emotional impact of the recognition of their ancestral connections to Africa, many development chiefs themselves see their positions as part of an important racial justice project. Beryl Dorsett, a former assistant secretary for elementary education in the U.S. Department of Education and deputy superintendent in Brooklyn's School District 17, traveled to Ghana as head of a group of sixty-five African American teachers from New York City in 1994. While there, she met a teacher and his father. Eventually Dorsett was enstooled as the development chief of the father's village, Apatrapa. The town also named a school in her honor. Dorsett, who is head of the international division of National Association of Negro Business and Professional Women's Clubs (NANBPWC) brought some of her colleagues in the association to the village in 1997. After consultation with local residents, the women embarked on several development initiatives. Dorsett founded a nongovernmental organization called Apatrapa Women in Development. She also established a child sponsorship program to provide tuition and school supplies to students enrolled in the school named in her honor. Ellen Stubbs and Mary Singletary, also members of the association, built a health clinic. Through the NANBPWC, they dug two wells for the village. While the NANBPWC website describes Africa as its homeland in some of its discussions of its activities West Africa, the overarching theme is the empowerment of black women worldwide. Rather than focusing on ancestral links, their projects highlight black consciousness more broadly conceived. Unfortunately such approaches do not capture popular attention the way that other formulations focused solely on the search for roots seem to.

EMBODYING AFRICA

The story of one of the most publicized roots-seekers of recent years certainly follows the narrative scope set down by Haley. It begins, however, not in the dusty archives in which Haley researched his genealogy but rather, as befits the new millennium, with lab results.[3] In 2005 the well-known African American actor Isaiah Washington received genetic ancestry testing results in front of a crowd gathered to celebrate the winners of the Pan-African film festival awards. After feeling initial trepidation, Washington had agreed to undergo the testing. For many African Americans today, their DNA provides the impetus to travel to Africa. The rise of genetic ancestry testing has meant that race has become fully embodied in the individual. Genetic ancestry testing also pulls at the seams of the racial collective by focusing on ethnicity. One must now not only embrace her generic African roots but rather must determine her specific ethnic origin. With this knowledge, one can add her individualized mission with regard to Africa.

Such was the case with Washington. He recounts the experience and his resulting engagement with Sierra Leone in the book, *Man from Another Land: How Finding My Roots Changed My Life*. Although the book has received nowhere near the same acclaim as *Roots*, it nonetheless is an important public representation of diasporic engagement with Africa. As such, I provide a brief analysis of some of its key points.

When Washington first received his results, he describes being overcome with emotion. As he recounts in his book,

> I felt reborn that night. No longer did I need cowrie shells hanging from my locks, African jewelry, African dance classes, or African drumming circles. There would be no more need to hang portraits of Negresses or Moorish chiefs or wear kente cloth around my neck. All the external things that I thought I needed to connect me to Africa were now unnecessary. Africa had been inside me all along. She was inside by DNA. She was beckoning me and guiding me my entire life through my dreams.
>
> (Washington and Lavette 2011, 73–74)

For him, race became something literally located within his body. It was also something that would guide the direction of his life as he soon after committed himself to development projects in Sierra Leone, a decision that he argues was foreseen. As a child, Washington had a recurrent dream of running through a forest in which he ended up every time in what he describes to be an African village. In addition, he describes himself as embodying the spirit of a great African freedom fighter. He writes, "Even at a young age, I was always trying to break barriers, aspiring to do things that people told me I couldn't, or others thought were strange or unattainable. I was willing to stay the course, take the unbeaten path no matter what got in my way, when others would give up and go home" (ibid., 5) After receiving his DNA results, he reinterprets the source of this drive. "I share a storied history, the same DNA with great Africans and men of incredible courage," he explains. "Men like Sengbe Pieh—Joseph Cinque as he was called during his historical trial—who had the bravery to lead the *Amistad* revolt. That history, that DNA, reflects a past of great accomplishment that eventually led me to my own place in history" (ibid., 10). For this reason, he decided that he must travel to Sierra Leone, a goal which became for him a spiritual calling. He describes the moment he had the decision to go as follows: "I closed my eyes and began to meditate . . . 'This is it,' I thought to myself. 'This is what I was born to do. This is my purpose'" (ibid., 74).

After much planning, Washington finally traveled to his newfound ancestral homeland. He describes arriving in Sierra Leone:

> It was May 22, 2006, when wheels touched down and the team and I arrived at Lungi International Airport Freetown, Sierra Leone. I was so happy, I could not stop smiling. At times, everything seemed to be in slow motion as if I were watching a movie, except it wasn't a movie, it was happening, and to me! I felt like a little boy about to unwrap a gift I had been hoping and wishing for all year long.   (112)

On his third day in the country, he traveled to the Bunce Island slave castle. His experience there, while saddening, ultimately left him feeling glad for the experience. He explains:

> We learned of slaves who willed themselves to death while on the island and others, trying to escape, who were killed by sharks in the deep waters surrounding the castle. I stood in the center of a corral where three hundred slaves lived chained together with only a small trough of rice to eat placed between them. I felt hurt by the humiliation they endured. I found myself feeling disgusted as I looked through a display window depicting the castle where the slaveholders sat around sipping wine and spirits as they chose which slaves they wanted to buy or molest.
>
> Somehow, after hearing all the horrific statistics and facts, I still felt a sense of pride. Yes the slave castle was designed by the oppressor,

but it was built by the oppressed. And it's still, hundreds of years later, standing for the world to see and understand the atrocities that took place there.

As I stood on Bunce Island I felt I was a living testament to the indomitable spirit of my great-great-great-great-great-grandmother.

(Ibid., 138–39)

Washington provides an almost textbook description of emotional catharsis. But this trip was also the beginning of his philanthropy in Sierra Leone. Washington was made a chief of the village of Ngalu and given the name Gondobay Manga II. Washington started the Gondobay Manga foundation to fund development projects in Sierra Leone. For him, as for Haley, his connection to Africa led to economic investment. In 2008, in recognition of his efforts, Washington was granted dual citizenship in the country. He notes that he was the first African American to be granted citizenship in an African nation on the basis of DNA. All of this, again, seems preordained. While in Sierra Leone, he learned that local folklore has it that "a man from another land" will return to Sierra Leone one day to help rebuild it. Seeing himself as the embodiment of this mythical figure provides a momentous ending to the tale of personal transformation.

Washington's description of his reaction to the discovery of his ancestry, his catharsis at Bunce Island, and his fulfillment of destiny by becoming a chief all point to his understanding of his connection to Africa as a deeply personal one that allows him to fulfill his individual destiny. Learning about his genetic code has functioned not to integrate himself within a racial community but rather to make him distinctive. He is not just black and, ultimately, not just Mende, but is Chief Gondobay Manga II. His embrace of Africa, then, is an acceptance of his distinctiveness, one born of race, but one that marks his singularity. It is an identity imprinted within his body, stamped inside of his cells, and written into his genes. At the same time, this identity inspires his philanthropic efforts. His endeavors, however, remain firmly within the realm of neoliberal economic development.

The experiences of some development chiefs and diaspora tourists suggest that competing notions of the African diaspora relationship have taken hold under late capitalism. The dominance of the autonomous liberal individual within public narratives about diasporic engagements with Africa is not an inconsequential development. The high visibility of these formulations arises from the fact that they fit well within the late capitalist framework. They maintain public focus on individual actors instead of on the work of groups. They construct roots-seekers as autonomous subjects and not as members of racial communities. And they provide a means to address African development issues through individual philanthropic gestures rather than through a confrontation with global structures of inequality. The unfortunate outcome of this focus is that it obscures the highly political engagements with Africa that remain part of the wide range of black diasporic public life. It conceals the ways that finding one's African roots *can*, in fact, lead to a flourishing of a radical black racial consciousness.

NOTES

1. See also Clarke 2006 for a discussion of the significance of *Roots*.
2. "'Roots' Takes Hold in America," *Newsweek*, February 7, 1977.
3. See Nelson (2014) for a fuller discussion of the role of DNA testing in contemporary constructions of black identities.

REFERENCES

Awuah, Joe. 2012. "American Boy Enstooled Chief." *Daily Guide*, February 28.

Bob-Milliar, George M. 2009. "Chieftaincy, Diaspora, and Development: The Institution of Nkosuohene in Ghana." *African Affairs* 108, no. 433: 541–58. doi:10.1093/afraf/adp0.

Clarke, Kamari Maxine. 2006. "Mapping Transnationality: Roots Tourism and the Institutionalization of Ethnic Heritage." In *Globalization and Race: Transformations in the Cultural Production of Blackness*, ed. Kamari Maxine Clarke and Deborah A. Thomas, 133–53. Durham, NC: Duke University Press.

Comaroff, John L., and Jean Comaroff. 2009. *Ethnicity, Inc.* Chicago: University of Chicago Press.

Haley, Alex. 1973. "Black History, Oral History, and Genealogy." *Oral History Review* 1:1–25.

——. 1976. *Roots*. Garden City, NY: Doubleday.

Holsey, Bayo. 2008. *Routes of Remembrance: Refashioning the Slave Trade in Ghana*. Chicago: University of Chicago Press.

——. 2010. "Rituel et Mémoire au Ghana: Les Usage Politiques de la Diaspora." *Critique Internationale* 47 (April–June): 19–36. doi:10.3917/crii.047.0019.

Ferguson, James. 1990. *The Anti-Politics Machine: "Development," Depoliticization, and Bureaucratic Power in Lesotho*. Cambridge: Cambridge University Press.

Massaquoi, Hans J. 1977. "Alex Haley in Juffure." *Ebony*, July, 31–42.

Meriwether, James Hunter. 2002. *Proudly We Can Be Africans: Black Americans and Africa, 1935–1961*. Chapel Hill: University of North Carolina Press.

Nelson, Alondra. 2014. *The Social Life of DNA: Race and Reconciliation After the Genome*. Boston: Beacon Press.

Touray, Omar A. 2000. *The Gambia and the World: A History of the Foreign Policy of Africa's Smallest State, 1965–1995*. Hamburg: Institut für Afrika-Kunde.

Washington, Isaiah, and Lavaille Lavette. 2011. *A Man from Another Land: How Finding My Roots Changed My Life*. New York: Center Street.

8

"The world is a ghetto"

Post-Racial America(s) and the Apocalypse

PATRICE RANKINE

The thigh bone is connected to the white suburbanites who turn their heads away from the calamity of Detroit . . .
—Charlie LeDuff, *Detriot: An American Autopsy*

Detroit is Holland is America is the world. And the world is a ghetto.

I am teetering between stability and an abyss. It is the posture of a possible suicidal plunge, or the step back after being talked off of a ledge. To some extent, what I am experiencing is the customary vertigo from a life-altering experience—a move that they say is a stressor on par with death. I have made a career change after fifteen years at the same university, and housing, relationships, and my frame of mind remain precarious. My thoughts vacillate regarding whether it would be best to live in Holland, Michigan, one of *Forbes* magazine's "Prettiest American Towns," in walking distance from the demands of my new position as dean for the arts and humanities at Hope College; or if it would be better to settle in Grand Rapids, a city that itself might be reemerging from its own abyss, its downtown featuring an autumn art fair (ArtPrize) and a spring Dionysia dedicated to ecstasy after the winter frost (LaughFest).[1] The choice seems straightforward enough, town or city, sustainability or sprawl, but for me it brings an added level of existential angst, a sickness unto death, even beyond the loss of leaving behind another life.[2] We are in "post-racial" America during the second decade of the third millennium, *anno dominis*, and I am a black man—on a ledge.

JULY 5, 2013: "WHAT TO THE SLAVE IS THE FOURTH OF JULY?"

As we drive through Grand Rapids to the west of the Grand River toward my temporary apartment near the Comstock Park neighborhood, my mother and father, who have come for the Fourth of July to help me move, pass horrified glances my way.[3] "I have never seen such poverty among white people," my mother opines. This is a woman from Bob Marley's Trenchtown, in the shanties of Jamaica. Land of "them belly full, but we hungry."[4] She has seen poverty in all hues. Yet there is something surreal about this. In fact, statistics corroborate my mother's armchair science. In 2013 one in seven Michiganders lived in poverty.[5] One should always trust the wisdom of one's mother. To one side of the Grand River, beyond the affluent boulevards of East Grand Rapids and at the edge of an abyss, reside some poor, poor people—black, white, and brown alike. Poverty is integrating; these might be among the most integrated neighborhoods I have ever seen, akin to Brazil's favelas. (I have lived in Kingston, Jamaica; Brooklyn, New York; and Lafayette, Indiana, and I've traveled throughout South America and Europe.)

Let us recall that in Grand Rapids, we are thirty miles from my new job in Holland, Michigan, nationally acclaimed as one of the prettiest towns in America (Giuffo 2013). According to Holland's mayor, Kurt Dykstra, who most resembles a Ken doll, though even further perfected and more handsome, Holland has the most rapidly growing economy in Western Michigan.[6] In other words, Holland, Michigan, is on the other side of the brink. First settled in the 1847 by Albertus C. Van Raalte, who was also the founder of Hope Academy (1851) and Hope College (1866), Holland was a Dutch outpost that to this day retains its historical significance.[7] I have traveled throughout Europe and the Americas and have scarcely seen a more segregated place. In fact, downtown Holland has next-to no racial or ethnic diversity, so it is unfair to call it segregated; ethnicity simply does not exist here. Holland, Michigan is 22.7 percent Hispanic—little of this population evident downtown, all on the brink . . . at the precipice toward the abyss.[8] As an astute resident ensconced in Holland's inner circle pointed out to me, it is telling that there is not a single ethnic restaurant among the vibrant downtown businesses that attract tourists to this idyllic place. And don't even think about soul food, Caribbean food, or any of that, though a local lawyer tells me that the barbeque on the outskirts of town is not bad. Downtown Holland, however, is virtually an ethnicity-free zone.

Despite the lack of diversity in Holland's heart, the city has captured the American imagination because it is not only one of the prettiest towns in America but it also sustains this pristine downtown. Holland celebrates Tulip Time every May with Dutch dances and food and festivities. While many small towns in America are struggling to attract and maintain businesses, brandishing empty storefronts at every-other stop, Holland's 8th Street bustles all summer long, and the heated sidewalks and street-side fire pit make winter just as warm, as I experienced in February 2013, when I first visited the town. Holland has the distinction of not only being featured in Forbes magazine, but editor James Fallows also featured the city in his August 10, 2013 *Atlantic* article, "Welcome to Holland," where he highlighted the city's summer charm.

The thirty-five miles from Holland to my temporary abode in Comstock Park, Grand Rapids, put me outside of the sphere of sustainability and onto a daily highway commute. It is a commute that burns the gas that costs almost four dollars a gallon that, along with the credit and housing crises, put America in its post-2008 plunge, out of which we are still climbing. We are between stability and an abyss. And yet here is my dilemma: in Grand Rapids, at least there is a downtown with ethnic and racial diversity, a culture of young artists, and museums and restaurants and street fairs with jazz and blues and funk and salsa. Grand Rapids, its poverty notwithstanding, is a city with its gait toward the future.

POST-RACIAL?

Despite the tone of my opening gambit, this essay is not my "talking cure," my therapy session, or my attempt to come to terms with my trauma— which is the severing from my past, my personal dilemma, or the melancholia of watching America's demise—through writing. Or maybe it is. If successful, my piece should help a broader audience than myself to account for where we are as Americans racially, socially, and spiritually. As a place attentive to vocation and the spiritual formation of its students through a Christian mission, Hope College's faculty, staff, and students are in a unique position to address the big questions of our time, and yet I find us intellectually and theologically at a remove from the heart of the matter. Our hearts are not in it; Holland's heart is not in it. The social realities of our time necessitate a set of discourses—political, economic, educational, and spiritual—that are driven in part by an attempt to come to terms with disparities that inevitably fall along lines of class, race, and ethnicity—and all of this in what we are told are post-racial times.

My analysis exposes as shallow and materialistic—though profoundly learned—the post-racial rhetoric of Touré's America, which he presents in *Who's Afraid of Post-Blackness* (2012), while I question the deeper reach of Charles Taylor's *The Secular Age* (2007) and other texts oft-cited within Hope College's particular approach to post-millennial Christianity. I include in this James Davison Hunter's *To Change the World* (2010), which calls for "presence" as a way to activate Christian love in a time of crisis. Where is God in the poorest neighborhoods of Grand Rapids, in the bankrupt Detroit, or on the South Side of Chicago? What is missing on both ends of the spectrum—that is, both from Touré's shallow analysis and from the profound but esoteric neo-Christian theology—is a more elusive, profoundly felt sense of *purpose* and calling that a care for all humanity—black, white, brown, yellow—underpins. What is missing is precisely what Taylor calls for: a response to despair.

BETWEEN STABILITY AND THE ABYSS

American cities and citizens are in an age of despair 150 years in the making, at least. I realize and appreciate that many Americans do not recognize the despair. This is because we have successfully isolated ourselves from much of reality, through the culture of barbiturates, anxiety medication, sleeping pills, and recreational drugs—all symptomatic of the crisis.[9] We dull the pain of a collective depression only to sense it creeping back over us, in time. It is no coincidence that the cities that I have mentioned, Holland and Grand Rapids, are under the same bureaucratic jurisdiction as the city of Detroit. That is, they are in the state of Michigan. The geographical isolation of cities in Western Michigan (South Haven, Saugatuck/Douglass, Holland) can feel at a remove from Detroit, 180 miles away, or even Grand Rapids, at only 30 miles distance. Whatever the psychological and physical detachment that "white flight" might afford, however, these isolated enclaves are linked historically, politically, and financially to the cities they left behind. The affluent can separate ourselves so much.

I live temporarily in Grand Rapids, but Detroit is the city in Michigan that has most captured the American imagination, the largest city to file for bankruptcy in the history of this New World experiment—perhaps in all the Americas. In *Detroit: An American Autopsy*, Charlie LeDuff makes the case that Detroit is not only emblematic of America in the early twenty-first century but also factually tied to broader systemic problems. In more than symbolic or tropic ways, Detroit's decline is America's decline, just as its rise had historical, political, and financial ties to the rest of the country. LeDuff, for example, traces to Detroit the rise of the American credit system: "In 1919, the young and hungry men of GM devised an ingenious scheme to supplant Ford as the number-one carmaker in the world. Credit" (2013, 147). The masses that had meandered to Detroit during the Great Migration were, of course, tied to factory work. Credit would not be a problem because "the assembly line would live forever" (36), until it didn't. And then came the problems. For LeDuff, the development of the credit crisis that reached its apogee in 2008 was itself almost a century in the making. For the American worker, the trust in credit over the "nobility of work" and "an honest day's labor" (36) was the starting point of a plunge into despair.

LeDuff is preternaturally aware of the racial dimension to the historical, political, and economic realities of postindustrial American cities such as Detroit, although he sometimes trades on race as easy currency. At one point in the book, LeDuff traces his own lineage to a black progenitor who traveled to Detroit from Louisiana. (LeDuff is a French name that betrays its bearer's Creole heritage.) Although of lighter hue, LeDuff's grandfather was black, according to the "one-drop" rule within the United States, but in Detroit left his segregated past behind and passed as white.[10] There is nothing post-racial about LeDuff's analysis. Race is at the root of the story of Detroit, and thus race is in its decaying branches. LeDuff frames his discussion of Detroit in profoundly racialized terms. Historical facts validate his nuanced and ironic posture, whether we look to statistics regarding who were sold subprime mortgages or we analyze data regarding who could leave Detroit after its decline and who remained.

LeDuff connects Detroit's decline to patterns of movement during the Great Migration. "Michigan," he proffers, "may geographically be one of America's most northern states, but spiritually, it is one of its most southern" (45). The same racial map helps us to understand other Michigan cities. In *A City Within a City: The Black Freedom Struggle in Grand Rapids, Michigan*, Todd E. Robinson presents Grand Rapids, Michigan, in similar terms through case studies of African Americans who migrated in the 1960s from the South to the "furniture city."[11] Robinson argues that African Americans did not find in Grand Rapids a more egalitarian racial landscape; rather, they faced a "racial conservatism" that closed them out of jobs, housing, and social and political inroads to more stable lives. From the looks of things, blacks in Grand Rapids, Michigan, in the early twenty-first century are still catching up.[12]

A similar conservatism influences the core of Holland, although my evidence here is primarily anecdotal. I could have easily lived in Holland, in fact. A grand historic home was quickly removed from the market in March 2013, within a short time of its viewing by one particular black man on the ledge. The house was neither sold nor listed as pending sale.

It was simply removed, no longer listed.[13] Coincidence? Perhaps. Members of Holland's inner circle often tell me about homes that are available for sale but have not—or will not—list publically. Many homes are sold without ever reaching the market. In other words, Holland is in many respects not a free-market economy. The inner network being what it is, in Holland there are not equal opportunities for the outsider, minorities, and those not in the know. While I cannot characterize the framework as itself actively racist, nor do I have the data to apply Robinson's category of "racial conservatism" to Holland, many of the anecdotes that blot the pages of Robinson's history of Grand Rapids are eerily familiar to those that I have heard from individuals willing to address the issue.

For Detroit, LeDuff trades on the racial realities to convey the despair in terms of cruel irony. Examples of a return of the past abound. LeDuff himself does not like being called Mister Charlie, a common moniker that Detroit's once-Southern citizens impose, because it is "an old slang term from antebellum times, a name given by slaves to their white oppressors" (69). LeDuff recognizes the past closing in on the present. And yet distinctions between black and white are suppressed, if not because we are in post-racial times then certainly because we are post-ethical. The "big three" automakers go to Washington, D.C., to ask for a bailout, these captains of industry who pushed Detroit and the nation to the brink. According to one of LeDuff's informants, the "big three . . . ain't nothing but Detroit." How were they any different from Kwame Kilpatrick, the philandering, race-baiting, black mayor, who embezzled millions from the city's coffers? People "don't realize that Detroit is a code word for nigger and they ain't nothing but niggers anymore" (78).

A tautology, by way of Charlie LeDuff: Post-racial is that state where race ceases to exist as a result of the fact that we are all niggers, and thus none of us can truly be a nigger. Language, after all, is about making distinctions, calling one thing "day" and its opposite "night." By citing the informant who says we are all niggers, LeDuff is, of course, addressing the credit crisis that came to a head in 2008, which had nothing to do with race, and yet was all about race, as noted in the overwhelming percentage of minorities, black and brown, who signed onto subprime mortgages only to watch them balloon out of control, and the one-time homeowners not able to get out of debt.[14] In LeDuff's account, the big three automakers acted no less unethically than did Kwame Kilpatrick.

Synecdoche: Part for the whole. Symbolically, emblematically, and tropically, Detroit figures for so many American cities, and their primarily segregated suburbs and shelled-out city centers. Detroit is in chiastic relationship to Holland, with its ethnicity-free, sanitized downtown to Detroit's majority black squalor. At the same time, Detroit is Holland is America is the world. And the world is a ghetto. Historically, politically, and economically, Detroit is the result of a set of realities that can be seen in many other cities across America—and for that matter, the Americas, Europe, and Africa. To cite LeDuff again, an "autopsy" of Detroit's demise reveals a clear causal—and not simply anecdotal—relationship: "The thigh bone is connected to the white suburbanites who turn their heads away from the calamity of Detroit, carrying on as though the human suffering were somebody else's problem" (15). And yet there is no hiding place, in the end. I ran to the mountains, and the mountains cried out.[15] Holland is a ghetto pretending not to be a ghetto. That is, Holland sweeps its poverty outside of its pristine downtown, the pretty brick-paved and music-filled 8th Street. I have heard that some at Hope College warn the students not to wander too far from 8th Street for fear of what they might find a short distance removed from the beautiful brick and limestone buildings.

In *The World Is a Ghetto: Race and Democracy Since World War II*, Howard Winant argues against "the ironic view" that "we are now in a post-racial, color-blind world" (2001, 1). Winant opposes this post-racial view and advances a solid set of propositions:

> that racial hierarchy lives on; that it correlates very well with worldwide and national systems of stratification and inequality; that it corresponds to glaring disparities in labor conditions and reflects differential access to democratic and communicative instrumentalities and life chances. My view is that the race-concept is anything but obsolete and that its significance is not declining. We are not "beyond race." (2)

Winant, a historical sociologist, sees the problem—and its origins—in global terms, across time. "Race" is not invented but rather imported from context to context, place to place, across geographical and temporal space. Here again, the reality must be explained in historical, political, and economic terms: "The interaction (and tension) among processes of capital accumulation, techniques of state-building and political rule, and general understandings that explained (or rationalized) the conflicts this emerging system entailed, were all deeply shaped by race" (39).

Winant's profound unearthing of the roots of race through historical sociology corroborates Charles Mills's treatment from the perspective of political philosophy, where, for example, John Locke's understanding of property is deeply rooted in the transatlantic trade and confinement of black, African bodies (*The Racial Contract* 1999); Lewis Gordon's analysis from philosophy through the African American existential response to harsh realities, not only through spirituals, the blues, and other expressions of despair but also in logical treatises and considered reflections (*Existentia Africana* 2000); and again through the sociology of Paul Gilroy's modernity, even the postcolonial melancholy of race among people who add the word "sand" in front of nigger and re-inscribe race on global frontiers, whether in Guantanamo Bay or Baghdad (*Postcolonial Melancholia* 2005), and the list goes on.[16] Whichever approach we take, these analyses expose the partial-thinking, myopic (cyclopic) gaze of Touré's post-black, however learned his references.

The premise of Touré's book stems from a conversation Michael Eric Dyson had with Oprah Winfrey at a fundraiser for then-presidential candidate Barack Obama in 2007, in which Dyson notes, much to Oprah's glee, that Obama "is rooted in, but not restricted by, his Blackness" (Touré 2012, 18). Such malleable "rootedness" allows Touré to claim skydiving from airplanes, where he communes with his Maker, to be as "black" as being president of the United States. This is a fair enough proposition, and I have elsewhere delighted in Suzan-Lori Parks's definition of a "black" play as any play ranging from Shakespeare to *The Glass Menagerie* to August Wilson.[17] I am not interested in racial essentialism. Too often we hear of children teasing their well-spoken counterparts as "talking white." Racial constructions regarding what blackness is and is not, or what whiteness is and is not, can be constricting and, in fact, often constitute *racism* itself. At the same time, there are roots to racial constructions, deeply buried in the past. Where exactly is Touré's analysis of blackness rooted? Is it rooted in an attempt to come to terms with where we are through where we have been? Touré's treatment is certainly not a historical analysis akin to what LeDuff offers, the sociological contextualization of Winant or Gilroy, or even Frederick Douglass's questioning of what the Fourth of July means to the Negro. For Touré, there is no suffering, no despair, no existential angst—for that matter, no white flight, no racial conservatism, and no remnants of laws and practices that, in the case of America, divided a nation. Out of context, blackness—race—is as ridiculous as Santa Claus in springtime.

Touré's milieu is a rarified, elite cadre of successful African Americans, a group that Eugene Robinson astutely distinguishes from others in *Disintegration: The Splintering of Black America* (2011). The other groups are a mainstream middle class, an underclass mired in poverty, and a group constituted by mixed-race and immigrant populations. Touré takes the part for the whole, but he does so without a true analysis of the constituent parts that make up the whole. (Here again is synecdoche.) At the same time, at the heart of Touré's misplaced analysis is the warning against reducing racial identity to stereotypes: We should not essentialize race. Being black, white, brown, or yellow is not any one thing, and yet each thing-in-the-world, each phenomenon, is rooted in historical realities and circumstances that the bliss of American forgetfulness cannot easily erase.[18]

Houston A. Baker Jr.'s treatment of race helps to restore subtlety and purpose to Touré's superficial reading of reality. In *Betrayal: How Black Intellectuals Have Abandoned the Ideals of the Civil Rights Era*, Baker reprises the idea of "race" people, men and women steeped in ethical traditions that lead to brighter futures for a wider array of people. Baker riffs on the idea of race people as a counter to the kinds of arguments that Touré raises in *Who's Afraid of Post-Blackness?* In fact, Baker exposes the idea of post-black as nothing more than ardent American individualism. He attributes the post-racial perspective to many black leaders who came subsequent to Martin Luther King Jr.: "The appearance of this cadre of black public intellectuals, in fact, can justly be read as epiphenomenal, secondary, and derivative" (2008, 11). The "epiphenomenon" is the abandonment of group politics for individual perspectives. Beginning with an extended homily of Martin Luther King Jr.'s "Letter from Birmingham Jail" and his broader ethics, Baker goes on to indict the moral bankruptcy of much of modern American intellectual discourse. Baker reminds his readers, "By 1968 King had become not only a tacit ally of Black Power but also a powerful model of the race man" (9). Race men and women realize that without broader gains, their individual successes are easily stymied. White, black, brown, and yellow race men and women joined together during the civil rights movement. They realized that what affects the part of the body politic affects the whole. "The thigh bone is connected to the white suburbanites who turn their heads away from the calamity of Detroit . . . " Detroit is Holland is America is the world. And the world is a ghetto.

Baker takes on topics as varied as the "deep apartheid of residential housing to the starkly racialized gulag of the nation's private prison-industrial complex." How does one claim a post-racial society when 58 percent of the prison population in America in 2008 was made up of blacks and Hispanics?[19] The broader American population hovers around 15 percent African American and 25 percent Hispanic. The statistics bespeak a situation so dire that in 2013 the U.S. attorney general, Eric Holder, called for a review of policies that target segments of the population, such as Stop and Frisk, and the War on Drugs. (Holder's comments are ubiquitously available; see, e.g., Wilkey and Reilly [2013].) This is post-racial America during the first decades of the twenty-first century.

VOX POPULI VOX DEI: "THE VOICE OF THE PEOPLE IS THE VOICE OF GOD"

The public certainly is not learning about the complexity and paradox of an American success story like Holland, Michigan, through Fallows's articles in the *Atlantic*, notwithstanding his late-summer corrective replete with readers' comments about the challenging realities that the reporter offered in his closing piece (see Fallows 2013a). To be fair to Fallows, his articles were a triumph of travel journalism, and Americans do not want to hear about despair in the summertime. It is worth noting that while a portion of society enjoys repose in those radiant months, many neighborhoods swerve into abysmal levels of violence during the sweltering season (see, e.g., Yaccino 2013). Grand Rapids officials, bafflingly, posted a statistical decline in violence during the summer of 2013, when I read about a drive-by shooting almost daily.[20] Fallows is not the *vox populi*; he is not at the heart of the problem. In world cities such as Grand Rapids, Michigan, and Sao Paulo, Brazil—world ghettoes, to use Winant's language—the *vox populi* is, to an extent, in hip-hop, that youth culture inclusive of youthful swagger, a certain fashion sense, and sonic expression through beats and rhymes (rap music).[21] Holland, Michigan, as one instance of a place that has its own manifestations of poverty, despite Fallows's summertime idyll, has its own rap culture, with Internet sensations such as Jake "SpinnDizzy" Mogck and Rediculis Rap Sux, but there seems to be no organic hip-hop movement that would include a distinct style and accompanying political and social messages. My turn to hip-hop might further alienate some readers, if my indictment of white suburban ethics has not done so already.

As Jamaican immigrants to New York City at the end of the 1970s, my sister and I understand hip-hop as part of a cultural milieu, but for many it brings the negative connotations of low culture, gangsta rap, and racial stereotypes. Even LeDuff is wont to refer to Detroit's disgraced leader, Kwame Kilpatrick, as the "hip-hop mayor," owing no doubt to the extent to which Kilpatrick drew from stereotypes in the public domain to contextualize his own activities. At its best, however, hip-hop has been at the heart of cultural expression for American youth since the late 1970s, and here it might serve to add some other frequencies to Fallows's essays.

So I turn briefly to hip-hop to further flesh out—to legitimate and punctuate—the sense of despair at the center of the statistics. In Grand Rapids, three rappers, who happen not to be recognizably African American, have gained some national recognition for their level of skill and their sociopolitical sincerity: Rick Chymes, Brandon "SteDDy" Aguirre, and Ed Nino. The titles of SteDDy's CDs suggest the process toward change, and the dead ends along the way: *Road Work* (2007) and *Caution Tape* (2010). SteDDy's "Uncovered" (2008), similar to LeDuff's analysis, frames the state of despair many people feel in terms that are not necessarily post-racial. Rather, SteDDy's analysis cuts across class. The refrain defiantly intones, "This is not for people who live in the ghetto; this is not for people who live in the suburbs." Drawing the accepted lines of "have" and "have-not" (the suburbs, the ghettoes), SteDDy articulates a post-2008 political landscape in which the haves sometimes lose what they have, "work[ing] for a paycheck" until they "come to a train wreck." He goes on to tell a now familiar story about a worker who had economic means but lost his job during the global financial downturn. That is, if there is a post-racial landscape, it is hardly the utopian dream of Touré's narrative; rather, it is a post-2008 apocalypse in which black, white, brown, and yellow meet at a point of abysmal despair. This is the context of Rick Chymes's "1000 Miles from Nowhere." The apocalypse is an apt metaphor for the outlook of many in the hip-hop generation of the early twenty-first century. Ed Nino's "The End," from his *Welcome 2 Jericho* CD (2010), studies the situation and, similar to the prophets of old, intones that "there will be a war when the storm meets the seas." Ed Nino's images an equalizing end, or at least the meeting of the minds that marks a beginning: "mankind, genocide, back to stage one."

Grand Rapids is Holland is Chicago is the world. And the world is a ghetto. The sonic expression of Grand Rapids rappers is connected in sentiment—the anxiety, the economic disparity, and the despair—to the concerns of young people in Brazil's burgeoning cities. Popular rappers include Criolo Doido (Kleber Cavalcante Gomes), from a Sao Paulo favela (Favela das Imbuias), and the hugely successful Emicida (Leandro Roque de Oliveira), whose CDs have an Internet and iTunes presence. While Criolo's albums, "No Na Orelha (In your ear) (2011) and "Ainda Ha Tempo" (There's still time) (2006), express the general anxiety of youth, with sugary sweet beats and party anthems, Emicida's lyrics contain all of this but add profound social commentary. His name, in fact, prefigures the extent to which he aims to be the emcee (*Emici-*) with a political phi-losophy, one that addresses the homicidal realities of Sao Paulo (*-cida*). "Samba do fim do Mundo" (Samba for the end of the world) is eerily similar to Ed Nino's in its apocalyptic outlook on the social realities of living in a Brazilian city at the dawn of the twenty-first century. The sweet, melodic hook of the samba belies the cutting critique of Brazil's failed *rede social*, the "social network" that should offer health care, education, and police protection to the citizen. "We cannot be afraid; things have to get better" (E preciso nao tem meido; e preciso ser maior), intones the dance-able, female chorus. But they never do. In May 2013 I heard a Brazilian commuter bewail the failed infrastructure in Salvador as she mounted the Lavador, the "elevator" that takes commuters from the lower city to the upper city (*cidade baixa* and *cidade alta*): "This madness is always 'improv-ing,' but it never gets any better." (Sempre vai melhorar, este porqueria. Nunca melhora.) Similar to the prophet Ed Nino, Emicida warns that the individual response to this "machine"—through the powerful trope of a "*miseria cartao postal*," a despair that makes the individual "go postal"—is the condition to which decaying social structures never get better.

In American terms, the poet Emicida would be considered "black," but Brazil's (farcical) "post-racial" paradise divides and conquers along dif-ferent lines. I call Emicida a poet, more than simply a rap practitioner, because of the power and reach of his tropes. "9 Circulos" (2012) invokes Dante's *Inferno* to characterize Brazil's abyss, with its own dire statistics, divided along class and racial lines. The title of his 2013 album, *The Glori-ous Return of the Person Who Was Never Here* (O gloriso retorno de quem nunca esteve aqui), hints at a deeper irony reminiscent of Brazil's high-est literature, its social satire never accepting of reality in the way that Touré's prose does. Emicida's paradox—how can one "return" if one was never here?—recalls the title of a novel by Machado de Assis, Brazil's most important writer, who was the mixed-ethnicity son of a slave. The title is *Posthumous Memoirs of Bras Cubas* (1997). How can a person write "mem-oirs" if he is dead? The paradox points to the broader existential condi-tion of Brazilian identity, a colony that was also not a colony (because the Portuguese king established his empire in Brazil in the beginning of the nineteenth century), populated by blacks and Portuguese (to name only a few groups) who were no longer black or Portuguese. Emicida's poetic—and empathic—take on the lives of Brazilian young people is akin to that of Ralph Ellison's *Invisible Man*, which contains the racial paradox of being a person—while also a non-person—within America's segregated landscape of 1952. For Brazil, as for America, much has stayed the same since 1952, which is *not* to say that nothing has changed (see Lyman 2013). The prologue of *The Glorious Return*, "Millionaire in Dreams" (Milionario do sonho), a spoken-word piece, a capella, frames the entire CD around a crisis: "It is difficult for a Brazilian child without social support to become a whole person" (2013a).[22] Emicida tempers his reality with the hopes of dreams; we are millionaires in our dreams: "There is always a world that has not yet been made, always a world for us to make. The world has not ended" (ibid.).

HOPE IN DESPAIR

The trope of apocalypse, whether conceived in terms of the end of the world or the remaking of it, is consistent throughout the foregoing citations. Emicida reaches for the dream of "a world that has not yet been made", and although in "Milionario do sonho" "the world has not ended," other lyrics point definitively to a sociopolitical apocalypse. The imagery is not a coincidence. Ed Nino's allusion to the apocalypse, or America with its "walls of Jericho" tumbling down, may stem from his roots in Western Michigan, a deeply religious social context.[23] One particular lyric from Ed Nino shouts out the Reformed Church in America and other manifestations of faith within this particular historical context. There are connections here from Grand Rapids back to Holland, Michigan, home of the founding of the Dutch Reformed Church in America under Albertus C. Van Raalte, and later the Reformed Church in America (to which Hope College is affiliated) and the Christian Reformed Church (parent to Grand Rapids' Calvin College). For Emicida, the religious context wavers between references to the Afro-inflected traditions of the slaves brought to Brazil from West Africa, whether their practices are reflected in Candomble or Umbanda (local Yoruba- and Christian-inflected practices in Brazil), to the Catholic worship of the Portuguese and other Europeans. In the social experiment of modernity, where these faiths mix together with syncretic harmony, Emicida wonders "which Orixa is going to clean me up."[24] He reaches to the same need for cleansing as his counterparts in the United States. Though it is "2012" and "the world is ending," nevertheless, "police here kill more than Tuskegee," a sure reference to the Tuskegee experiment in the United States in which black men with syphilis were deliberately left untreated in a social experiment they knew nothing about. The world did not end for everyone in 1932–1972, but it did for many involved in the Tuskegee experiment during those years. The life chances of many, as we have also seen in the foregoing analysis, do not always appear to have improved immensely. As Emicida sees it, police still kill young black and brown people in Brazil with the same sinister betrayal as that felt by the black men infected with syphilis in Tuskegee.

Within the Brazilian context, Emicida calls to whichever God will help. As Tupac did in the 1990s, by Michael Eric Dyson's assessment in *Between God and Gangsta Rap* (1997), Emicida and other modern-day prophets, through their references to the apocalypse, that futuristic, eschatological period when Jesus returns to judge the living and the dead, are addressing theodicy's conundrum. Where is the God of justice, they desperately ask, in such an unjust world? Theology is of course the study of God, an inevitably futile attempt to put to order and reason a boundless magnificence, a mystery that, ultimately, cannot be known. For early Christians, the Nicene Creed codifies belief in terms of the dogma of a triune God—father, son, and Holy Spirit. According to John, Jesus is the embodiment of the Logos in theology: "The Word (*logos*) became flesh and dwelt among men" (John 1:14). But is this God still dwelling with us, in the form of the Holy Spirit, a spirit of grace? Where is this grace for the shirtless babes that I see wandering somewhat aimlessly on a summer's eve on the streets of Grand Rapids? Does the spirit of grace exist for the children of Detroit? As the intergenerational masses took to the streets of Brazil during the summer of 2013 to protests the rising costs of public transportation, heath care, and generally poor infrastructure, was the spirit of grace with them?[25] Dyson wrote of Tupac that his lyrics reached for God's justice in a seemingly unjust world. Has God blessed Holland, Michigan, and no one else?

The young poets of Grand Rapids, Sao Paulo, and other proverbial ghettoes throughout the world reach for God out of an abysmal, apocalyptic reality, for which the only possible responses are hope or despair. They strive to ascertain whether their hope is founded in any reality or if we have in fact hit rock bottom. In *To Change the World,* James Davison Hunter characterizes the current age in terms of secularization, or the retreat of belief from the public sector, but the extent to which young poets in the hip-hop framework grope for meaning within the context of our lived condition is compelling, perhaps even quickening. We might well live in a secular age, where God is only one of a number of options, the others including the drugs of the addict that Emicida characterizes. Nevertheless, Emicida and others attempt to find God not in their space of refuge, but in the world, whence God seems to have disappeared, at least if we judge by what we see. Though characteristic rather than comprehensive, the few rappers I have discussed resonate with one another in their analysis of a ghettoized world, of rich and poor, where the "haves" are separated from the "have-nots," more often than not, in economic as well as racial terms. The rappers I have discussed as the *vox populi,* a journalistic presence that reports of recovery and beach-town resorts often drown out, are also resonant with Hunter's sense of things: "Indeed the sense of ourselves as being both frail and courageous, capable of facing a meaningless, hostile universe without faintness of heart, and of rising to the challenge of devising our own rules of life, can be an inspiring one, as we see in the writings of Camus for instance" (9).

Emicida might range from "frail to courageous" in a single ballad. He reaches out of the abyss and finds a cloud of witnesses who attest to the realities he bemoans, the dismal lack of opportunities stemming from poor educational systems and the immorality of leaders. In post-apocalypse Detroit, the racialized mantra of "welfare queen" or the image of lazy, shiftless masses that worked so well to divide an electorate in the 1980s will no longer suffice to explain reality.[26] As LeDuff laments, we might characterize the times in terms of a moral crisis of virtue and vice: the pride, gluttony, lust, sloth, greed, wrath, and envy of our leaders. The racialized tropes of the past will no longer serve, though the reality of race is a clear and present phenomenon, a thing-in-the-world.

O FIM: NAMING THE PHENOMENON

"La'tasha Hardings [sic]. Remember that name . . . Cause a bottle of juice . . . is not something to die for."
—Tupac Shakur, "Something 2 Die For" (1993)[27]

In the end, beyond the statistics, on the other side of hope and despair, are living breathing people. As Ralph Ellison put it in his essay "Change the Joke and Slip the Yoke," beyond archetypes and statistics is the living, breathing person (see Ellison 1964). Ellison makes a case for literary, poetic treatment of phenomena, of things-in-the-world. The foregoing analysis should serve to some extent to frame the available sociological data and statistics. The *vox populi* of such persons as Emicida and Ed Nino stand in a gap between the triumphant statistics of a city like Holland, Michigan, and the paradoxical, puzzling numerology of the declining crime rate in Grand Rapids, Michigan. Whatever the statistics, individuals attest to the fact that we are not in post-racial times, after all. Disparities continue to plague society, and they too often fall along racial lines. The violence that plagues many corners of American society drives the desires of many to get away, to leave at our earliest convenience or be pulled down into the abyss. Put otherwise, white flight was not an unreasonable response for a time, but in the end there is nowhere to run: "The thigh bone is connected to the white suburbanites who turn their heads away from the calamity of Detroit." The people who ran from declining cities were climbing out of their own abyss. As Houston Baker reminds us, however, the response to despair on the part of the individual cannot be severed from the broader realities. In the 1960s race men and women standing together fought against unjust law. The civil rights movement of our times might not be so much in contesting laws and policies that divide a nation, but rather in identifying practices that must end: Stop and Frisk, No Child Left Behind, War on Drugs, Stand Your Ground, and so on. Trayvon Martin, remember that name. Because a bottle of iced tea and a bag of Skittles are not something to die for, even if you are wearing a hoodie.

"I am an invisible man," a black man in Western Michigan on a ledge. I am teetering between stability and despair. I take some solace in knowing that the world is a ghetto—that is, that the startling disparities that I am seeing on my commute to and from Holland are not isolated phenomena. Rather, just as the economic catastrophe of 2008 was a worldwide phenomenon, so too is its collateral damage. I listen to Emicida, Ed Nino, and others, knowing that although they do not know me and might not recognize each other, they speak across geographical spaces to a calamity that cannot be denied. Whatever mythology frames America's grand narratives, the voice of the people is the voice of God. Real leaders do not offer vacation paradise, but hope in despair.

Vanessa Greene. Alfredo Gonzalez. Jim Gentile. Jack Nyenhuis. Elton Bruins. Maxine Debruyn. Christine Statema. Sarah Wilson. Karen Nordell Pearson. Tracey Nally. John Knapp. Kendra Parker. Remember these names. Because the hope that we can provide to countless others is something for which we can live. The way out of despair is composed of individual steps away from the ledge. I am not alone. These are people who recognize reality and are not afraid to name the phenomena. In *To Change the World*, Hunter calls for a "presentness" from ethical people, a being-with that helps those struggling with despair. The individuals I have named understand presence and, like me, are not satisfied with an idyllic vision of the world we see.

Wherever I decide to live, whether Holland, Michigan, where my presence might make a difference, whatever its personal toll on me, or in Grand Rapids, Michigan, where I might gain strength from those who for generations have faced similar struggles, there is a great cloud of witnesses, ancestors, and new friends across the racial divide, who will help make the difference. They evidence a quiet movement a half decade in the making. These are the race men and women who have proven that they are not afraid to speak truth to power. They have offered hope in my despair and in many cases have done so for generations for many others at Hope College. A college or university is at its best a city on a hill, a place where we live together, study, and name and transform phenomena, the things-in-the-world around us, as honestly, scientifically, and eruditely as possible. Given Hope College's historical foundation in Christian faith, the dream of theodicy, "justice for all," must not be too far in the future.

NOTES

1. Holland, Michigan, was listed fourteenth among *Forbes* magazine's fifteen prettiest towns on August 16, 2013. The website connected to the ArtPrize festival describes ArtPrize as follows: "ArtPrize® is a radically open, independently organized international art competition with an unprecedented $200,000 top prize decided entirely by public vote." The 2013 festival marked its fifth year. See http://www.artprize.org/about. LaughFest is an "annual festival [that] was launched in March 2011 and has featured Lewis Black, Wayne Brady, Jim Breuer, Hannibal Buress, Bill Burr, Rodney Carrington, Bill Cosby, Mike Epps, Jim Gaffigan, Whoopi Goldberg, Chris Hardwick, Kevin Hart, Pete Holmes, D.L. Hughley, Gabriel Iglesias, Anthony Jeselnik, Joel McHale, Kevin Nealon, Brian Regan, Amy Schumer, Martin Short, Sinbad, Betty White and many, many more nationally touring artists and acts. LaughFest features laughter in all its forms from comedy, performance, and improv to film and a variety of seriously funny stuff." See http://www.laugh festgr.org/about/laughfest/.

2. The phrase "sickness unto death" is taken from the Bible, from John 11:4, at the point where Jesus tells Lazarus's family, who are lamenting Lazarus's death and entombment, that his "sickness" is not "unto death." Søren Kierkegaard uses the phrase as the title of his 1849 treatise on despair.

3. The reference in the subhead is to Frederick Douglass's 1852 address, delivered on July 5, in which he speaks about the frustrating distance between the promises of the Bill of Rights and the reality of American plantation life at that time.

4. The refrain is from the song of the same title from Bob Marley's *Natty Dread* album, released in 1974.

5. For the statistics, see www.spotlightonpoverty.org. The statistics also show that Michigan's unemployment rate hovers between 1–3 percent above the national average.

6. Although it is unclear where Mayor Dykstra derived the statistic, the broader Western Michigan economy is listed by some agencies as the fastest growing economy in Michigan. See www.rightplace.org.

7. The Albertus C. Van Raalte Institute, affiliated with Hope College, has recently published a number of books on the history of Hope College. See, for example, Jacobson, Bruins, and Wagenaar (2001); and Bruins and Schakel (2011).

8. The percentage is from the United States Census Bureau from 2010. See www.census.gov. The percentage for Michigan from the same source is 4.4 percent. Holland, Michigan is 3.6 percent African American, compared to 14.2 percent for the state of Michigan.

9. Despite criticism that the book is more a personal memoir than a national, sociological study, Wurtzel's *Prozac Nation* (1995) is one of the early attempts to deal with prescription medication as an epidemic. For a nuanced approach that does reveal higher prescription drug use among the highest and lower income brackets, see Maris (2012).

10. For a thorough treatment of the one-drop rule and the invention of whiteness and blackness in the New World, see Malcolmson's *One Drop of Blood* (2001).

11. See also Jelks's *African Americans in the Furniture City* (2006).

12. The median household income in Grand Rapids in 2011 was $36,408, compared to $45,981 for the state of Michigan. See city-data.com. There are more African Americans than white who are unemployed and uninsured in Grand Rapids. Black male and female mortality rates continue to be higher than that of white counterparts. For the 2011 report from the Grand Rapids African American Health Institute, see http://www.graahi.org/Portals/0/Documents/2011MinorityHealthReport.pdf.

13. Sources tell me that the owners of the home took the house off of the market because they could not find a buyer. "Making housing unavailable" is a violation of the Fair Housing Act, but the causal relationship (when and why this particular house was made unavailable) is difficult—if not impossible—to prove, as is "discrimination in the sale, rental, and financing of dwellings, and in other housing-related transactions, based on race, color, national origin, religion, sex, familial status (including children under the age of 18 living with parents or legal custodians, pregnant women, and people securing custody of children under the age of 18), and disability." See "Fair Housing—It's Your Right," *U.S. Department of Housing and Urban Development*, http://portal.hud.gov/hudportal/HUD?src=/program_offices/fair_housing_equal_opp/FHLaws/yourrights.

14. That minority homeowners were disproportionately affected by the subprime mortgage crisis is not in debate. Several sources corroborate the claim, including Democracy Now, the Levy Institute, and HUD statistics. See particularly Carol D. Leonning's June 10, 2008 article in the *Washington Post* and Daniel Gross's *Slate Magazine* article of October 7, 2008.

15. See Luke 19:40, where Jesus says that if the people keep quiet, "the stones will cry out."

16. George Yancy's article "Walking While Black in the 'White Gaze'" in the *New York Times* forum "The Stone" is poignant, citing racial provocations from David Hume and Immanuel Kant to Thomas Jefferson. Yancy's is an existential urgency nauseating for the extent to which race has not gone away.

17. See Rankine (2013), *Aristotle and Black Drama*, where I cite Parks's "The New Black Math" and discuss Wilson's "The Ground on Which I Stand."

18. Ralph Ellison compellingly riffed on this topic of bliss in his second novel, published posthumously as *Juneteenth* (1999) and republished as *Three Days Before the Shooting* (2011). Ellison's antiphonal characters are Alonzo Hickman, a black preacher and trumpet-player, and Bliss, his adopted son, the result of his brother's interracial affair, and a man who has denied his racial ancestry.

19. See "Criminal Justice Fact Sheet," *NAACP*, http://www.naacp.org/pages/criminal-justice-fact-sheet. See also the Department of Justice statistics for 2012, published in July 2013.

20. On the decline in the murder rate, see Tunison (2011). The news wire mLive.com can be searched to corroborate the reports of drive-by shootings.

21. Although I have not kept up with the research on hip-hop since my own personal interest in my teens and twenties, Tricia Rose's *Black Noise* (1994) is still authoritative and relevant in terms of its historical and critical analysis of the emergence of hip hop culture from rap, street graffiti, and break dancing.

22. This phrase resonates with Tupac's "I was raised in this society, so there's no way you can expect me to be a perfect person." In "Pac's Theme," from his 1993 CD.

23. There is a delicious irony in Holland / Grand Rapids: residents report themselves to be deeply religious, but Holland / Grand Rapids is also by one measure a top-ten area for the viewing of pornography. See Martinez (2013).

24. The Orixas are akin to Saints in Catholic worship, deities—ancestors—who are not themselves God but intercede on behalf of adherents.

25. Although the *New York Times* did not begin reporting of the street protests in Brazil during the summer of 2013 until weeks had gone by, I was in the

unique position of traveling through and being in these cities throughout May and June 2013 and have compiled many reports from *O Globo* in Rio de Janeiro. Transportation, education, and health care were the main areas of complaint for the street protestors, *manifestates*, in Portuguese.

26. "Welfare queen" is a ubiquitous term for which a quick Internet search yields numerous hits. Despite what is commonly known now to be the case—namely, that there is a false, mythical, and inflated view of relationship between blacks and welfare—attempts to extend the stereotypes can be cited as late as 2012. As it relates the 2012 presidential campaign, see Jones (2012).

27. Printed lyrics of Tupac's song mistake the name of Harlins (for Hardings), who was shot and killed by a Korean grocery store owner in 1991 in Los Angeles. The incident was one of the touchstones for the Los Angeles riots of 1992.

REFERENCES

Baker, Houston A., Jr. 2008. *Betrayal: How Black Intellectuals Have Abandoned the Ideals of the Civil Rights Era*. New York: Columbia University Press.

Bruins, Elton J. and Karen G. Schakel. 2011. *Envisioning Hope College: Letters Written by Albertus C. Van Raalte to Phillip Phelps, Jr. 1857 to 1875* (Historical Series of the Reformed Church in America). Grand Rapids, MI: Eerdmans.

Criolo Doido. 2006. Ainda Ha Tempo. SkyBlue Music. CD.

——. 2011. No Na Orelha (In Your Ear). Oloko Records. CD.

Douglass, Frederick. 1852. "What to the Slave Is the Fourth of July?" Keynote Address. Rochester, New York. July 5.

Dyson, Michael Eric. 1997. *Between God and Gangsta Rap: Bearing Witness to Black Culture*. New York: Oxford University Press.

Ed Niño. 2010. "The End." Welcome 2 Jericho. 3 Sense Entertainment. CD.

Ellison, Ralph. 1952. *Invisible Man*. New York: Random House.

——. 1958. "Change the Joke and Slip the Yoke." *Partisan Review* 25, no. 2 (Spring).

——. 1964. "Change the Joke and Slip the Yoke." In *Shadow and Act*. New York: Random House.

——. 1999. *Juneteenth*. New York: Vintage Books.

——. 2011. *Three Days Before the Shooting*. New York: Modern Library.

Emicida. 2012. "9 Circulos" ("9 Circles"). Casp and Nave Beatz. CD.

——. 2013a. "Milionario de Sonho" ("Millionaire in Dreams"). O Gloriso Retorno de Quem Nunca Esteve Aqui (The Glorious Return of the Person Who Was Never Here). Laboratório Fantasma.

——. 2013b. "Samba do fim do Mundo" ("Samba for the End of the World"). O Gloriso Retorno de Quem Nunca Esteve Aqui (The Glorious Return of the Person Who Was Never Here). Laboratório Fantasma.

Fallows, James. 2013a. "American Futures: Grand Finale Holland-Palooza." *Atlantic*, September 3. http://www.theatlantic.com/national/archive/2013/09/american-futures-grand-finale-holland-palooza/279293/.

——. 2013b. "Welcome to Holland." *Atlantic*, August 10.

Gilroy, Paul. 2005. *Postcolonial Melancholia*. New York: Columbia University Press.

Giuffo, John. 2013. "America's Prettiest Towns." *Forbes Magazine*, August 16. http://www.forbes.com/sites/johngiuffo/2013/08/16/americas-prettiest-towns-3/.

Gordon, Lewis. 2000. *Existentia Africana: Understanding Africana Existential Thought*. New York: Routledge.

Gross, Daniel. 2008. "Subprime Suspects." *Slate* October 7. http://www.slate.com/articles/business/moneybox/2008/10/subprime_suspects.html.

Hunter, James Davison. 2010. *To Change the World: The Irony, Tragedy, and Possibility of Christianity in the Late Modern World*. New York: Oxford University Press.

Jacobson, Jeanne M., Elton J. Bruins and Larry J. Wagenaar. 2001. *Albertus C. Van Raalte: Dutch Leader and American Patriot*. Holland, MI: Hope College.

Jelks, Randal Maurice. 2006. *African Americans in the Furniture City: The Struggle for Civil Rights in Grand Rapids*. Champaign: University of Illinois Press.

Jones, Imara. 2012. "Romney's Campaign Wedge: Taxpayers vs. Welfare Queens." *Colorlines News for Action*, August 30. http://colorlines.com/archives/2012/08/romneys_back_to_the_future_campaign_plan_taxpayers_vs_welfare_queens.html.

Kierkegaard, Søren. 1941. *The Sickness unto Death*. Trans. Walter Lowrie. Princeton, NJ. Princeton University Press.

LeDuff, Charlie. 2013. *Detroit: An American Autopsy*. New York: Penguin Group.

Leonning, Carol D. 2008. "How HUD Mortgage Policy Fed the Crisis." *Washington Post*, June 10. http://www.washingtonpost.com/wp-dyn/content/article/2008/06/09/AR2008060902626.html.

Lyman, Rick. 2013. "50 Years After March, Views of Fitful Progress." *New York Times*, August 23. http://www.nytimes.com/2013/08/24/us/a-time-to-return-to-and-reflect-on-the-march-on-washington.html?pagewanted%253Dall.

Machado de Assis, Joaquim Maria. 1997. *Posthumous Memoirs of Bras Cubas*. Trans. Gregory Rabassa. New York: Oxford University Press.

Malcolmson, Scott L. 2001. *One Drop of Blood: The American Misadventure of Race*. New York: Farrar, Straus and Giroux.

Maris, David. 2012. "Who Is Popping All Those Pills?" *Forbes*, July 24. http://www .forbes.com/sites/davidmaris/2012/07/24/1-in-3-american-adults-take -prescription-drugs/2/.

Marley, Bob. 1974. "Them Belly Full (But We Hungry)". Natty Dread. Island, Tuff Gong, CD.

Martinez, Shandra. 2013. "Most Porn-Loving Religious Cities: How Holland/ Grand Haven Cracked the Top 10." mlive.com, May 24. http://www.mlive .com/news/grand-rapids/index.ssf/2013/05/most_porn-loving_religious _cit.html.

Mills, Charles. 1999. *The Racial Contract*. New York: Cornell University Press.

Rankine, Patrice D. 2013. *Aristotle and Black Drama: A Theater of Civil Disobedience*. Waco, TX: Baylor University Press.

Rick Chymes. 2013. "1000 Miles from Nowhere." The 5iveit LP. Rick Chymes. MP3.

Robinson, Eugene. 2011. *Disintegration: The Splintering of Black America*. New York: Anchor Books.

Robinson, Todd E. 2013. *A City Within a City: The Black Freedom Struggle in Grand Rapids, Michigan*. Philadelphia: Temple University Press

Rose, Tricia. 1994. *Black Noise: Rap Music and Black Culture in Contemporary America*. Middletown, CT: Wesleyan University Press.

SteDDy. 2007. Road Work. CD Baby. CD.

——. 2008. "Uncovered." Freedom of Speech. Chaotic Mine Records. CD.

——. 2010. Caution Tape. CD.

Taylor, Charles. 2007. *A Secular Age*. Cambridge, MA: Harvard University Press.

Touré. 2012. *Who's Afraid of Post-Blackness?: What It Means to Be Black Now*. New York: Free Press.

Tunison, John. 2011. "Why Grand Rapids Police Say Murder Rate Is Declining." mlive, January 6. http://www.mlive.com/news/grand-rapids/index .ssf/2011/01/grand_rapids_declining_murder.html.

Tupac Shakur. 1993a. "Pac's Theme." Strictly 4 My N.I.G.G.A.Z. Interscope Records. CD.

——. 1993b. "Something 2 Die For." Strictly 4 My N.I.G.G.A.Z. Interscope Records. CD.

Wilkey, Robin and Ryan Reilly. 2013. "Eric Holder: 'Broken' Justice System Needs 'Sweeping' Changes, Reforms To Mandatory Minimum." *Huffington Post*, August 12. Web.

Winant, Howard. 2001. *The World Is a Ghetto: Race and Democracy Since World War II*. New York: Basic Books.

Wurtzel, Elizabeth. 1995. *Prozac Nation: Young and Depressed in America*. New York. Riverhead Books.

Yaccino, Steven. 2013. "A Violent Weekend in Chicago Despite a Recent Trend of Decreasing Homicides." *New York Times*, July 8. http://www.nytimes.com/2013/07/09/us/a-violent-weekend-in-chicago-despite-a-recent-trend-of-decreasing-homicides.html.

Yancy, George. 2013. "Walking While Black in the White Gaze." *New York Times*, September 1. http://opinionator.blogs.nytimes.com/2013/09/01/walking-while-black-in-the-white-gaze/?_php=true&_type=blogs&_r=0.

9

The Long Road Home

ERIN AUBRY KAPLAN

When I was coming of age in the 1970s, I was acutely aware that I was coming into a new age of American blackness. The first long age had begun with slavery and lasted hundreds of years. The very notion of being black and American at all—Du Bois's famous conundrum—continually fought for some life, first during slavery, afterward during Jim Crow and the attendant violence of lynching, and the thousand other knife points of social and personal oppression in which people didn't necessarily die but were distorted and stifled. In the 1960s, as the last of Jim Crow crumbled, mass consciousness shifted off its old foundation and a new, more militant and unapologetic blackness was suddenly possible for the first time. Expressions of anger and open reproach of whites that once could get you lynched or at least fired became culturally acceptable, even cool. The pendulum swung back toward the middle and by the late 1970s, as I was entering high school, we seemed to be cautiously settling into something more holistic: a blackness still wary of its place in the white American project but less daunted by it, socially critical but self-aware, still marooned at the bottom rung of most economic indicators but expectant and acquisitive—we wanted color TVs and Malibu Barbies like every other American. This new, post–second reconstruction New Negro was multifaceted in a way nobody had been before. For me and my friends, blackness was no longer fundamentally an albatross or a condition to overcome, it was who we were: Living black was something to be revealed to the world, not reviled. Perhaps most importantly, no matter what happened from now on, blackness would always keep its head up, not reflexively duck it down or modify its voice for the sake of its own survival. The structured invisibility that had crippled every black generation before mine had yielded to a new visibility that made it reasonable for me to assume a decent future rather than require that I constantly argue for it. This shift did not mean the country had achieved racial justice—far from it—but a new deal was in the air because we finally had a clear starting point from which we could theoretically travel in infinite directions. American blackness, a notion that had been vigorously suppressed for some 350 years, was finally getting under way.

It was a short run. Forty years later, blackness is being declared "over." Post-black, post-racial, whatever one wants to call it, in the early twenty-first century the political and cultural powers that be are declaring blackness has outlived its usefulness in American life and must be retired along with typewriters and telephone landlines. Bizarre as it is, the position has a certain logic: blackness has indeed achieved a visibility I couldn't begin to imagine in the 1970s. We have elected a black president, Barack Obama, twice. Hip-hop is America's pop music and its biggest commercial export, so ubiquitous that people no longer comment on the phenomena of whites, Asians, and other ethnic groups becoming rap artists or slinging around the words "nigger," "ho," "bitch" and other terms of so-called urban endearment. The mainstreaming of interracial unions has created a movement to declassify "black" as a race at all and replace it with "other" or "mixed race," not just on federal census forms but in daily life. Blackness that was once so fixed in American society seems to have become fluid and malleable, with post-blackness the ethnic version of postmodernism that says blackness, untethered to history and a sordid American past, is pretty much whatever we make it. From this vantage point, the absence of black is the new black. The tortured thing that once enslaved us all is now setting its own standards and setting us all free. Really, what could be more encouraging?

But the hopeful posture of post-blackness is a fraud, an elaborate marketing campaign that has everything to do with streamlining blackness as a concept and nothing at all to do with the complex reality of black people themselves. To begin with, the core premise that blackness somehow shackles America is bogus; it is white supremacy that shackles us, and always has. Nor is post-blackness a new phenomenon. From the moment slavery ended and for quite some time before, whites worried about how Negroes could ever live freely in a white society that reviled them so. Blacks as slaves was one thing; blacks living as full Americans was virtually unimaginable, even to the Great Emancipator himself. Post-slavery was our first official post-racial period in which the radical and dangerous new idea of American blackness had to be immediately curtailed with laws and court rulings and social custom and practice. The Klan was simply the most graphic enforcer of this new arrangement.

Today we preach post-racialism of a very different, gentler kind. Negating blackness wears not the face (or white robes) of oppression but of enlightenment—with no more blackness, the reasoning goes, there is no more racism. We are all simultaneously released from its dreadful legacy. But the goal of modern post-blackness is ultimately the same as the Klan's: to make—or to keep—black people invisible and therefore inconsequential. But instead of flaming crosses on our lawns or Jim Crow laws ordering us to the back of the bus, we now get altruistic, quasi-academic talk about how we are all equal and how invoking a black identity only obstructs that equality. Post-racialism posits that it is color that separates us, therefore black people need to stop talking about being black because blackness at its heart is divisive and nonprogressive. Divesting oneself of blackness today is like going green—it requires some individual sacrifice, sure, but you've got to do it or risk doing serious harm to the whole planet. You've got to take one for the team.

The push for post-blackness is not just conservative or Republican, by the way. Whites of all political persuasions, from tea party-ers to diehard revolutionary Communists, long for race to be finally "over," some for ideological reasons, some because they sincerely believe that claiming blackness really does inhibit American progress, including their own. Blackness is unpatriotic. Post-blackness believers are also somewhat puzzled by black people who, given the chance *not* to be black, don't take it. Why not? Why on earth claim "black" when it attaches to so many problems, when the whole experience has been largely one of rejection, displacement, heartache, oppression, repression, violence, and mountains of bad statistics that dog us to this very minute? Of course blackness has its good points, including defining the entire enterprise of American culture for the last 150 years—I mentioned hip-hop, but that's just the latest iteration of it. With that breadth of influence, black people themselves do feel like something of an afterthought, an unnecessary consideration. And then there are those among us who are simply race-weary, who don't want to shed their identity but want less to stay in the fight for meaningful visibility that never seems imminent. Our intragroup version of post-blackness is, and in some ways always has been: Can't we be meaningful on our own? What does it matter what white folks call us as long as we know who we are?

But it matters. Not because what white folks think defines us—we are hopefully post-*that*—but because the matter of being fully black and American is not defined yet. It is still becoming. Du Bois knew it, early post-black experimenters like Zora Neale Hurston knew it, all of the black conservatives and centrists who sanction a new, limited kind of blackness know it. They know the reason why everybody is debating post-blackness and not post-whiteness or post-immigrant or post-gay or post–Native American, even though Native Americans are the most severely diminished population in the country—for that very reason, we must preserve them and what they stand for. Not us. Preservation is exactly what nobody thinks black people need, because despite all our troubles and our own diminished status, we are quite present in American society (too present, in the minds of many folks). Which means that, by any objective measure, we are not over. If blackness was truly over, whites would not still be regularly reenacting major Confederate battles or calling for President Obama's head each time he commits the cardinal sin of giving Republicans and other latent Confederates exactly what they want. We know that there is no post-blackness so long as whites continue to create the terms of black existence and blacks continue arguing against those terms, as many of us are attempting to do in the pages of this book. Post-blackness's "choice" of not being black is profoundly false, but in a society that is also post-fact, especially in matters of race, the lie is routinely ignored. And why wouldn't it be? The meaning of race is something Americans have preferred in every era to invent or idealize in order to comport with American ideals (or other kinds of ideals) that are fundamentally undermined by slavery and the dehumanization of blacks for generations afterward that has become so efficient and so effective, we don't even think it as dehumanization anymore. Consider the fact that race—a word so consciously abstract that is itself dehumanizing—has been long downgraded to a "social issue," like abortion and family values, as eternal fodder for talk show debates that never really get resolved and aren't meant to. And we have by and large accepted that arbitrary downgrade because we have gotten so used to such things.

The ultimate legitimacy of post-blackness depends not on what conservatives say, but on whether blacks will capitulate to yet another illegitimate belief about themselves. The power of post-blackness counts on us growing tired and giving up and acquiescing to the latest assault against a long and almost numbing string of assaults against our integrity as people and full Americans. Acquiescence is always tempting because we have so many real and pressing things to tend to; the call for post-blackness, in the very troubled and complex scheme of things today, might look mild by comparison. It is just a phrase, after all.

But the idea behind it is hardly mild. It is serious. Annihilation is not a game, just as my buoyant sense of a new black beginning in 1977 was not a game, either. That new beginning moved, flashed like the high sun on the surface of a river. I saw it; it was real. It is still real but still elusive. I am slightly younger than President Obama and have not lived as expansively as I assumed I would when I was fifteen and looking fairly hopeful into the future: but for all his success, neither has he. Black Americanness is still coming of age. It has not run its course because the course is still being built, because we are all still cautiously finding our way along it and obstructions are still materializing. When we do get to an end of the course, that will not be post-blackness. It will be a pause, a breath, before the beginning of another age. We will continue.

10

Half as Good

JOHN L. JACKSON JR.

A young child scribbling on a chalkboard perched atop an easel in the hallway of a two-bedroom apartment, just at the entrance to our kitchen. That's one of the earliest memories I can conjure up. I'm writing my ABCs and spelling out three-letter words, fingertips and palms caked white. For as long as I can remember, probably from about my second birthday, this was my afternoon routine, a ritual mandated by my stepfather, who would periodically make surprise stops at that chalkboard, ever so briefly, on his way out the door, or to the bathroom, just to confirm that I was demonstrating the kind of progress in my "lessons" that he expected.

He was determined to make sure that I was better prepared for school than all the other kids on the block. More to the point, he had convinced himself that I already was. The chalkboard was just sealing the deal, speeding things up. The man loved to pump me up with positive reinforcement about my exceptional intellectual abilities, my God-given gifts—only further enhanced by the judicious enforcement of my daily chalkboard regimen.

"This boy is a smart one," he would say almost daily, making the declaration to me, my mom, and anyone else within earshot, family or not. It was a belief that he faithfully espoused since before he had any real data to go on. "He is a bright one. Bright, bright, bright!! If he hits those books like I ask him to, he can do anything. Sky's the limit."

I can actually recall him saying "sky's the limit" on more than one occasion, which is a common-enough phrase, I know, but for some reason, it always felt a little weird coming from him. No matter how many times he repeated the words, they would always sound foreign to his West Indian tongue. But I got the point. He had high hopes for me, high expectations, and whenever I fell a little short, even early on, if I couldn't distinguish, say, C-A-T from C-O-T on that tattered and peeling chalkboard, he had little patience for it—and no qualms about showing his disappointment in actions and not just words.

By the time I started kindergarten, given my at-home pre-K training camp, I was more than ready for public school. And I did well, both at the first elementary school I attended (with mostly Afro-Caribbean and African American classmates) on 55th Street, a few blocks from Church Avenue, in Brooklyn, and at the second one (with a majority of Jewish and Italian kids) just a fifteen-minute drive south in Canarsie, a mostly lower-middle-class neighborhood in the same borough. We moved into that New York City housing complex down in Canarsie, the Bayview Houses, when I was still in the second grade, a move prompted at least in part by the perennial parental search for safer neighborhoods and better schools.

I practiced spelling more than math on that rickety old chalkboard, but I started to do some basic adding and subtracting, and my stepfather expected me to devote as much attention to that as I had always done to reading and writing. And my first few years of school showed the bountiful benefits of all that preschool prep. It was all mostly just review for me in the first few years, especially since the chalkboard drills never stopped. I was supposed to finish my homework and then practice all of that material—and more—at the board. I didn't move on to using composition notebooks exclusively until well into the third grade, my chalkboard finally stored in the back of a closet until my sister, five years younger, would be ready to start the same at-home program.

With all of my board-writing at home, I continued to do well in my classes, so much so that the principal of PS 272 gave my parents the option of allowing me to skip the second grade altogether, and my junior high school, John Wilson, was poised to place me in an accelerated program that would condense three years of middle school work into two. My parents said "no" to both ideas, not really giving either serious consideration. "Let him just stay on schedule," they said. And so I soldiered on, having my early schoolwork monitored periodically at home and my recreational activities directly and proportionately linked to study time.

For every hour of reading I got through, I could watch thirty minutes of television. That was the rule. And I absolutely LOVED TV, still do, so I was committed to reading—only so that I could watch as much network TV as possible, overdosing on situation comedies but organizing my 1980s around hour-long detective shows like *Remington Steele* and whatever that Bruce Willis and Cybil Shepherd vehicle was called. I wanted to be Michael J. Fox from *Family Ties*, and I risked life and limb in high school by rummaging through my stepfather's closet (he had to be at work by six in the morning) and wearing his fanciest and most colorful sweaters to high school, trying to put them back in his closet, just so, as soon as I got home—those sweaters, no doubt, the sartorial influence of both Fox's Alex P. Keaton and *The Cosby Show*'s Heathcliff Huxtable.

I read and read and read, and so I watched more and more TV. Honestly, I don't think I ever really enjoyed reading, maybe specifically because it was simply a paperly means to a televisual end, but I did it. And it wasn't like anybody just took me at my word when I said I'd read something. My parents recognized that I wasn't above trying to game the system, so I had to write out fairly detailed summaries each day and leave them on the kitchen table for folks to peruse at their leisure. And my stepfather would always look at them, no matter how late he got home, even once in a while waking me from my sleep in the middle of the night to get clarification on a passage. He hated bad handwriting or sentences that weren't well proofread. "Write this over. It is too sloppy. And please take your time, John. When you rush, you make mistakes."

Sometimes he or my mom would even go back to the book, which I always had to leave on the table alongside my recaps, and quiz me further about specific parts of the reading (usually only if a summary seemed underwhelming to them, like the superficial byproduct of mere skimming). All of this helped to keep me safely at or above grade level. And during parent-teacher conferences, teachers would corroborate some of my stepfather's aforementioned assessment. I was a smart kid, they said. Make sure he keeps it up.

And there were other incentives besides TV shows and the flattery of grade school teachers. If I came home with a 100 percent on a test, I would be rewarded with a dollar. Or maybe an extra thirty minutes to play outside. There were inducements all over the place, positive and negative.

When I received a score in the 90s on something, I would hear tongue-in-cheek (mostly) questions about why I hadn't gotten the full 100—100s were the goal, with the occasional 104 or 105 (from successfully answered extra-credit questions) sometimes bringing even more bonuses. And anything less than a 90? Well, I didn't bother to bring those home, or if I did, they just stayed in my bag, since dipping below that 90 cutoff was considered a kind of household failure, and my stepfather's response could get pretty dark pretty quick. And I got the point. I had to be the best. I was supposed to be the best. I needed to outcompete everybody in my classes. "What did the chiney girls get?" he'd ask.

I was about five when my mom married my stepfather, a charismatic immigrant from Trinidad and Tobago who was raised in a culture where all Asians were called "chiney" and who had little more than a high school education, which was part of the reason why he focused on my early schooling like a dog with a bone. He valued the importance of education and knew how relatively difficult it was to get ahead without it. He was going to make sure that I didn't fall into the trap of dropping out. And the real working assumption was that I couldn't just get average grades if I wanted to be successful. I had to be at the top of my class. A standout. The exception. There certainly wasn't any extra household money squirreled away for college tuition, so I had better show these schools that it was worth their while to pay my way.

When I was growing up, we never really talked about racism in my household, and certainly not as the reason for why I had to do well. In fact, I never heard my parents talk about race at all. When we moved to Canarsie, there were ample opportunities for them to wax xenophobic—or at least frustrated and incredulous—about the ethnic whites in our housing project complex or in the coveted single-family brick houses just across the street. But if they did talk, I didn't hear it. Or at least I didn't take enough note to recall it these many years later. They didn't have any white friends, mind you, not as far as I could tell. Coworkers they were cordial with, sure, but nobody they went out with or had over for dinner. They didn't have many black friends either (based on the same criteria), but they didn't go out of their way to talk about white people one way or the other.

Many academics have written about the differences between how African Americans and black immigrants from the West Indies or Africa deal with race/racism in the United States—with various theories for why those differences exist and how they impact black people's lives and life chances. Many of those studies would find this relative lack of race talk in my family predictable, given that my mother and stepfather were both from the Caribbean, but I clearly grew up thinking of myself as an African American more than a second-generation Afro-Caribbean, and not just because my biological father and his family were from somewhere in the Deep South. For most of the black kids I went to school with, West Indian or not, we were raised on New York City hip-hop music, and we mostly ignored its fundamentally transnational roots, so our sense of self was American, urban, and generally countercultural. The United States was our reference point, and though the extent of our race talk generally consisted of little more than retelling the jokes that Eddie Murphy and Richard Pryor popularized about differences between how blacks and whites behave in similar circumstances, we read ourselves quite fully into the saga of America's sordid racial history.

So my parents didn't spend a lot of time schooling us on race. They didn't seem to talk about it much. Probably still don't, though the subtle invocations are much easier for me to see as a grown up. And although my stepfather didn't talk about race, he had a kind of natural fearlessness, an aura of invincibility, that I believed would have met racism—and any would-be racist—with a swift kick in the ass (or just a couple of lashes from his belt). But it was clear to me, even early on, that I didn't have the luxury, as far as he was concerned, of being mediocre. He couldn't intimidate some admissions officer into punching my ticket for Harvard or Yale. And part of his strict mandate about studying and getting high grades was predicated on his assessment of the challenges that growing up as a young black man in America would bring.

Some African Americans still wax nostalgic about how much harder black people used to work. You know, "back in the day." It is a subplot in the story about segregation's golden age of black-on-black harmony and mutual benevolence. Racism was so awful and humiliating, they claim, that blacks had no choice but to stick together and give everything their all, to work as hard as they possibly could. Being unexceptional was the kiss of death for a black person in "a white man's world." Even when you worked hard, chances were that you got little in return, especially compared to whites. Those who were exceptional might still not get much more than the white world's castoffs. But underachieving—or just plodding along in uninspired mediocrity—was hardly a real option.

Not every black person in 1960s America heroically marched with Martin Luther King Jr. or achieved singular greatness thanks to strong black social ties and the neighborly supervision of other people's children. Black people could always be mediocre; the only issue was that in a white supremacist state, mediocre blacks "proved" the rule of racial inferiority. They made the race look bad. Mediocre whites were individual underachievers, but racism demanded that mediocre blacks stand in for the inherent, God-given limitations of their entire race. Plus, whites controlled most of the important social and economic institutions in the country, and the weaker members of their social networks could still benefit from those connection. Blacks didn't have nearly the same kind of social power or access to it, so they didn't have the luxury of being average if they still wanted a chance to thrive and succeed. We had to be "twice as good as whites," some elders explain, just to get the jobs that white Americans didn't even want.

My stepfather never said that I had to be twice as good as white people. His racial references for achievement were my "chiney" classmates, those "model minorities." In fact, he didn't really talk much about white people at all. He wasn't much of a talker in general, but he especially didn't seem to have much to say about white people (at least not around me). But his assumptions about what I would need to commit to as a young person seemed to pivot on that belief that I had to constantly push myself, work harder. I might have been smart in his estimation, but that alone didn't guarantee a thing, which is why he was such a stickler about me and my chalkboard. If I lost my focus, if I slipped in terms of my disciplined approach to learning, all the natural ability in the world didn't matter. I would be in trouble, especially since I had no powerful social network to fall back on.

I have to admit that I didn't (and still don't) feel exceptionally bright. As a teenager, I remember thinking that all parents must believe their kids to be budding geniuses. I didn't think I was stupid. But some of my classmates seemed no less intelligent, including some of the ones who didn't pass many of their classes—or even attend them consistently. What I had mastered was how to get good grades from teachers, though after I successfully passed the test to get into Brooklyn Technical High School— one of New York's selective public high schools—my parents exhaled ever so slightly, and I was able to coast, which meant that the 100s were fewer and farther between.

The "twice as good as whites" rhetoric was about recognizing that American society was a place where whites and blacks could perform the same actions and come out with very different results. That might be considered one textbook definition of racism. "Twice as good" implied that "average" meant different things for blacks and whites.

But there is another (related) argument afoot in certain sections of the black community, some of its biggest proponents being various black neocons and comedian Bill Cosby. But it isn't just them. I hear versions of the claim whenever I speak to black audiences about my anthropological research on class differences in contemporary Harlem, and not just the older audience members who lament the state of black youth today. Exhibit A: the most misogynist and violent forms of hip-hop music they can find. The claim is simple and turns "twice as good" on it head. Some people believe that there is a new mentality on the rise in black America, a mentality oblivious to the pitfalls of black mediocrity, a mentality that couldn't be more different from everything "twice as good" talk was supposed to inspire.

There was a time when blacks championed high achievement, the argument goes. They didn't have what they deserved, so they fought harder to get it. Nowadays, African Americans have grown quite comfortable with having less, content in their generally second-class citizenship, less angry about their social marginalization. They once fought tooth and nail for equal rights; now they seem resigned to their own continued inequality. Some would say they even embrace it. They once protested and marched and faced down dogs for the right to vote. However, now they seem to have lost just about all of that reverence and respect for the ballot, even in an Obama era when more young blacks where convinced to head to the polls.

We might call this a version of the "culture of poverty" argument, the notion that poor people of color possess a belief system that promotes underachievement and dysfunction, placing a premium on behaviors that are maladaptive and self-destructive. These cultures reward bad behavior with social legitimacy, street cred, and underachievement. The "code of the street" in black neighborhoods, they argue, is an even more warped version of mainstream American avarice, selfishness, and ignorance.

What's the logic of their argument? Blacks think they should be handed everything. Forget about being twice as good. For the twenty-first-century black person, "half as good" is more than enough. The country doesn't deserve any more from them. Detractors maintain that they are so busy focusing on race and what racism did to them and their forefathers, what it supposedly continues to do, that they don't just pull themselves up by their proverbial bootstraps and take responsibility for their lives. They are constantly on the lookout for scapegoats, for external forces that justify and explain away their underachievement: I didn't get good grades because the test is biased. I didn't get the job because the employer must be racist. The bank won't give me a loan because the loan officers are racist. It is raining in my neighborhood because the clouds are bigots. Someone or something is always out to get them.

Now, there are all kinds of statistical regressions that folks have used to show that, other things being equal, there are still a ton of ways in which racism accounts for social differences. Think of the audit studies where, say, identical resumes have black- versus white-sounding names at the top, and the Biffs end up getting called in for job interviews much more often than the Leroys (with the same qualifications), in ways that are statistically significant and hard to explain by chance alone—or by invoking any factors other than race/racism.

This position (that blacks have gone from promoting the idea of "twice as good" to embracing the idea that "half as good" is fine, that less should be more than enough) is absurd and brilliant at the same time. First of all, it sets up a scenario wherein talking about racism at all is only ever a crutch. People who see racism must be the "half as good" blacks, the ones looking for handouts, celebrating their victimhood. Critical analysis and social critique be damned, to see race or racism is to be lazy—and racist. Period. It means just trying to kick back on your heels and waiting for "the white man" to give you everything you want. "Why should I have to work hard?" the thought-bubble in black people's heads is supposed to be saying. "My forefathers built this country. They worked enough for all of their offspring. We are owed our forty acres and a mule. Our reparations. So, I am not going to do a hard day's work until I get what's already long overdue, my back pay."

Proponents of this position might admit that few people speak so self-consciously and in such crystal-clear terms about their own motivations

and social traits. Culture doesn't always work that way, they'd scold. I'm
an anthropologist; I should know that. The "half as good" position is just
something blacks have come to internalize, to take for granted. It informs
their actions even when they can't articulate their commitment to it. They
know that they don't want to work, but they still need money and food
and fancy TVs and expensive sneakers and flashy rides and everything else.
They want their bling, but they don't want to do a thing to earn it. This is
exactly why there is such a hyperdemonization of "the welfare state." The
"culture of poverty" folks have long argued that food stamps and welfare
and other government handouts help to grease the wheel for this mentality, for this "half as good" mindset, without even knowing it. Those programs are Trojan horses of psychological self-destruction. With affirmative action and other governmental efforts to reward blacks for not doing
anything, they don't have to be nearly as good as their white counterparts
to get the job or the college seat or the government contract or anything
else. According to this theory, blacks are smart enough to know that they
don't have to be as good as whites to succeed, and they have thoroughly
internalized this realization.

So, the argument closes, if these blacks think they should get everything
without doing anything and you combine that with Americans' penchant
for lavishing praise on their children for mediocrity, for even just average
accomplishments, then you get a perfect storm of racial underachievement, lowered expectations, and do-nothing entitlement.

There is hardly a public intellectual around who hasn't weighed in on
this debate from the right or the left, either taking the position of boot-
strapologists or dismissing the argument as another attempt at "blaming
the victim," making blacks the too-easy cause of their own social marginalization. But I don't think blacks are clamoring for "half as good" success,
even if many self-respecting self-help gurus might say that the name of the
game is precisely to get more while exerting less. By that logic, if "half as
good" were true, it might even be a rational response to America's racial
lineage. But as I see it, blacks are not clamoring for half-as-good-opportu-
nities. If anything, they feel that "twice as good" might sometimes get you
less than it should.

Just take my own tribe: black academics. A few years ago I wrote a piece for the *Chronicle of Higher Education*'s online site that absolutely terrified me. A series of odd coincidences and scheduling serendipities found me breaking bread with some of the most successful blacks in the academy over the stretch of just a few weeks. Scholars at the very top of their fields in the humanities and the social sciences. They have won all kinds of prestigious awards. Their work is cited liberally within their disciplines and beyond. They are tenured at some of the most prestigious institutions in the county. And every one of them felt underappreciated, disrespected, and dismissed as scholars. They had achieved everything that they could have in their chosen fields, and they felt like many of their white colleagues still treated them with little more than contempt, envy or utter indifference. It was disheartening to hear. These senior scholars of color described themselves as ignored by administrators, maligned by others in their fields, and somewhat alienated from the centers of their disciplines—even when they were arguably the very centers of their disciplines.

The first time I heard such a tale, over lunch at a coffee shop in California, I tried to dismiss it as an isolated incident, one person's idiosyncratic experience. Maybe he was just being hypersensitive. Or I could have caught him on a bad day. But then I sat across from a few more senior and very successful scholars (in Michigan and Massachusetts, in New York and North Carolina) with similar stories to tell (of humiliating slights that they interpreted as race-based disrespect), and I had to admit that something more was going on than just thin-skinned bellyaching.

Most of these scholars were sharing their stories with me (as their junior colleague) for my own good, in hopes of steeling me for a similar (potential) future of professional discontent. Their point: No amount of publishing productivity or public notoriety exempts you from the vulnerabilities and burdens that come with underrepresentation in the academy. Being "twice as good" as most of their white colleagues (by objective and generally agreed-upon criteria) still wasn't enough to spare them from the sting of race-base stigma.

These scholars weren't lamenting the stain of "affirmative action," the fear that their successes were tainted by other people's assumptions that their achievements were based on something other than purely meritocratic deservedness. That's the Clarence Thomas critique of affirmative action. Only one of the senior black faculty I ate with during that stretch seemed plagued by such a concern. The others were arguing something close to the opposite: that they had genuinely succeeded at a game decidedly stacked against them, that most people in their fields knew and understood that, but that the thanks they received was a tacit (or not so tacit) attempt to ignore them anyway, to demean them with cool disinterest and a series of daily exclusions from important departmental discussions or real leadership roles at their respective universities. What explains all that? And was I doomed for the same fate?

My stepfather might have given me my early taste of academic success, but my mother gave me my temperament, a mix of smiling (often), being nice to people, and trying not to let others get under my skin. Or at least not letting on when they do. Young black boys love their mamas, and I am certainly a version of that cliché. And her everyday sensibilities rubbed off on me much more than my stepfather's did. He was gruff and stern, always in a glare that hinted at a hot rage just beneath the surface. But I tend to be much more "open-faced" than that, which is my mother's influence. She is still very quiet and deferential and polite. Always polite.

Long before anyone told me about inspirational speaker Earl Nightingale's take on the seemingly endless powers of a "good attitude" and before Wharton professor Adam Grant's counterintuitive claim that, even in business (as it has always been in matters of spirituality, at least as far as Christianity is concerned), it is better to give than to receive, I have always tried to be a generous and empathetic person. At least I want to think I am. If anything, that is one of the things that separates me from some—though not all—of my colleagues. There are at least two kinds of academics when it comes to empathizing with students. Most faculty can have empathy for students that they think of as being just like them. Maybe based on their ethnic affiliation, their regional background, or any number of other factors, they see themselves in those students and can be more than willing to give them the benefit of the doubt on things, in subtle ways, maybe even without knowing it. They lobby for them to get a second chance. Or some special recognition. I have seen that at just about every single place I've ever taught. And it doesn't matter if the academics in question are left-leaning, right-leaning, male, or female. Everyone does it. But only a smaller subset seems to muster the same kind of empathy for (and investment in) folks that they see as different from them in some substantial way. Clearly, race is one of those rubrics, but it isn't the only one. And some faculty are sometimes a little less likely to go the extra mile for these students. More prone to matter-of-fact pronouncements. Doing things "by the book" instead of thinking off-script about what these students need in more humane and creative ways, something they would be much more likely to do with folks just like them.

And I do think that being "twice as good" as whites (or only benefiting from affirmative action in ways that allow blacks to get away with being "half as good" as white scholars) explains my path in the academy. I think that what modicum of professional success I might have in this occupation is almost exclusively a function of the fact that I try (though I don't always succeed) to take everyone I meet very seriously. It is an ethnographic disposition, I'd argue. All human beings are more than adequate ambassadors of their cultural worlds. It doesn't matter how smart they are (or aren't); if you listen long enough and carefully enough, a good ethnographer can always learn something by listening and looking. If not, the failure is the ethnographer's, nobody else's. And I think that sometimes people just respond generously to that, to the sense of being listened to.

I always tell myself that I smile too much. That I wish I had more of my stepfather's cold stare. But I also realize that smiling, genuinely and warmly smiling, is a kind of magic bullet, especially for black men in America. Not too long ago, I did a kind of experiment. I am constantly telling students that "everything is ethnography," that an anthropologist is always on the clock, seeking out new ways of spying and interpreting cultural practices and processes. So I went against the grain of my general tendencies and tried not to smile as a kind of ethnographic experiment, just to see how it would effect my social interactions. I conducted this little test as part of a job interview. I didn't really know anyone on the search committee, at least not very well (academic jobs are usually vetted by a committee), and I decided that I would actively try not to over-smile during my interview session. I wouldn't scowl, but I would try to stay emotionally and facially neutral. I couldn't help but forget once or twice (during the almost thirty-minute interview), a smile or two broke out across my face at a couple of times for a few fleeting seconds each, but I tried to suppress them immediately, as soon as I realized. I did all I could to look serious. Not angry, but not smiling either. I crossed my right leg over my left. I sat back calmly. I answered their questions soberly but substantively (I thought), and then I left. I don't know how I was read, but I fear that I might have been seen as arrogant. Maybe even a little standoff-ish and "uppity." Who knows? It wasn't a controlled scientific experiment, so I can't isolate all the variables and search for some statistically signifi-cant correlation between features of my performance/personhood and the committee's decision that I wasn't a good fit for the job. But I felt that I could feel their coolness during our group conversation, and I couldn't help but wish that I could go back in again and test that response against the one that my more smiley self might have garnered.

I want to think about my liberal use of smiles as an example of interper-sonal empathy and generosity, but maybe I am reading myself too gener-ously. At my most cynical and self-critical, I call it the postmodern version of "shucking and jiving," doing what I have always done in all-black spaces, but now doing so in all-white or mixed quarters: trying to do whatever I can to put people at ease, to listen to what they have to say, to shower them with inviting (and unselfconscious) smiles. Is this the twenty-first-century equivalent of the Yes Man? Even if one positions one's would-be smiles around an actual "no" to the powers that be?

I must not have wanted that job if I was willing to do what I just described. But it still stung when I didn't get the nod. When I was told that I wasn't right for the post, I thought of my more senior black col-leagues and the disrespect they'd talked about. Like everyone else, my world is full of tiny and not-so-tiny slights, major and minor humiliations just about every single day, a barrage of looks, comments, emails, reactions, decisions, and personal or professional rejections—intended and inadver-tent—that belittle at every turn. At least it feels that way, like my daily life is organized around the reeling dash from one disrespectful dismissal to another. The world's playlist constantly ending up back on a version of the same tune, "John, don't believe your own hype. You're not as good as people pretend you are. And don't you ever forget it." This little ditty does battle with my stepfather's earlier accolades. It is probably an outgrowth of those very accolades, nurtured by my nasty little subconscious.

I spent my twenties and thirties hoping that I could credentialize myself into a kind of protective cocoon against such onslaughts. I may not have been "twice as good" as anybody, but I was going to try my damnedest to have the discipline to reach my goals: BA. MA. PhD. Tenure. Named Professor. None of it is foolproof. And at the end of the day, it might all be based on nothing more than how often and easily you smile, on whether or not someone is twice or half as good at that.

II

"Whither Now and Why"

Content Mastery and Pedagogy—
A Critique and a Challenge

DANA A. WILLIAMS

On April 2, 1960, at Johnson C. Smith University, W. E. B. Du Bois delivered a speech he titled "Whither Now and Why," in which he questions what the aims and ideals of the Negro will be if he achieves equal American citizenship: "Are we to assume that we will simply adopt the ideals of Americans and become what they are or want to be and that we will have in this process no ideals of our own?" (2001b, 193). The former leads to a disassociation with any memory of Negro history and a severing of any tie to Africa, essentially to racial and cultural suicide (194). Having ideals of our own, however, involves "the possibility of black folk and their cultural patterns existing in America without discrimination; and on terms of equality" (195). In "Bourgeois Fugue: Notes on the Life of the Negro

Intellectual," Houston A. Baker Jr., like Du Bois, anticipates the moment when African Americans will develop a cultural apparatus to measure itself and the world. Having long ago shed the skin of a Western aesthetic valuation and having made significant contributions to African American cultural theory, Baker laments the "self-styled 'raceless' and post soul aesthetic" (2011, 46–47) that consumes the more bourgeois segments of black intellectual life and contends that the best thing that could happen now "would be the birth of a real and caring black bourgeoisie, one [E. Franklin] Frazier would approve and that Howard University [both men's alma mater and mine] would salute as a model for a bold and vigorous African and African diaspora curriculum" (47). Taking Baker's challenge seriously, I began to think very deliberately about the myriad reasons my colleagues and I had yet to build that model. One of the reasons I returned to Howard as a faculty member in 2003—completely unfazed at the too-frequent comments from many of my black peers at Louisiana State University that my choice was a sentimental "career-ending" move—was, in fact, because I too believed that such a model was possible and that it was most likely to emerge as a purposeful intellectual and cultural enterprise at Howard. My belief was not undergirded in mere hope and speculation; there was an indisputable legacy as proof and intermittent contemporary efforts as evidence. For example, under the direction of Eleanor W. Traylor, the humanities division of the College of Arts and Sciences reimagined its "Introduction to Humanities" courses to situate African, Native American, and East Asian narratives and film at the center of the tradition of "great" texts. More than an exercise in textual inclusion, the course revision abandoned the old frame of grappling with questions that inevitably seek to reveal the difference between constructed categories like "evil" and "good" and sought instead to ask new questions that embraced worldviews from "marginal" cultures and adopted Alain Locke's notion of critical relativism.[1] But this achievement, as an institutionalized practice, is more anomalous than it is standard. The reality is that not even Howard has managed to free itself from the disciplinary loyalties and ideological affinities that limit serious engagement with African ways of knowing and being in ways that enliven humanity or even the study of humanities.

Adherence to discipline (and attending methodologies) and to ideologies that tend to inform the traditional Western academy, in short, trouble the waters that might birth the kind of curriculum Baker calls for. Not yet ready to concede defeat, the question I ask myself repeatedly echoes Du Bois'—whither now and why—now that the Western world is turning toward a more global reality, where does Howard, as a thought leader historically and rhetorically committed to meaningful exchange with the diaspora, go from here. No less important, though, are the questions *how do we get there* and *why does going there matter.*

My own disciplinary training is in literature, African American literature in particular. And since I think it important to avoid presumptuously assuming the posture of an academic trained in Africana Studies methodologies, I limit my "close reading" here of the challenge of disciplines and ideologies in large part to literature and humanities fields. In its broadest interpretation, "the humanities" concerns itself foremost with the exploration, analysis, and exchange of ideas that inform the human experience and its condition. It derives from the late fourteenth- and early fifteenth-century Italian and English Renaissance traditions of "humanists" to describe the intellectual pursuits of those who emphasized the primacy of classical literature (and grammar and rhetoric), history, and philosophy in formal educational systems.[2] As the study of humanities disciplines expanded in time and space, it claimed to inspire a global, cultural dialogue, yet its essential motivation undeniably has been to study the languages, history, and cultures of the ancient Mediterranean world— notably, to the exclusion of the world that predates it.

This exclusion lasts well into the twentieth century until postmodernism begins to question the rigid categories that traditionally defined and shaped humanities disciplines. At Howard, the intervention and redefinition comes a little earlier. Even prior to the aggressive revision that takes place in the early 1990s of the "Introduction to Humanities" course alluded to earlier, a 1968 syllabus of the year-long course notes: "Some of the greatest literature in the world has been written outside of and before the birth of 'Western Civilization.'" It then offers this common disclaimer: "But just as we cannot study all kinds of art, we cannot even study all kinds of literature. So we shall concentrate on a few of the books of the Western tradition which have had the greatest influence on your world and which have given men everywhere a little wisdom and a lot of pleasure."[3] Ever aware of and frustrated by the intellectual dodge, though still unrepentant of it fully, the syllabus confesses that "The Shipwrecked Sailor" is an obvious source for Homer's *The Odyssey* and that the earliest iteration of *The Odyssey*'s genre, a traveler's tale, is from Egypt. But the humanities' principal concern is declared in the course title: "Basic Ideas of Western Thought." I like to imagine our progenitors as being coy here—suggesting that Western thought ideas are "basic." I can even find support for this speculation. Following the description of the traveler's tale is this line: "Another kind of tale . . . had to do with a journey down into the region of the dead," referring, of course, to those tales collected in *The Book of Coming Forth by Day and Night*, called *The Egyptian Book of the Dead* by Western scholars. I make the distinction here even with the nomenclature to tease out a nuance that makes my point that Howard humanities scholars were well aware of the ways Western thought oversimplifies the complexity of African culture. The naming of *The Egyptian Book of the Dead* presumes a finality in death, while the naming of *The Book of Coming Forth by Day and Night* understands the book not as one of "death" but as religious texts that from the New Kingdom onward were placed in the tomb on the coffin as part of the rituals that helped the dead navigate the journey in the afterlife—the "dead" have a region where they are fully alive in both the past and present moment.[4]

By 1992 faculty in the departments of Classics, English, Philosophy, and what was then Modern and Foreign Languages (now World Languages and Cultures—naming matters) had redesigned the course as two independent offerings with the overt and deliberate intent of decentering the West, the first and second rise of Europe specifically, as the point of departure and reference for the study of the laws of nature and man's relation to his society in ancient civilizations. The center shifted, literally. And it is in large part because of that shift that I was able to claim in an honors humanities seminar I taught during the spring 2012 semester that the class would help students understand and recover worldviews that not only offer alternate responses to the broad thematic questions that inform the study of the humanities—what is the nature of ultimate reality; what is the nature of man; what is man's relation to ultimate reality?—but that it would also offer new methodologies for studying the human experience.

The premise that undergirded the course was not mine by design but no less mine in belief—it was John Henrik Clarke's.[5] In the foreword of the *African World History Project: The Preliminary Challenge*, he writes, "When Europe was born, Africa, particularly Egypt, had had a ten-thousand-year walk in the sun politically and culturally and was now tired from its long journey. . . . The challenge of the Nile Valley created Egypt"; the challenge of Egypt and the Mediterranean islands influenced Rome and Greece, and the challenge of Rome and Greece clearly influenced Europe (2002, x). In short, I haughtily announced to my students at the start of the semester, to link the humanities to the European Renaissance was an error at best and self-defeating at worse since man's determination to study the laws of nature and to establish civil and religious systems to govern the universe predates European "humanists" by at least ten thousand years. Any study of the humanities characterized by "deep thought" requires all participants—the instructor, the pupil, and the texts alike—to commit to achieving deep understanding and to giving full consideration of the oldest of civilizations and then to understanding how the traditions, thoughts, beliefs, and values of those civilizations have been transformed and reimagined by more "modern" peoples. This is the challenge—to achieve deep understanding and to give full consideration of the oldest of civilizations and to bring knowledge about those civilizations forward, bridges intact, into a contemporary moment. To do this for "early" civilizations is perhaps an unsustainable pursuit for even a single department. But, at least in part, it is what Classics departments claim to do, though they somehow manage to cut off the nose to spite the face consistently and then to hide the head in the antiquities room of the proverbial world museum, masking too often as the Western academy. The nose, in this instance, is classical Africa, with "knowledge" that precedes Greece and Rome serving as the face. Acknowledging the Africanist presence in classical civilizations is then given the least amount of exhibition time or space possible in the academic space as museum, when it is exhibited at all; or the "noble" scholar as curator relegates it to the room with Asiatic antiquities or, more boldly and perhaps honestly, simply ceases to feign interest in anything other than ancient Mediterranean cultures.[6]

To master content and to build a bridge for a single continent and its civilizations is perhaps unreasonable, still, for a department, though theoretically this is precisely what African Studies departments claim to aim to do, but their subject positioning as a construct of the Western academy makes it similarly impossible. The disciplinary and methodological affinities are too strong and too limited, and the implications are too dangerous. One hope, then, might be a turn to Black Studies, which is the only academic discipline that emerges out of the community and has commitments, at least in theory, beyond the university. But Black Studies has yet to fortify its methodology, though it has made great strides in doing so at Howard especially, in ways that enable the discipline to rise and meet the challenge before us.[7] Indisputably, Howard's Afro-American Studies department is without peer. Unlike other Black Studies departments (and programs) where faculty have degrees in other disciplines with a "certificate" or emphasis in Black Studies, Howard's department has five full-time faculty with PhDs in the field. The only faculty hire in recent years without a degree in African American Studies is one of few African American scholars with a PhD in Egyptology. Courses in *medu necher*, or Egyptian hieroglyphs, are offered each semester—the vision and commitment to building a team of young scholars who will finally enable us to allow black peoples on the continent and throughout the diaspora to be in conversation with ourselves with little regard for the white gaze are real.[8] But until the model that is emerging in Afro-American Studies at Howard takes full form and becomes the standard bearer, and perhaps even after, the only real solution, if we can call it that, is for there to *be* a Negro university, to use Du Bois's language, for only a Negro university can facilitate the work of a team of scholars at the university in all fields to do the work that must be done if we are to access what Wole Soyinka, in the aptly titled collection of essays *Of Africa*, articulates as the dynamic possessions that Africa enjoys and that the rest of the world does not already possess in superabundance—African humanism.

As Africa's gift to the world, that humanism, in its unadulterated form, involves "ways of perceiving, responding, adapting, or simply *doing* that vary from people to people, including structures of human relationships" (Soyinka 2012, vii), and that reject oppressive hierarchies. These ways of knowing "all constitute potential commodities of exchange," Soyinka argues, and can be "recognizable as defining the human worth of any people—and could actually contribute to the resolution of the existential dilemma of distant communities, or indeed to global survival, if only they were known about or permitted their proper valuation" (ibid.). This humanism, then, is universal. But how could it be, since it is deeply informed by culture? What lies beneath such a question is the assumption that a universally applicable conceptualization of what it means to be human and in community with others without violence or judgment cannot be informed by blackness. Surely it must be *post* something— post-racial, post-black, post-colonial, post-Africa. That humanism can be informed by culture (a black culture at that) is the very foundation upon which the Negro university that Du Bois imagines must build.

The Negro university, Du Bois tells us in "The Field and Function of the Negro College," must use the history of the Negro in Africa and America to interpret all of history and to "understand the social development of all mankind in all ages. . . . And this is a different program than a similar function would be in a white university or in a Russian university or in an English university, because it starts from a different point" (2001a, 125). Taking Africa as the starting point, Du Bois makes clear, is not so much an uncritical embrace of cultural nationalism as it is a recovery of the full arc of human history.[9] The real challenge we must now face or concede that we are disinterested in meeting is to be a Negro university with the notion of African humanism as a way of seeing and being in the world decidedly at its core.

I am reminded here, of course, of the "Towards a Black University Conference" that the Howard student association sponsored in 1968, which called for the total rejection of a university-sanctioned (if not mandated) acculturation "into a society which debilitates black people" (quoted in Davis 1969, 46). While the intent was never to make Howard *the* Black

University, a clear goal was to "define the structure and mechanics" of *a* black university (ibid., 46).[10] So why, nearly fifty years after that historic conference, do we still await Howard's (and its peer institutions') response to a call to develop the mechanics necessary to have blackness inform an understanding of universal experiences and to recognize that no history of the world can be understood without full appreciation of the history of Africa, especially as it relates to the development of mankind through the ages? The tendency as faculty is to obfuscate the challenge of first determining and then articulating and executing this structure and mechanics with a need for administrative cooperation. We must acknowledge the administrative impediments that distract us from the work we have been called to do as the scapegoats impediments can be and often are. To be clear, I do not exempt myself from this critique. When it became clear just how hard it would be to master the content necessary to help my students understand the ways African cultures and traditions have responded to the big questions related to the human condition, I conceded and retreated to the texts that I know best, those of African American literature. Instead of meeting the challenge of developing the "Introduction to Humanities" course that would allow me and my students to access the bounty of African humanism, I decided to focus exclusively on the novels of Toni Morrison and to settle with accessing the mere residue of the rich traditions and culture from which her fiction draws. Unable to walk them through Kemet's "walk in the sun" and the way it influenced the Mediterranean islands and then Rome and Greece and then Europe and then America, I couched the course's "radical" pedagogy in its methodology. The goal shifted from walking them from classical Africa to the Negro arrival in the Americas to a still noble pursuit of establishing a line of inquiry that would cultivate a life-long desire to achieve content mastery and to minimize my and my students' present lack. I used guiding questions or "thinking prompts" (drawn heavily from the 1968 syllabus but retooled to suit my purpose) that constantly reminded students that ideas, concepts, and questions about humankind and its relation to the world that have been fundamental to and recurrent throughout world history have genealogies that exist outside of the history of Western thought. By all accounts, it was a successful class—it even won the best syllabus award in the humanities that year—but I am painfully aware of the ways it, too, was an intellectual dodge made necessary by my own lack of content mastery. My point here is that we can only demand of the university what we demand of ourselves.

Few would deny that we all participate in the slow death march that leads to cultural suicide, even if we could argue about the ways we do so. Any attentive scholar could similarly argue convincingly that historically black colleges and universities have made their decision—their goal, as a matter of practice, is to continue to strive for full integration into American society and, naively, to adopt its decreasingly relevant ideals. So, the question of where Howard, as a thought leader historically and rhetorically committed to meaningful exchange with the diaspora and as the institution I call home, will go from here is paramount indeed. Will we accept the challenge of content mastery and build a team of scholars committed more to the liberation of African peoples on the continent and all over the world—and, by extension, liberation for all of humanity—than to vulgar careerism and to delusions of disciplinary meaningfulness? There is only one way for those of us who are most at home in academic spaces to get there—and that is through mastery of and deep thought about our respective areas of study in the broadest sense. The final question, then, is why going there matters. And that answer is even simpler—because we are the only people who can free us.

NOTES

1. Locke's critical relativism called for an evaluation of world cultural values or ideas about humanity while avoiding the two extremes inherent in such an evaluation—relativism and dogmatism. In its acknowledgment of values as relative to their culture, critical relativism would situate values in the contexts out of which they are birthed and, concurrently, acknowledge with reciprocity and tolerance the diversity of values and cultures that populate the world, all the while subjecting cultural values to objective criticism.

2. Academic disciplines traditionally associated with the humanities include classics, history, languages, literature, linguistics, performing arts, philosophy,

religion, and visual arts. Humanities disciplines privilege the analytical, critical, and speculative in terms of methodology and have their roots in the Western academy as a part of the course of study for the cultivated man—courses of study related to grammar, poetry, rhetoric, and moral philosophy were signs of the educated, the civilized. When education became more broadly accessible among the ancient Greeks, we see the concept of the seven liberal arts emerge (grammar, rhetoric, and logic; arithmetic, geometry, astronomy, and music). By the fifteenth century, Renaissance humanism begins to privilege literature and history, and ancient Rome and Greece become the pivots on which all humanities study turns.

3. I am grateful to Carrie Cowherd for sharing these syllabi with me as I prepared to teach an honors humanities seminar and as I continue to think about revising humanities course offerings at Howard.

4. I am indebted to Mario Beatty for teasing out this recognition with even more clarity than I asserted in my initial effort.

5. I take some care to note that, for many years, my familiarity with Clarke as a representative thinker was limited to my awareness of his contributions in African American literary studies. I am deeply indebted to Greg Carr for introducing me to Clarke's seminal importance to African American cultural and intellectual history, writ large. I don't imagine I would have ever encountered a non-literary Clarke or the *African World History Project* at all, absent the frequent and meaningful exchanges between me and Carr. My understanding of Africana studies methodologies is significantly informed by these exchanges, by his published writings on the subject, and by his too infrequently published public lectures that easily number more than fifty annually.

6. Ironically, following recommendations made by an internal commission at Howard on academic renewal that it reimagine itself, the Department of Classics at Howard, the only free-standing Classics department at an historically black college or university, proposed to become "Ancient Mediterranean Studies." The board of trustees, however, rejected this proposal, and Classics' fate is, to date, still unclear.

7. I am thinking especially of Carr's work on developing conceptual categories to inform methodology as outlined in *Lessons in Africana Studies* and his "What Black Studies Is Not: Moving from Crisis to Liberation" (2011).

8. *Medu necher* and Coptic languages are offered by Afro-American Studies. Classics continues to offer Greek and Latin, while the Department of World Languages and Cultures offers courses in no fewer than eight African languages annually. In short, the whole history of the world can be engaged carefully, without the liability of nonculturally informed interpreters.

9. The "irony" of cultural nationalism is that it anticipates globalization by at least fifty years. It abandoned fidelity to the nation-state as concept almost at its inception, understanding boundaries as politically and economically driven constructions. Similarly, it seems ironic to suggest a look to Africa to grapple with the challenge of an increasingly more global world. The irony dissipates with the growing awareness that the turn to Africa is not a turn to place but a turn to non-essentializing worldviews that inform place. Soyinka's attempt to provide *Ifa* as one such model in *Of Africa* is an astute one and should be purposefully considered. It must also be extended to include other non-oppressive traditions that articulate full understandings of humanity.

10. Acklyn Lynch, one of the faculty who helped design the conferences sessions, makes this point to George Davis in an issue of *Negro Digest* dedicated to the discourses the conference raised (1969).

REFERENCES

Baker, Houston A., Jr. 2011. "Bourgeois Fugue: Notes on the Life of the Negro Intellectual." In *From Bourgeois to Boojie: Black Middle-Class Performances*, ed. Vershawn Ashanti Young with Bridget Harris Tsemo, 41–48. Detroit, MI: Wayne State University Press.

Carr, Greg. 2011. "What Black Studies Is Not: Moving from Crisis to Liberation in Africana Intellectual Work." *Socialism and Democracy* 25, no. 1 (March): 178–91.

Clarke, John Henrick. 2002. Foreword to *The Preliminary Challenge: African World History Project*. Ed. Jacob H. Carruthers and Leon C. Harris, x–xvii. Los Angeles: Association for the Study of Classical African Civilizations.

Davis, George B. 1969. "A Step Forward? The Howard University Conference." *Negro Digest*, March, 44–48.

Du Bois, W. E. B. 2001a. "The Field and Function of the Negro College." In *The Education of Black People: Ten Critiques, 1906–60*, ed. Herbert Aptheker, 111–33. New York: Monthly Review.

——. 2001b. "Whither Now and Why." In *The Education of Black People: Ten Critiques, 1906–60*, ed. Herbert Aptheker, 193–203. New York: Monthly Review.

Soyinka, Wole. 2012. *Of Africa*. New Haven, CT: Yale University Press.

12

Fallacies of the Post-Race Presidency

ISHMAEL REED

Legitimate grievances against police brutality tipped into excuse-making for criminal behavior. Racial politics could cut both ways as the transformative message of unity and brotherhood was drowned out by the language of recrimination. And what had once been a call for equality of opportunity, the chance for all Americans to work hard and get ahead was too often framed as a mere desire for government support, as if we had no agency in our own liberation, as if poverty was an excuse for not raising your child and the bigotry of others was reason to give up on yourself. All of that history is how progress stalled. That's how hope was diverted. It's how our country remained divided.

—President Barack Obama, August 29, 2013

President Barack Obama, the leader of the post-race movement, raises a straw idea when he accuses blacks of making excuses for criminal behavior. I don't find the blacks in my district, who meet monthly to hear reports of crime in our neighborhoods, making excuses. One doesn't hear black leaders on the left like Jesse Jackson, or Louis Farrakhan on the right, making excuses. When it comes to African Americans, the president's favorite words are "dysfunction" and "disproportionate." Commenting on the verdict acquitting George Zimmerman of the murder of Trayvon Martin, the president suggested that young blacks were disproportionately into crime. This principle of disproportionality has often been used to hide white dysfunctional populations. Such demographics, which include white underclass people, seem only to achieve a dopamine boost by having blacks look bad. The media have made hundreds of billions of dollars by satisfying this perverse craving of the dysfunctional. Blacks have complained, protested, and staged boycotts against media (whom they regard as their enemy) for over one hundred years.

Some years ago a study about substance abuse during pregnancy among Californians led to two news reports. One held that black women were "disproportionately" abusers of substances during pregnancy. Black women were 6 percent of California's population at the time. Another held that substance abuse was a problem for white women.[1] The actual number of abusers for white women was 35,000, precisely the number of Ugandans afflicted with AIDS at that time. A crosshatch, to be certain, but still smarting of epidemic proportionality. Within the past few years, a study appeared reporting that the typical substance abuser in California is a white woman.[2] However, United States jails everywhere are full of black and Hispanic women incarcerated for nonviolent drug offenses.

In the world of drug abuse reportage, the media continues to classify crack as a black drug even though most abusers of crack have been whites. Few whites have been sentenced for crack or other drug crimes.[3] One can say that policemen who have blatantly planted evidence on black suspects, testified about them in court, racially profiled them, and beat and tortured them are not only documented in interminable news reportage but are also virtually stock characters of multiple media crime shows. It seems a matter of "everybody knows." Prosecutors are also guilty of engaging in misconduct in cases involving blacks. Same with judges, as in the notorious conspiracy to criminally sentence young people in Pennsylvania, an occurrence so well known that it still makes Harrisburg weep! Blacks receive harsher sentences than whites for the same crimes. White suspects and white defendants are privileged over black suspects and black defendants.[4]

Like the media, whose bills are paid for by multinational corporations and think tanks financed by some of the same entities, the president seems to blame black male behavior for the country's social problems. Yet, if the president wants black fathers resident and responsible in black homes, he might accomplish the mission by granting clemency to the thousands of black men in prison for drug crimes. He might model such clemency on President Carter's granted pardons to those mainly middle- and lower-middle-class conscientious objectors who fled to Canada in order to avoid the draft. Even the president's attorney general has lessened the pressure on white marijuana smokers in several states with low black populations (Perez 2013).

The president must know about racism in the criminal justice system. Columnist Charles Blow attributes the actions of the New York City Police Department and its notorious Stop and Frisk policy, which has been declared unconstitutional by a federal judge because it singles out black and brown citizens, as contributing to the exodus of blacks from that city (2011). Flimsy academic pseudo-science has also contributed to the racial profiling of black and brown youth in the United States. New York mayors from the Giuliani administration forward have been influenced by the work of the late James Q. Wilson, coauthor of *Crime and Human Nature: The Definitive Study of the Causes*. Wilson's coauthor was the late Richard Herrnstein, who posited mental inferiority of blacks. Wilson is Scots-Irish and the late Herrnstein was Jewish. Both Wilson's and Herrnstein's ethnic groups have been disparaged with charges of feeblemindedness and savagery by bigots in a former era.

Then there is Wilson's "broken windows" philosophy that provided a racist foundation for New York's Stop and Frisk policy (Guiliani 2012). Wilson cried a monstrous "wolf," predicting an apocalyptic crime wave perpetrated by super predators of color. It was a publicity-seeking hoax worthy of P. T. Barnum, a non-empirical clown show and a hoax. Nevertheless, it birthed the "Super-Predator" as media fodder and policy catalyst. Fear of a violent juvenile crime wave led some to predict a new cohort of these "super-predators" Conservative academics such as Wilson and John DiIulio and a small band of mainstream criminologists such as Alfred Blumstein and James Fox forecasted societal disaster (Krisberg 2005). Wilson predicted "30,000 more young muggers, killers, and thieves" (Wilson 1995); DiIulio foresaw another 270,000 violent juveniles by 2010. He warned of a "crime bomb" created by a generation of "fatherless, Godless, and jobless" juvenile super-predators (DiIulio 1995). Theirs was coded language for black American youths, already under-resourced by U.S. design, intent, and policy.

The media hyped the story, and many elected officials exploited it. The citizenry was told about a generation of babies born to "crack-addicted" mothers, babies who would possess permanent neurological damage, including the inability to feel empathy. The scientific evidence supporting this claim was nonexistent (Krisberg 2005).

Racial profiling isn't caused by the personal behavior of blacks but by the behavior of so-called demography experts such as Wilson, politicians like former New York City mayor Michael Bloomberg, whose policy of Stop and Frisk singled out hundreds of thousands of black and brown men for public humiliation. Mayor Bloomberg argues that his goal is to protect black and brown citizens from their own. It is reminiscent of the response made by New York mayors during the 1930s, when Harlem blacks complained publicly about New York police brutality (Mathias 2013). The New York police force—unsurprisingly—responded that their protocols healthily benefitted Gotham's uptown blacks. A coalition of activist groups led by Adam Clayton Powell accused the notorious NYPD of using "Gestapo" tactics against Harlem blacks (Johnson 2003). Eventually, there was nothing for it but for Harlem to erupt in a chaos of broken glass, mad dashes of looting, and police brutality. The so-called black riot is the pseudonym of the popular lyrics of frustrated black oppression: "Y'all going to make me lose my mind up in here." Nothing has changed.

Moreover, in an analogous vein, one would expect in recent years that corporate feminists would be savvy with respect to the racial as well as gender and sexuality history of the United States. One would expect them, as general activists for rights and liberty, to protest stop and frisk practices against black and brown women. Wasn't the early advocacy of their feminism that one's feminism is paramount, regardless of race, creed, or place of national origin? (Weren't black women interrogated by their white feminist sisters: "Do you consider yourself first a woman or a black person?") Black and brown women have complained publicly that the

NYPD uses the stop-and-frisk policy to molest them sexually (Ruderman 2012). Where are their voices?

President Obama, while announcing that black youth are "disproportionately" into criminal behavior, audaciously fails to mention or address the fraud perpetrated against black mortgage holders by the powerful banking system. His attorney general is not so double-voiced. Yet, neither federal voice from the White House or its cabinet is reluctant to let us suspect that no banks or bankers will be charged with criminal behavior. Ha! They are too big, non-colored, to go to jail . . . and they are not disproportionately young.

Next the president criticizes blacks for their dependency; he shows ignorance of the historical relationship between blacks to both private and public sectors, which give whites the advantage. Thousands of middle-class blacks have fathers in the home. But that didn't prevent banks, including some large and well-established firms, from depriving them of hundreds of billions of dollars in assets by deliberately directing them into toxic loans in a manner that was, in my opinion, practically criminal (Weissmann 2011; Asher-Schapiro 2013). Even the *Wall Street Journal* reports that over 60 percent of such households were eligible for conventional loans (Brooks and Simon 2007).

The attitude of U.S. banks toward blacks hasn't changed since the 1860s when ex-slaves were encouraged to place their assets in the Freedman's Bank (Osthaus 1976).[5] That bank failed because missionaries, who didn't know anything about banking, operated it. The Freedmen's Society brought on Frederick Douglass as president when the bank was failing, then blamed him for the bank's failure. (What led Douglass to believe he had the savvy to manage a bank is anyone's guess.) Because the bank failed, thousands of emancipated blacks lost all of their savings. Douglass commented that the Freedman's Bank was "the black man's cow but the white man's milk." For a brief period, the freedmen, with their many small deposits, had made the bank a success, but the benefits went to white speculators and real estate dealers in Washington. To a certain degree, the bank provides a case study in the perversion of a philanthropic crusade into a speculative venture.

The U.S. banks' seduction of toxic loans to blacks has resulted in the loss of hundreds of billions of black American dollars. (Not, to be sure, without degrees of black complicity and co-conspiring.) This constitutes a financial catastrophe that wasn't caused by the personal behaviors of blacks in general. Such fiscal disaster has led to analogues of the removal of populations that occurred in Europe before World War II. When the then-superpowers agreed among themselves which populations should be removed, they militarized and financialized toward action. It did not matter that their target populations had occupied a "national" territory for generations. Uncomfortable "races" and "age demographics" became imaginary "predators" to be wiped out.

What happened in Europe—just the other day—is what happened in the United States in cities like New York, Oakland, and San Francisco, where black populations have declined due to the rise in the cost of housing, the foreclosure policy of banks, and the repopulation of desirables, which in the United States is referred to as "gentrification." Advocates of gentrification like *New York Times* man Sam Roberts have praised the repopulation of New York with fertile whites, and his colleague, David Brooks, has praised whites with "high fertility rates" for voting for George Bush.[6] It was Roberts who wrote that blacks were prone to commit violence (Roberts 1993).

Often working in tandem with the private sector, the public sector has also been hostile to the acquisition of assets by blacks. Take for example Franklin Delano Roosevelt's New Deal programs. Blacks were denied access to these programs because FDR made a deal with the Dixiecrats that they were left out. Between 1945 and 1955, the federal government transferred more than $100 billion to support retirement programs and fashion opportunities for job skills, education, homeownership, and small-business formation. Together these domestic programs dramatically reshaped the country's social structure by creating a modern, well-schooled, home-owning middle class. At no other time in American history had so much money and so many resources been targeted at the generation completing its education, entering the workforce and forming families.

But most blacks were out of all this. Southern members of Congress used occupational exclusions and took advantage of American federalism to ensure that national policies would not disturb their region's racial order. Farmworkers and maids, the jobs held by most blacks in the South, were denied Social Security pensions and access to labor unions. Benefits for veterans were administered locally. The GI Bill adapted to "the southern way of life" by accommodating itself to segregation in higher education, to the job ceilings that local officials imposed on returning black soldiers and to a general unwillingness to offer loans to blacks even when the federal government insured such loans. Of the 3,229 GI Bill-guaranteed loans for homes, businesses, and farms made in 1947 in Mississippi, for example, only two were offered to black veterans.

(Katznelson 2005)

"What about New Deal spending programs? They were channeled away from the poorest people, including millions of blacks, who lived in the South," writes Jim Powell (2003), a senior fellow at the Cato Institute. While whites began receiving Social Security in 1935, the majority of blacks, including domestic and agricultural workers, didn't receive Social Security until 1950. The GI Bill and the mortgage interest deductions are considered the main engines for middle-class prosperity, yet the majority of blacks have been denied both. Both the Great Society programs and the War on Poverty benefited whites the most, as has Affirmative Action. Describing the Great Society programs and the War on Poverty as black programs is more propaganda from the media and race-baiting political demagogues. Whites were the main beneficiaries of both programs. The Federal Housing Administration began granting white borrowers low-interest money in 1934, permitting them to accumulate trillions of equity, which allows them to begin businesses and pay college tuition. The FHA's attitude toward blacks has been the policy of red lining (Reed 2013b).

It is obvious that the post-race president needs to be schooled on dependency. Maybe after a briefing he would criticize members of the Tea Party for their need for dependency. One Tea Party leader, who publically and unapologetically called for the vandalism of Democratic Party headquarters across the country (and whose directive was heeded), was exposed in the *Washington Post* as living on government-issued disability checks, and Tea Party-aligned congressman Paul Ryan was found to have received Social Security survivors benefits (Rucker 2010; "W. W." 2012). But if the post-race president were to criticize white dependency, he'd be on the receiving end of his enemies, including Rush Limbaugh, regarded by some as the true leader of the Republican Party.

Lastly, the president has accused blacks of dividing America, yet the hysterical, some might say psychotic, reaction to the election of a black president has led to growing secessionist movements in several states and launched a demand for his impeachment. None of these actions has a black author. What does the president mean when he says racial politics could cut both ways as the transformation message of unity and brotherhood was drowned out by the language of recrimination? Where is the recrimination coming from? The majority of Republicans who believe that he was born in Kenya? A hostile media that for the first time in American history has actually created a political party, the Tea Party, which, according to a report issued by the NAACP has prominent Holocaust deniers and racists among its membership, a party that is motivated by hatred of a black president?[7] *Newsweek*, formerly managed by Tina Brown, credits Roger Ailes for creating the Tea Party. He was one of those who designed the Willie Horton ad that, by raising the specter of the black boogeyman, contributed to the election of George H. W. Bush (Dowd 2000). His boss is Rupert Murdoch, whose newspaper, the *New York Post*, was sued by Sandra Guzman, who says she was fired for objecting to the cartoon of the president as a murdered chimp on the sidewalk, which puts the Murdoch operation to the right of Adolf Hitler, who wrote that blacks were only "half ape." Although the *New York Post* lied and said that the cartoon had nothing to do with the president, the cartoonist eventually resigned (Byers 2013; Burkeman 2009; Bloomgarden-Smoke 2013).

So vile have the racist attacks on the president been that in my book *Going Too Far*, I have compared him to the Catholic priest in *The Exorcist* because his presidency has drawn out the demonic depth of American racism. Not only has Fox News become a conduit for all of the frenetic and loony attacks on the president, but CNN actually televised a debate for the Tea Party.[8] CNN did this in partnership with the Tea Party Express, despite the latter organization's former head having referred to the president as an "Indonesian Muslim turned welfare thug" on live television (Good 2010; Graham 2009) Karl Marx and Friedrich Engels wrote: "The ideas of the ruling class are, in every age, the ruling ideas; i.e. the class which is the dominant material force in society is at the same time its dominant intellectual force. The class which has the means of material production at its disposal has control over the means of mental production" (1968).[9]

MSNBC impaneled five commentators after the president made yet another assault on black personal behavior in his remarks at the 2013 March on Washington. It only highlighted the marginalization of the opinions of traditional black Americans, especially those of black men like Roland Martin, who was fired for alienating the audience (Feldman 2013). Four commentators were white and the moderator was Touré, the black American author of *Who's Afraid of Post-Blackness*, a brilliant and provocative book that has been endorsed by a media that apparently believes that there is a conspiracy among Black Nationalists to prevent Touré from listening to Beethoven. After the president's speech, Chuck Todd both on MSNBC and a panel assembled the next day congratulated the president for his "post-race" speech. White men have most of the power in the media. They are the scriptwriters, producers, directors, and owners of the media, which define the black experience often with disastrous results. In fact, I have compared the treatment of black men in the media with that of the treatment of Jewish men in the Nazi newspaper *Der Sturmer*, whose cartoons I exhibit in the outtakes of the film, *Black Boogeyman*. This comparison might seem outlandish to those who haven't compared the two media, but W. E. B Du Bois cited the same Nazi newspaper when comparing the depictions of blacks by Southerners (Lewis 2001). He called such stereotypes propaganda. Things haven't changed since the 1930s, when Langston Hughes complained that most of the plays about black life were written by white men. So white male commentators took the lead in their appreciation of the president's speech, hailing it as a post-race speech, which means that they liked the black dysfunction parts. Regardless of the evidence that blacks have been shortchanged by both private and public sectors, official spokespersons for the ruling class, including right-wing academics whose quack studies about black behavior influence public policy, continue to blame the social problems of the society on the moral failures of blacks who are subjected to tough love lectures rendered by other people, including some whose moral standards don't measure up to those they demand (Reed 1995).

What about white dysfunction, the sleeping dog that politicians and media business people allow to lie? When I heard on Current TV that hundreds of white kids had died of overdoses in Boston, it shocked even me.[10] The media have paid little attention to white "dysfunction," possibly because it would be a real turnoff for those whom they wish to buy their advertisers' products. During the week that the president commented about black dysfunction, the *New York Times* ran a headline about the abundant heroin supplies among whites in New England (Seelye 2013).

Although he hobnobs with the rich, the president apparently hasn't heard the new line coming down from the McMansions through their well-funded messenger, Charles Murray, whose scapegoats for the failures of American society now includes the white working class. The only place stable families can be now found, according to him, is among the 1 percent (Hacker 2012).

The post-race fantasy has traction because it has millions of dollars behind its construction. One of the Manhattan Institute's backers is Chase Manhattan Bank.[11] This is why Institute Fellow John McWhorter was catapulted to the front ranks of black opinion makers. His assignment has been to ridicule, sometimes with a sort of quaint old-styled rhetoric and sarcasm that one associates with George Will. He has criticized others and me in neocon publications like *Commentary* and the *New Republic*, both of which endorsed *The Bell Curve*, which has become a kind of test for where neocons stand on race (Naureckas 1995; McWhorter 2012, 2004). He criticized my account of my negative experiences with the police as though racial profiling was something that blacks make up.[12]

His colleague at the Manhattan Institute, Heather Mac Donald (2001), believes that racial profiling is a myth even though a report from the Department of Justice (2003) during the Bush administration acknowledges its existence. The attorney general has exposed the racial disparities in the criminal justice system, disparities that are destroying the black family as blacks and browns are singled out by a rigged system that applies harsher sentences to blacks and makes them vulnerable to the profit-making private prison system, which is demanding longer sentences as a method of recruiting cheap labor. Moreover, the president can be accused of singling out blacks for scolding.

While giving black audiences the back of the hand, the president praises Latinos. Before one audience he said, "Diversity has always been America's strength. We are richer because of the men and women and children who've come to our shores and joined our union. . . . And nowhere is that more true than with the Latino community. Right now, there are 54 million Americans of Latino descent—one-sixth of our population. Our neighbors, our co-workers, our family, our friends. You've helped us build our cities, grow our economy, defend our country" (Salazar and Solis 2011). Yet the Hispanic teenage birth rate in 2012 was higher than that of blacks. There are more Hispanic children living in poverty than black children (U.S. Census Bureau 2013). (And 40 percent of those who live in poverty are white.) But the teenage birth rate for blacks has declined significantly, from 118 per thousand in 1991 to 47 per thousand in 2011 (Hamilton and Ventura 2012).

Aren't tough lovers supposed to congratulate those whom they regard as dysfunctional offenders when they do something right? I get offended when I see progressives argue against people who make careers off of baiting black single mothers without pointing out the drastic reduction of teenage births among black teenagers. Progressives are at a handicap when debating black dysfunction careerists like the tough love circle at Harvard and the enemies on the right who gain political power and ratings for their communications businesses by scapegoating blacks because these progressives subscribe to the same myths about black immorality as the right. When those whose minds are made up before all of the evidence is presented are not comparing what they feel is the lack of personal responsibility on the part of blacks, or are not holding up Hispanics as a model minority, then they cite the success of Asian Americans. Writer Scott Nakagawa has even criticized William Schneider of MSNBC for using Asian Americans—which consists of at least thirty-eight culturally distinct groups—as a model minority in reports clearly aimed at shaming blacks. He contends that such a labeling conceals the problems afflicting some Asian American communities, like sex trafficking and poverty (Nakagawa 2014). Using Asian Americans to embarrass blacks is something that novelist Frank Chin (1972) noticed a couple of decades ago.

So why does the president, a brilliant man, ignore the facts when criticizing dysfunction in the black community, and why is he silent about dysfunction in the white community? Why does he hold Hispanics as a model minority for others to emulate when the Hispanic minority is plagued with gang violence, unmarried motherhood, and dependency? During the week when he made remarks about the George Zimmerman verdict—where, according to Zillah Eisenstein (2013), white women jurors chose race or gender—there were stories about abundant supplies of heroin causing an epidemic in New England. Current TV reported "hundreds" of deaths of white youths in Boston as a result of heroin overdoses.

How did the issues of black Americans get moved to "the back burner," as one progressive put it? One of the methods used against those who view fair treatment of blacks as unfinished business has to do with what I called in a published essay, "The Roving of Black Americans" (Reed 2013a). Blacks who had the high moral ground were removed from that summit by charges of bigotry, which involved collective blame. First, white women from the north charged Stokely Carmichael with misogyny, a charge that has dogged black males since then and, according to some, might be the result of this later smearing by Gloria Steinem and her proxies (Litman 2011; Wallace 1990). I don't make the charge here, but the singling out of black men for charges of misogyny has diminished their influence on the left. bell hooks (1999) has criticized the middle-class feminist movement for holding black men to a different standard for misogyny, and Harriet Fraad (2013) writes that although the feminist movement began as an "integrated" working class movement, it was coopted by "educated, privileged" women. One can see this "it's-all-the-man's-fault" attitude in a passage from *The Norton Anthology of African American Literature*. An editor writes:

In a sharp departure from many of their male precursors, Morrison, Walker, and their black female contemporaries did not focus on the traumatic encounters of blacks and whites across the color line. The interracial conflicts at the heart of narratives by black male writers from Frederick Douglass to Ralph Ellison to Amiri Baraka did not take center stage. Racism remained a major concern. But for these writers, the most painful consequences of racism were played out in the most intimate relationships. Making hitherto private traumas public soon proved controversial. Women writers were accused of bashing black men and, worse, of being disloyal to the race. For examples, Shange's for colored girls who have considered suicide/ when the rainbow is enuf, a "choreopoem" that was clearly indebted to Baraka and the Black Arts movement for its poetic technique, became the object of controversy when it was staged for Broadway in 1977. (Gates et al. 2014)

As someone who is Ntozake Shange's colleague and the first to print and excerpt from "Colored Girls..." and as someone who has published black women writers both in Africa and the United States, I can assure the editors of this Norton anthology that such a description diminishes the range of writings by black women today, and that although feminists might cite Zora Neale Hurston, the women in her fiction can be just as duplicitous as the men—try reading "The Gilded Six-Bits" (1975). Ms. Hurston also wrote a minstrel show that had Africans committing cannibalism. As far as black male writers limiting their writings to attacking whitey, as one high-profile black literary diva put it recently (a simplistic and ignorant assessment), Richard Wright, Ralph Ellison, Claude McKay, Amiri Baraka, and others aimed some of their sharpest barbs at black men. Wright was physically attacked for criticizing blacks. Feminists also have asserted that black male writers received all of the glory, when Richard Wright and Chester Himes were in financial difficulty toward the end of their lives. I know, because Chester Himes lived in my house. It's all there in John A. Williams's "The Man Who Cried I Am," about how black male writers like Langston Hughes and others were perused by right-wing forces like the FBI and House Un-American Activities Committee. Yes, black men can be wrong when it comes to women, but in comparison to the men belonging to other American ethnic groups, black men are amateurs. I don't know of any black man who supports honor killings or who has sold his children into slavery, but the idea of the black male as the oppressor must be comforting to the men who are responsible for thousands of black, yellow, brown, and red men and women being eliminated from Medicaid, resulting in the deaths of thousands—the men who have caused the suffering of millions by the iniquitous Welfare Reform Act because such a line lets them off the hook. Moreover, if the editors are so hot on black women's fiction, why are Elizabeth Nunez, Jill Nelson, J. J. Phillips, and Carlene Hatcher Polite (whose novel *The Flagellants* is considered by some to be the novel that heralded the arrival of the black feminist novel) omitted? Why is Gates's critic Thulani Davis not included? But in the end the black feminist fiction to which the editors refer may no longer be at the "center." Currently, the African American Studies Department at Harvard seems to be lending its prestige to David Simon's (*The Wire*) and Quentin Tarantino's (*Django Unchained*) interpretations of the black experience. *The Wire*, written by Simon, a black dysfunction entrepreneur, was hailed by a black Harvard professor as saying more about urban life than any sociological treatise (Chaddha and Wilson 2010).

Next blacks were collectively charged with anti-Semitism. This charge was made by the second-most-powerful post-race advocate today next to the president, Henry Louis Gates Jr., in the *New York Times* (Gates 1992). How did blacks demonstrate their anti-Semitism? When Senator Joseph Lieberman ran for president, he was the first choice among blacks. When Rev. Al Sharpton entered the race, he was the second choice. And it was only a matter of time before the *New York Times* smeared blacks with the charge of homophobia (Flanagan and Schwarz 2008).

This set a prevailing attitude among whites that blacks were the real racists and their issues were undeserving of attention. This allowed the ushering in of a series of New Blacks. Or in other words, the civil rights of others, many of them prosperous middle-class whites, became "the Civil Rights of our Time," as though the classical questions of black oppression had been solved. This attitude spilled over into popular culture. In *Bonfire of the Vanities*, Tom Wolfe constructs a civil rights movement that cons patrons with the help of Jewish leniency. In the play *Six Degrees of Separation*, patrons are instructed to discontinue donations of conniving civil rights hustlers and save their sympathies for white gays. In Rebecca Gilman's *Spinning into Butter*, a black student complains about a hate crime; he made it up. In Jonathan Reynolds's *Stonewall Jackson's House*, blacks were better off in slavery. A liberal critic for *Newsweek* recommended the play for a Pulitzer Prize. In Mark Medoff's *Prymate*, a black actor plays an ape. Two incest movies, *The Color Purple* and *Precious*, depict black welfare recipients cheating, eating bad food, lying around watching TV, and having sex with their children. Although there have been a series of fictional works that C. Leigh Innis calls "Black Boogeyman" books, which he says "sell better than sex," *Precious*, which was fronted by two black producers (who were not considered producers by the Oscars because they became "producers" after the film was made) introduced the "Black Bogeywoman."

Obama's comment about blacks making "excuses" echoes the line set by the corporate media, that blacks make excuses instead of "working hard" to "get ahead." Perhaps the president was influenced by the post-race circle at Harvard where Henry Louis Gates Jr. blames the problems of the underclass on their personal behavior.

Was the leader of the post-race Joshua Generation and first black president nurtured by a circle of Harvard professors who believe that the personal behavior of an element they call "the underclass" is the cause of their problems? Do members of the Joshua Generation believe that the walls that prevent blacks from moving forward have come "tumblin' down?" Other post-racers believe that the classical racial impediments have been dismantled and that more attention should be paid to the oppression of others. Tavis Smiley is correct when he says that the president has spoken more about the oppression of the lesbian, gay, bisexual, and transgender movement, dominated by middle-class spokespersons, which ignores the fact that black and Puerto Rican transvestites paved the way for their success by battling the police in San Francisco and Stonewall (Reed 2013b). Yet, even among the oppressed, there are hierarchies; in a race-conscious country where citizens are ranked according to the degree of skin pigmentation, having white skin is an advantage. Even though gays have been called, among other things, "the new blacks," white gays have an easier time obtaining mortgages in San Francisco than blacks do (Savage 2012).

This is the Harvard post-race circle that has a course devoted to *Django Unchained*, which accepts the Sambo thesis that passive blacks cooperated with their enslavement and needed a Talented Tenth superhero to rescue at least one of them, yet criticizes the Black Arts movement as "short lived" in the *Norton Anthology of African American Literature*, a volume that showed Gates's uncritical capitulation to feminist ideology (Gates et al. 2014). As if it were not bad enough with white fiction writers and TV writers fighting each other over who will write a black dysfunction novel, in a bizarre outburst in the *New York Times Book Review*, Gates read black male fiction writers out of the market on the grounds of "black sexism" (1987).

Maybe Harold Cruse was correct when he said that nontraditional blacks, African and Caribbean individuals, harbor the same prejudices against traditional black Americans as many whites (1967). Granted, the president is an American, but his father was a Kenyan and his experience as a black male American was atypical. Joy Reid, one of the few black conservative commentators on television, compared the president's attitude toward blacks with those of her African immigrant parents, who complained about blacks who don't work hard. She made this reaction to the president's speech on September 8, 2013, while appearing on Melissa Harris Perry's show. In an example of Cruse's comment, on the same show a Trinidad-born commentator endorsed Bloomberg's Stop and Frisk measures and insisted that the Central Park Five were guilty even after they were exonerated. An African-born commentator said that she had no problems with the Bloomberg administration. This, after a federal judge had declared Stop and Frisk unconstitutional for singling out black and brown men for such searches, yet the president floated the name of the Stop and Frisk enforcer, Raymond Kelly, for head of Homeland Security.

Not all Caribbean- and African-born commentators have tough-love attitudes toward traditional African Americans, but the voices of those immigrant writers and intellectuals who credit traditional African Americans for paving the way for their success are drowned out by a media that uses the others against traditional blacks. One of the latter is the great novelist Elizabeth Nunez, but her considerable gifts are overshadowed as the result of the commercial demand for "Black Boogeyman" books, theater, and film.

I remember a conversation I had with a very famous black writer who'd just received a major prize in recognition of his remarkable work. He'd been invited to a well-known black writers' conference. He'd accepted but then told me that he was going to cancel. I suggested that he not cancel. I told him that those who were praising him, given how the mainstream middle persons view black writing as a series of tokens, might abandon him, but a black readership will be with him until the end.

This is the true of the first black president. He is confronted by a rabid foaming-at-the-mouth opposition from the right, and criticism from the white left whose attitudes have been wishy-washy toward blacks even before Claude McKay made his famous charge in the Kremlin in 1922, charging the white left with white chauvinism. Blacks will be with this president until the last dog dies. He should respect them.

NOTES

1. Contrary to stereotypes, women who are older, wealthier, well educated, and Caucasian actually have the highest rate of alcohol use during pregnancy. Yet these women are less likely to be asked about alcohol or drug use than poor or minority women. Punitive efforts directed at pregnant women who use substances have disproportionately singled out poor and minority women

who use illicit substances and ignored better-off white women who drink and smoke (Lunde 2012).

2. "Few experts would have suspected that the biggest contributors to California's drug abuse, death and injury toll are educated, middle-aged women living in Central Valley and rural areas, while the fastest-declining, lowest-risk populations are urban black and Latino teenagers," wrote Mike Males on January 3, 2007, in the *New York Times*.

3. Despite racialized images of crack users, data from the National Institute on Drug Abuse (NIDA) reveals that people reporting cocaine use in 1991 were 75 percent white, 15 percent black, and 10 percent Hispanic. People who admitted to using crack were 52 percent white, 38 percent black, and 10 percent Hispanic. From a rational perspective, these numbers should not be surprising: whites are, after all, the majority and have a long-standing tendency to use drugs at rates higher than blacks. Nonetheless, in 2009, the U.S. Sentencing Commission released data showing no drug matches crack in terms of racially biased convictions. According to the data, 79 percent of 5,669 sentenced crack offenders were black, 10 percent were Hispanic, and only 10 percent were white (Gwynne 2013).

4. In their analysis of the causes of wrongful convictions, the California Innocence Project found that prosecutorial misconduct was a factor in from 36 percent to 42 percent of the convictions. See *California Innocence Project*, Californiainnocenceproject.org.

5. The Glass–Steagall Act, which met with the approval of President Bill Clinton, led to the same speculation by the banks. This speculation led to the subprime mortgage disaster that wiped out the assets of thousands of black families.

6. Brooks writes: "You can see surprising political correlations. As Steve Sailer pointed out in the *American Conservative*, George Bush carried the 19 states with the highest white fertility rates, and 25 of the top 26. John Kerry won the 16 states with the lowest rates." He later writes, "Politicians will try to pander to this group" (2004).

7. "New Tea Party Report: Exposing the Links Between Tea Party Leaders and Racism," *NAACP*, http://www.naacp.org/pages/tea-party-report.

8. "CNN, Tea Party Express to Host First-Ever Tea Party Debate, Sept. 12," *CNN Press Room*, September 8, 2011, http://cnnpressroom.blogs.cnn.com/2011 /09/08/cnn-tea-party-express-to-host-first-ever-tea-party-debate-sept-12/.

9. *The German Ideology* (Die deutsche ideologie) is a book written by Karl Marx and Friedrich Engels around April or early May 1846. Marx and Engels did not find a publisher; however, the work was later retrieved and

published for the first time in 1932 by David Riazanov through the Marx-Engels Institute in Moscow.

10. Mariana van Zeller, "Gateway to Heroin," *Vanguard* documentary, YouTube video, first televised by Current TV on June 20, 2011, https://www.youtube.com/watch?v=IwKqTAqm6Ww.

11. "The Manhattan Institute: Launch Pad for Conservative Authors," Institute for Public Accuracy, March 1, 1998. http://www.accuracy.org/item/49-the-manhattan-institute-launch-pad-for-conservative-authors/.

12. "Well, forgive me: this collective portrait of degradation bears so little resemblance to my own experience, or the experience of my friends and acquaintances, that I can only throw up my hands. Certainly, my friends and I can cite unpleasant and possibly racially tinged incidents here and there in the course of our lifetimes. But for none of us are these the anecdotes we come home with on a weekly, monthly, or even annual basis. Not once to date have I had a nasty, intrusive run-in with the police, despite being no stranger to nightlife in cities like New York, Philadelphia, and Oakland, and despite having driven a beat-up car in tony white neighborhoods on a regular basis when, as a graduate student, I earned extra money playing piano at parties" (McWhorter 2004).

REFERENCES

Asher-Schapiro, Avi. 2013. "Wells Fargo's Makeover." *Jacobin*, November 15. https://www.jacobinmag.com/2013/11/wells-fargos-makeover/.

Blow, Charles M. 2011. "Escape from New York." *New York Times*, March 18, A23.

Bloomgarden-Smoke, Kara. 2013. "Page Six Cartoonist Sean Delonas Is Taking a Buyout," *New York Observer*, June 6. http://observer.com/2013/06/page-six-cartoonist-sean-delonas-is-taking-a-buyout/.

Brooks, David. 2004. "The New Red-Diaper Babies," *New York Times*, December 7, 2004. http://www.nytimes.com/2004/12/07/opinion/07brooks.html?_r=0

Brooks, Rick, and Ruth Simon. 2007. "Subprime Debacle Traps Even Very Credit-Worthy," *Wall Street Journal*, December 3. http://online.wsj.com/news/articles/SB119662974358911035.

Burkeman, Oliver. 2009. "New York Post in Racism Row Over Chimpanzee Cartoon," *Guardian*, February 18. http://www.theguardian.com/world/2009/feb/18/new-york-post-cartoon-race.

Byers, Dylan. 2013. "N.Y. Post's Allan to Face Harassment Charges," *Politico*, October 29. http://www.politico.com/blogs/media/2013/10/ny-posts-col-allan -to-face-harassment-charges-176220.html.

Chaddha, Anmol, and William Julius Wilson, 2010. "Why We're Teaching 'The Wire' at Harvard." *Washington Post*, September 12. http://www.washington post.com/wp-dyn/content/article/2010/09/10/AR2010091002676.html.

Chin, Frank, and Jeffery Paul Chan. 1972. "Racist Love." In *Seeing Through Shuck*, ed. Richard Kostelanetz, 65–79. New York: Ballantine Books.

Cruse, Harold. 1967. *The Crisis of the Negro Intellectual: A Historical Analysis of the Failure of Black Leadership*. New York: William Morrow.

DiIulio, John J., Jr. 1995. "The Coming of the Super-Predators." *Weekly Standard*, November 27. http://www.weeklystandard.com/Content/Protected /Articles/000/000/007/011vsbrv.asp?nopager=1.

Dowd, Maureen. 2000. "Liberties; Acid Tongue in Cheek," *New York Times*, September 3. http://www.nytimes.com/2000/09/03/opinion/liberties-acid -tongue-in-cheek.html.

Eisenstein, Zillah. 2013. "White Female Jurors and Florida Justice." *Feminist Wire*, July 17. thefeministwire.com/2013/07/white-female-jurors-and -florida-justice.

Feldman, Josh. 2013. "Roland Martin Bashes 'Largely White Male Executives' At CNN Uncomfortable With 'Strong, Confident Minorities.'" *Mediaite*, March 29. http://www.mediaite.com/online/roland-martin-bashes-largely -white-male-executives-at-cnn-uncomfortable-with-strong-confident -minorities/.

Flanagan, Caitlin, and Benjamin Schwarz. 2008. "Showdown in the Big Tent," *New York Times*, December 6. http://www.nytimes.com/2008/12/07 /opinion/07flanagan.html.

Fraad, Harriet. 2013. "The Feminist Movement—What Happened and Why?" *Tikkun Daily*, February 20. http://www.tikkun.org/tikkundaily/2013/02/20 /the-feminist-movement-what-happened-and-why/.

Gates, Henry Louis, Jr. 1987. "Reclaiming Their Tradition" *New York Times Book Review*, October 4, 34–35.

——. 1992. "Black Demagogues and Pseudo-Scholars." *New York Times*, July 20. http://www.nytimes.com/1992/07/20/opinion/black-demagogues-and -pseudo-scholars.html.

Gates, Henry Louis, Jr., Valerie Smith, William L. Andrews, Kimberly Benston, Brent Hayes Edwards, Frances Smith Foster, Deborah E. McDowell, Robert G. O'Meally, Hortense Spillers, and Cheryl A. Wall, eds. 2014. *The Norton*

Anthology of African American Literature, 3rd ed., vol. 2. New York: W. W. Norton.

Giuliani, Rudolph W. 2012. "What New York Owes James Q. Wilson," *City Journal*, Spring. http://www.city-journal.org/2012/22_2_james-q-wilson.html.

Good, Chris. 2010. "Mark Williams Steps Aside as Chairman of Tea Party Express." *Atlantic*, June 18. http://www.theatlantic.com/politics/archive/2010/06/mark-williams-steps-aside-as-chairman-of-tea-party-express/58402/.

Graham, Nicholas. 2009. "'Tea Party' Leader Melts Down on CNN: Obama Is an 'Indonesian Muslim Turned Welfare Thug.'" *Huffington Post*, November 15. http://www.huffingtonpost.com/2009/09/15/tea-party-leader-melts-do_n_286933.html.

Gwynne, Kristen. 2013. "4 Things You Probably Didn't Know About Crack, America's Most Vilified Drug." *AlterNet*, August 2. http://www.alternet.org/drugs/4-things-you-probably-didnt-know-about-crack-americas-most-vilified-drug.

Hacker, Andrew. 2012. "The White Plight," review of Murray's *Coming Apart*, in *New York Review of Books*, May 10. http://www.nybooks.com/articles/archives/2012/may/10/white-plight/.

Hamilton, Brady E., and Stephanie J. Ventura. 2012. "Birth Rates for U.S. Teenagers Lows for All Age and Ethnic Groups." *NCHS Data Brief* 89 (April). http://www.cdc.gov/nchs/data/databriefs/db89.htm.

hooks, bell. 1999. *Yearning: Race, Gender, and Cultural Politics*. Boston: South End Press.

Hurston, Zora Neale. 1975. "The Gilded Six-Bits." In *Yardbird Reader*, vol. 4., ed. William Lawson. Berkeley, CA: Yardbird Publishing.

Johnson, Marilynn S. 2003. *Street Justice*. Boston: Beacon Press.

Katznelson, Ira. 2005. "Raw Deal, New Deal." *Washington Post*, September 27. http://www.washingtonpost.com/wp-dyn/content/article/2005/09/27/AR2005092700484.html.

Krisberg, Barry. 2005. "Reforming Juvenile Justice." *American Prospect*, August 14. http://prospect.org/article/reforming-juvenile-justice.

Lewis, David. 2001. *W. E. B. Du Bois, 1919–1963: The Fight for Equality and the American Century*. New York: Holt Paperbacks.

Litman, Amanda. 2011. "Black History Month: The Myth of the Black Superwoman Revisited." *Ms.* blog, February 16. http://msmagazine.com/blog/2011/02/16/black-history-month-the-myth-of-the-black-superwoman-revisited/.

Lunde, Erin. 2012. "Substance Abuse During Pregnancy." *Sonoma Medicine* 63, no. 4 (Fall): 23–27.

Mac Donald, Heather. 2001. "The Myth of Racial Profiling." *City Journal*, Spring. http://www.city-journal.org/html/11_2_the_myth.html.

Males, Mike. 2007. "This Is Your Brain on Drugs, Dad." *New York Times*, January 3.

Marx, Karl, and Friedrich Engels. 1968. *The German Ideology*. Moscow: Progress Publishers.

Mathias, Christopher. 2013. "Bloomberg Decries 'Dangerous' Stop-And-Frisk Ruling, Promises Appeal," August 12. http://www.huffingtonpost.com/2013 /08/12/bloomberg-stop-and-frisk_n_3744102.html.

McWhorter, John. 2004. "Still Losing the Race." *Commentary*, February. http://www.commentarymagazine.com/article/still-losing-the-race/.

——. 2012. "What a Florida Teenager's Death Tells Us About Being Black in America." *New Republic*, March 20. http://www.newrepublic.com/article /101840/trayvon-martin-race-injustice.

Nakagawa, Scott. 2014. "MSNBC Is Doing Asian Americans No Favors." *Race Files*, March 14. http://www.racefiles.com/2014/03/14/msnbc-is-doing -asian-americans-no-favors/.

Naureckas, Jim. 1995. "Racism Resurgent: How Media Let The Bell Curve's Pseudo-Science Define the Agenda on Race." *FAIR*, January 1. http://fair .org/extra-online-articles/racism-resurgent/.

Osthaus, Carl R. 1976. *Freedmen, Philanthropy and Fraud: A History of the Freed-man's Savings Bank*. Champaign: University of Illinois Press.

Perez, Evan. 2013. "No Federal Challenge to Pot Legalization in Two States." CNN, August 30. http://www.cnn.com/2013/08/29/politics/holder -marijuana-laws/index.html.

Powell, Jim. 2003. "Why Did FDR's New Deal Harm Blacks?" Op-ed, Cato Institute, December 3. http://www.cato.org/publications/commentary/why -did-fdrs-new-deal-harm-blacks.

Reed, Ishmael. 1995. "Talking Morals to the Underclass Is Like Slave Own-ers Talking Liberty." *Baltimore Sun*, July 9. http://articles.baltimoresun .com/1995-07-09/news/1995190025_1_loury-morality-black-underclass.

——. 2013a. "The Roving of Black Americans." *Black Renaissance Noire*, August 15. http://www.nyubrn.org/the-roving-of-black-americans-by-ishmael-reed/.

——. 2013b. "Who's Next? Are Gays the New Blacks?" *Playboy*, July/August.

Roberts, Sam. 1993. "Trying to Stanch Blood in an Urban War Zone." *New York Times*, November 15. http://www.nytimes.com/1993/11/15/nyregion /metro-matters-trying-to-stanch-blood-in-an-urban-war-zone.html.

Rucker, Philip. 2010. "Former Militiaman Unapologetic for Calls to Vandal-ize Offices Over Health Care." *Washington Post*, March 25. http://www

.washingtonpost.com/wp-dyn/content/article/2010/03/25/AR20100
32501722.html?hpid=topnews&sid=ST2010032402500.

Ruderman, Wendy. 2012. "For Women in Street Stops, Deeper Humiliation." *New York Times*, August 6, A1. http://www.nytimes.com/2012/08/07/nyregion /for-women-in-street-stops-deeper-humiliation.html?pagewanted=all& _r=0.

Salazar, Ken, and Hilda Solis. 2011. "Obama Praises Latinos, Jobs Act." *UPI*, October 12.

Savage, Charlie. 2012. "Wells Fargo Will Settle Mortgage Bias Charges." *New York Times*, July 12. http://www.nytimes.com/2012/07/13/business/wells -fargo-to-settle-mortgage-discrimination-charges.html.

Seelye, Katharine Q. 2013. "Heroin in New England, More Abundant and Deadly." *New York Times*, July 18. http://www.nytimes.com/2013/07/19/us/heroin -in-new-england-more-abundant-and-deadly.html?pagewanted=all&_r=0.

U.S. Census Bureau. 2013. "Income, Poverty and Health Insurance Coverage in the United States 2012," September 17. http://www.census.gov/newsroom /releases/archives/income_wealth/cb13-165.html.

U.S. Department of Justice. 2003. *Fact Sheet: Racial Profiling.* http://www.justice .gov/opa/pr/2003/June/racial_profiling_fact_sheet.pdf.

Wallace, Michele. 1990. *Black Macho and the Myth of the Superwoman.* New York: Verso.

Weissman, Jordan. 2011. "Countrywide's Racist Lending Practices Were Fueled by Greed." *Atlantic*, December 23. http://www.theatlantic.com/business/archive /2011/12/countrywides-racist-lending-practices-were-fueled-by-greed/250424/.

Wilson, James Q. 1995. "Crime and Public Policy." In *Crime*, ed. James Q. Wilson and Joan Petersilia, 488–507. San Francisco: Institute of Contemporary Studies Press.

"W. W." 2012. "Is Paul Ryan a Hypocrite?" *Economist*, August 13. http://www .economist.com/blogs/democracyinamerica/2012/08/paul-ryan-randianism.

13

Thirteen Ways of Looking At Post-Blackness (after Wallace Stevens)

EMILY RABOTEAU

I

Among the fifty prisons
the only flesh the naked eye could see
was black

II

The blackbird pronounced its broken wing a cliché
and flew off to Havana

III

I was of two nations
like a mulatto
who appears un-black

IV

Tired of eating shit
a black man sat
in the oval office
enjoying a cold bowl of plums

V

I do not know which is more terrible
the birth of our Blackness on the boats
or its death and rebirth as a ghost

VI

Oh, black hands of Ethiopia!
When shall you stretch forth
to close the incalculable distance?

VII

The blackboard is not black
The sky is not blue
The teacher erases the math
leaving a cloud of chalk

VIII

The woman is dead
The money is missing
The black man must have done it

IX

Here are the little girl's black patent leather shoes,
her jump rope, her children's bible,
and the chunk of concrete
that split her skull in the Birmingham blast

X

The composer knows
without knowing how,
the sorrow of the black keys
overcomes its own sound

XI

When the pie was opened
the blacks began to sing,
Give us now a piece of what we served unto the king!

XII

She rode through Harlem on a tour bus
Her camera misled her
in that she mistook a black church for a museum

XIII

For decades of decades it was dark and
in that darkness they dreamed a dream
of a blackness so vast it had no name

AFTERWORD

I often teach Wallace Stevens's imagistic poem, "Thirteen Ways of Looking at a Blackbird," to creative writing students as an example of perspective. In that poem, which contains thirteen stanzas, a blackbird appears
from thirteen different angles. Each stanza produces a different mood, or
sensation: mystery, doom, calm, beauty, fear, freedom, etc. . . . After reading the poem, I usually whip out a black umbrella or some other object,
and have each student come up with an associative stanza about it. I dis-
courage them from being too literal. Then I gather their work together
to create a class poem. When I was invited to write about post-blackness,
I immediately thought of this homage exercise and wanted to apply it.
Post-blackness, like blackness itself, is a slippery concept, open to interpretation. I'm not sure I understand what post-blackness is, nor what I think
about it, except that it seems to suggest we are past something that I don't
believe is past. My attempt was to go at it from different associative angles
without making any overt pronouncements about something so intricate,
perplexing, and important as race.

Conclusion

Why the Lega Mask Has Many
Mouths and Multiple Eyes

HOUSTON A. BAKER JR.

There is no post-racial, just post-humane.
—Professor Obery Hendricks[1]

When we issued a call for contributions to a collection of original essays addressing post-Blackness, my colleague, Professor Merinda Simmons, and I were equal opportunity collaborators. We agreed to invite contributors from a rich admixture: women and men, young and advanced, Black and White. We were as surprised by some of our invitees' refusals as we were pleased by the exuberant acceptances of others. The mixture of acceptance and refusal signaled for us not only the cache of post-Blackness but also the term's ideological, racial, and professional currents. Post-Blackness is a sea tossed by long waves of controversy. We sent invitations to race spokespersons who simply ignored us. Others offered demurring refusals. These refusals arrived mainly from scholars who are "not of color." They are known for and have made their most significant academic advances as experts on race. One of them entered the curious claim that analyses of post-Blackness should be left to "racial insiders." As a Black man and White woman in scholarly collaboration, we did not conceive our project as a collection designed exclusively for black, "raced" insiders. When our White invitee suggested such, he seemed unaware that he was "raced." Strange navigational lights flash on when "post-Blackness" and its public consequences are at sea.

Professor Simmons and I did not expect all invitees to respond. Nor did we expect all to accept. What we quickly realized, however, is that "post-Blackness" produces tides of anxiety. We were, therefore, exceptionally grateful to the many excellent scholars who accepted our call. In time, some scholars were compelled to withdraw. Others simply dropped off the collaborative radar without a "good-bye." Original essay collections demand patience and rely upon the intellectual acumen and generosity of courteous and committed contributors. We are grateful for our scholarly essayists, prose autobiographers, poets, and novelists.

The foregoing précis of our collaborative process may well represent the common fate for collections of original essays. However, we believe the knotty concerns of race and identity linked with post-Blackness generate uniquely fraught monetary and celebrity concerns. From its coinage more than two decades ago, "post-Blackness" has sparked entangling claims and counter claims, yielding melancholia and self-aggrandizement, proclamations of new dispensations, and meditative autobiographical recall.[2] There has also been a maelstrom of sociohistorical critique. Such criticism often manifests itself as a decided resistance to post-Blackness' founding proposition. That proposition unfolds as follows: There is a *past* blackness that serves only as a *period*, a prelude to a teleological and exultant *post*-Blackness. One imagines a philosophically intoned deliberation among those bold enough to announce an end to decades of retro-blackness. They might pose hypothetical questions such as: "How inadequate and limiting was that *old blackness*, and what really was it good for? Are we not now the new big thing?" Such hypothetical discursive registers seem marked by ennui and the self-referential sigh of T. S. Eliot's poetic speaker: "Well that's done: and I'm glad it's over."

Of course, overly self-conscious deliberations from post-Blackness first responders are on par with the inevitably expressed anxieties mediating transitions from one charting of creative and sociopolitical order to another. Harbingers of post-Blackness are, after all, men and women with vested interests. They crave acknowledgment as town criers of an end to "all that." But wasn't it the old-school modernist Ezra Pound who nearly a century ago announced that his cadre would "Make it new"? To me, the Pound connection ironically suggests that post-Blackness's messengers are, at least in the larger politico-aesthetic realm, a rear guard. Announcements of post-Blackness simply mimic both Poundian self-exaltation and American advertising's ubiquitous slogan: "New and Improved." As more than one essay in our collection argues, sharp, right-rudder deviations toward the "post" are eternally replete with psycho-commercial interests. Freud has his place in all of this, but so too does Madison Avenue. The phrase "first Black president of the United States" is coextensive with current annunciations of post-Blackness.

It is legitimate to say post-Blackness is meant to denote a fulfillment of faith connoted by Barack Obama's presidential campaign and election victory. No longer need one commit to the substance of things hoped for and the evidence of things unseen. Post-Blackness appears with aplomb to announce victory, satisfy our cravings, and soothe our anxieties about an inadequate Black past of deep misery and Black Nationalist fervor. The politics and aesthetics of the not-so-distant Black past were, after all, vociferous and ultra-Black; they unquestionably lacked a well-spoken Black commander in chief of the United States.

In 1967 the indomitable Gwendolyn Brooks captured the imaginative energies of Black Liberation and the Black Arts movements spanning the 1960s to the 1980s. She realized a revolution was afoot. In her poem "The Wall," she observes that the men and women manning the bridge and accelerating the momentum of Black arts, politics, and culture unabashedly issued "their yea and their Announcement that they were ready to rile the high-flung ground." Partisans and participants in this "yea and announcement" were dedicated to collective, Black, and engaged actions meant to ameliorate the silent abjection and horrific confinements of the Black American Majority. As a collective, partisan and participants worked in enduring traditions of race men and race women of countless Black generations.

On Obama's presidential campaign trail, Oprah Winfrey opined a yea and announcement quite different from Gwendolyn Brooks's. Winfrey declared that Obama was "the one." Her meaning was crystal clear. Barack Hussein Obama, in his singularity, had been sent in fulfillment of the faith of our fathers. He was Black salvation incarnate.

Wary listeners—some students of scripture—were inclined to discount Oprah's fanfare and cling to the Gospel according to Luke. In Luke 21:8, it is written that Jesus responded as follows to a clamorous assembly demanding that the man from Jerusalem name the precise day and time of Armageddon and Judgment: "See that you not be deceived, for many will come in my name, saying, 'I am he,' and 'The time has come.' Do not follow them!"

Obama's handlers were an edgy group. They were adept, if sometimes frenetic, in their following. If it was necessary to throw Black Liberation Theology and its Chicago minister, Rev. Jeremiah Wright, under the bus in order to elect "the one," so be it. The handlers achieved this removal of a Black holy hindrance to their nominee in remarkably punctilious fashion. The charismatic preacher was disappeared. And still, Obama's handlers persuaded the many among the Black electorate to raise a halleluiah chorus to "the one." The campaign slogan was hope; Obama was its signal embodiment. As the campaign's momentum escalated, one of my colleagues wrote to me as follows: "Do you realize that more than ninety percent of Black voters have committed to the faith that Obama will lead blacks beyond racism, violence, and poverty?" She continued: "When did we, as a people, forget that in politics there are no permanent friends, only perpetual and eternal interests?"

During the seemingly interminable run-up to Obama's 2008 election victory, detractors, celebrants, and media pundits everywhere went toe to toe in lamentation, hyperbole, and high prophecy on the prospects of a U.S. Black presidency. Extravagant claims for the change an Obama presidency would effect were met by counterclaims that Obama was inexperienced, bearing thin political credentials and limited acumen to confront the opposition awaiting him should he win the White House. Though seldom discussed in the open air of campaign speeches and debates, "race" was, in fact, the significant undertow of all the political rant and maneuvering of the run-up. Scholar Stephanie Li defines this controlled submergence of race as "signifying without specifying."

For example, a statement such as "he is the one"—a signification filled with scriptural resonance—is never allowed to become openly spoken as: "We never really *expect* (only hope) to see a Black Man, one committed to the perpetual and eternal interests of blacks, become president of the United States." Yet, in the gap between signifying and specifying, Obama's Black support was energized by his campaign's signature "hope," a signifier entirely lacking in designated and announced racial specifics.

In 2013, as President Obama moved toward the second year of his second presidential term, his national approval rating had plummeted from an all-time high of 69 percent to an all-time low of 40 percent. Myriad political events have worked against the president's ratings. An attempt here to rehearse what has gone irretrievably wrong with the world and word of Obama would be hubris. Such analyses are best consigned to other venues. What is certain for the present writing is that from Obama's inaugural address in 2008 to the grand cacophony and apologetics surrounding the botched launch of the Affordable Care Act, an array of events have clearly nullified claims for a messianic: "He is the one."

The presidency of Barack Obama may have motivated declarations of the birth of post-Blackness, but the men, women, and milieu of post-Blackness have not ameliorated one whit the racial humiliation and abject confinements of the U.S. Black Majority. Faith in the incarnation of the "the one" has proved as commensurate with reality as Ponce de Leon's magical map to the fountain of youth.

De Leon's fountain is now a theme park in Florida, a state that supports a Stand Your Ground statute. The statute masquerades as a prudent self-defense measure, but recently it enabled the killing of Black teenager Trayvon Martin. His killer was George Zimmerman, a community watchman turned vigilante. Zimmerman was acquitted of murder by an all-White jury that agreed he was "standing his ground" against an assaultive teenager walking home at night from a store with a bag of Skittles while talking on his cell phone. Stand Your Ground is an incentive to violence. De Leon's myth of promised youth and brave new worlds thus staked its claim in a state where the death of youth plays out as vigilante justice. By their very nature, myths resist empirical scrutiny, on-the-ground efficacy, and dubious long-term effectiveness.

The foregoing essays collected here are in some ways a studied demythologization of post-Blackness. A number of them expeditiously discount the empirical validity of post-Blackness through the calculations of simple mathematics. They forthrightly challenge the sample size of Touré's research for *Who's Afraid of Post-Blackness: What It Means to Be Black Now*. By the author's count, his research consisted of 105 interviews with "prominent" Black Americans. There are in excess of forty million Black American residents in the United States. Hence, Touré's evidence is drawn from a miniscule (to be precise: .0000026 percent) sampling that can hardly be called a sample at all. For the truly empirical, one can say that mean, variance, and randomness—not to mention size—have no place in Touré's interviews for post-Blackness. What he builds from the elite 105 is a leaky vessel that, one thinks, few would wish to get on board. Of course, what Touré is pitching is not a collective journey but an exemption. He explicitly argues that he must be granted an exemption to do precisely as he individually pleases. If we envision a hypothetical Selective Service for the Black Liberation Struggle, Touré and his post-Black cohort would demand "1–0" status, defined as "Conscientious Objector, perhaps available for alternate community service." The writer Greg Tate is author of a compelling book about those who want to be Black in their individualism and celebrity and financial profits but not in collective struggle with the Black Majority. Tate's title is spot-on for post-Blackness: *All But the Burden*.

What is most significant about Touré's opus are the words of his subtitle: "What it means to be black now." Point in fact. What it means for
Trayvon Martin and his family "now" is that Trayvon Martin is dead. In
the aggregate, the U.S. Black Majority understands that what it means
to be "black now" is perpetually to be under live ammunition fire in
the "hood" and to be harassed as a "person of interest" at Barneys in
New York because you are a person of color with resources to make
an expensive purchase. To be black now is to be a black teenage girl
in Dearborn, Michigan, seeking help after suffering an automobile col-
lision. The African American young woman, Renisha McBride, found
her way to the porch of a home in a predominantly White neighborhood of Dearborn in search of aid. The White male homeowner aimed
his 12-guage shotgun at her face and killed her. He says he was "standing
his ground."

To be black *now* for the Black Majority is to live shorter lives, work
disgusting menial jobs, suffer unemployment when such jobs fail, endure
explicit and implicit insults for the audacity of "appearing in public," and
move in city or country U.S.A. from "can in the morning" to "can't at
night" with a noose (metaphorical, or Jena specific) over your head.

Meanwhile, the first Black president of the United States has a 40
percent approval rating. Who really wants to be emblazoned as "the
one"?

Professor Simmons and I hope the present collection will speak with
integrity and gratitude the names of those within the foregoing pages.
Their generous responses not only trouble post-Blackness but also
bespeak the troubles that Blackness has seen and transmogrified for centuries. We have adopted for our sign the Lega mask of many mouths and
multiple eyes. The mask signifies multidirectionality, transtemporality,
and inescapable inscriptions of the trade winds and the windfall profits
that produced an abject black. An abject black violently abused across
archipelagos and landmasses of the New World. Even when they do not
specify, we know our collective writings look all ways, speak multiply, and
signify outrageously.

Lega/Lengola "Triple Face" Mask. Wood, white Kaolin, and encrusted patina. Early to mid-twentieth century, Democratic Republic of the Congo. Courtesy of Artenegro.

NOTES

1. Professor Hendricks's statement is in response to a photograph of white Georgia deputy sheriff, Chad Palmer, who—costumed in blackface and prison stripes—attended a private party as a Camden County prison inmate. In the photo, which went viral on social media, Sheriff Palmer pretends to be picking cotton. The year of the photo is 2013. See http://www.huffington post.com/2013/11/16/chad-palmer-blackface_n_4283978.html.

2. In 2001 Thelma Golden, curator of the Studio Museum in Harlem, mounted a show titled "Freestyle" featuring new black artists. Golden, in collaboration with artist Glenn Ligon, dubbed the mode of these new artists "post-black." The term set off heated exchanges among critics, artists, and journalistic opinion shapers. Was Golden announcing the demise of "blackness" as it had come radically to be defined during the Black Arts movement? Was she whimsically proclaiming the advanced guard of black art was post-racial? No one (not even Golden and Ligon) was certain about the semantic limits and expanses of the term "post-black." Certainly, it remains a marker that is troublingly evocative and thus a term to be critically troubled.

CONTRIBUTORS

HOUSTON A. BAKER JR. is Distinguished University Professor and professor of English at Vanderbilt University. He has served as president of the Modern Language Association of America and is the author of articles, books, and essays devoted to African American literary criticism and theory. His book *Betrayal: How Black Intellectuals Have Abandoned the Ideals of the Civil Rights Era* (Columbia University Press, 2010) received an American Book Award for 2009.

MARGO NATALIE CRAWFORD is associate professor of African American literature and global black studies in the Department of English at Cornell University. She is the author of *Dilution Anxiety and the Black Phallus* (Ohio State University Press, 2008) and the coeditor, with Lisa Gail Collins, of *New Thoughts on the Black Arts Movement* (Rutgers University Press, 2006). Her essays appear in a wide range of books and journals, including *American Literature, Want to Start a Revolution?, The Cambridge Companion to American Poetry Since 1945, The Modernist Party, Callaloo, Black Camera, NKA: Journal of Contemporary African Art, Black Renaissance Noire*, and *James Baldwin: Go Tell It on the Mountain; Historical and Critical Essays*. She is on the editorial board of the Society for Textual Scholarship, the *James Baldwin Review*, and the *Wiley Blackwell Anthology of African American Literature*.

BAYO HOLSEY is associate professor of African and African American studies and cultural anthropology at Duke University. She received her

PhD in sociocultural anthropology from Columbia University. She is the author of *Routes of Remembrance: Refashioning the Slave Trade in Ghana* (University of Chicago Press, 2008), which examines the public history of the trans-Atlantic slave trade in Ghana. This book won the Royal Anthropological Institute's Amaury Talbot Prize for African Anthropology and the Association for Third World Studies' Toyin Falola Africa Book Award. Currently she is completing a second book entitled *Tyrannies of Freedom: Race, Power, and the Fictions of Late Capitalism*.

JOHN L. JACKSON JR. is the Richard Perry University Professor of Communication, Africana Studies, and Anthropology at the University of Pennsylvania. His books include *Harlemworld: Doing Race and Class in Contemporary Black America* (University of Chicago Press, 2001); *Real Black: Adventures in Racial Sincerity* (University of Chicago Press, 2005), *Racial Paranoia: The Unintended Consequences of Political Correctness* (Basic Civitas, 2008), and *Thin Description: Ethnography and the African Hebrew Israelites of Jerusalem* (Harvard University Press, 2013). His latest film, codirected by Deborah A. Thomas, is *Bad Friday: Rastafari After Coral Gardens* (2012).

ERIN AUBRY KAPLAN is a Los Angeles journalist and essayist who has been writing about issues of concern to black communities since 1992. She is a contributing editor to the *Los Angeles Times* op-ed and became its first regular black columnist in 2005. She is also a former staff writer for the *LA Weekly*. Her collection of reportage and essays, *Black Talk, Blue Thoughts and Walking the Color Line: Dispatches from a Black Journalista*, was published in 2011 by Northeastern University Press.

STEPHANIE LI is the Susan D. Gubar Chair in Literature at Indiana University, Bloomington. Her books include *"Something Akin to Freedom": The Choice of Bondage in Narratives by African American Women* (State University of New York Press, 2010) and *Signifying Without Specifying: Racial Discourse in the Age of Obama* (Rutgers University Press, 2012). Her fourth monograph, *Playing in the White: Black*

Writers, White Subjects, will be published by Oxford University Press in 2015.

EMILY RABOTEAU is associate professor of English at the City College of New York, in Harlem. She is author of the novel *The Professor's Daughter* (Henry Holt, 2005) and the recently released memoir *Searching for Zion: The Quest for Home in the African Diaspora* (Atlantic Monthly Press, 2013), grand prize winner of the New York Book Festival. Her fiction and essays have appeared in *Tin House, The Believer, McSweeney's, Guernica*, the *Guardian, Salon*, and elsewhere. The recipient of a Pushcart Prize and the Chicago *Tribune's* Nelson Algren Award, she has also received literature fellowships from the National Endowment for the Arts, the New York Foundation for the Arts, and the MacDowell Colony.

PATRICE RANKINE is professor of classics and dean for the arts and humanities at Hope College, in Holland, Michigan. He is author of *Ulysses in Black: Ralph Ellison, Classicism, and African American Literature*, published in 2006 with the University of Wisconsin Press, which was named one of *Choice* magazine's outstanding academic books in 2007 and is currently in its second printing. His second book is *Aristotle and Black Drama: A Theater of Disobedience*, which Baylor University Press published in 2013. He is a member of the Archive of Performances of Greek and Roman Drama's Advisory Board at Oxford University, and his publications also include numerous articles, book chapters, and book reviews.

ISHMAEL REED is an internationally acclaimed poet, essayist, playwright, novelist, and recipient of a MacArthur Fellowship (genius award). His novels, *Yellow Back Radio Broke-Down* (Dalkey Archive Press, 1969), *Mumbo Jumbo* (1972), and *The Last Days of Louisiana Red* (1974), ushered in a bold and brilliant new vein of satire in African American literature. His most recent critique of racism and black neoconservatism in the United States is *Barack Obama and the Jim Crow Media: The Return of the "Nigger Breakers"* (Baraka Books, 2010).

RICHÉ RICHARDSON is associate professor of Africana Studies at Cornell University. She is the author of lectures, interviews, and essays. She is also an internationally acknowledged quilter of African American themes and images. Her book *Black Masculinity and the U.S. South: From Uncle Tom to Gangsta* is a major contribution to the University of Georgia Press series titled The New Southern Studies (2007), which Professor Richardson coedits with Professor Jon Smith.

HEATHER RUSSELL is associate professor of English and African and African Diaspora Studies at Florida International University. Her book *Legba's Crossing: Narratology in the African Atlantic* was published in 2009 by the University of Georgia Press. She has contributed essays, articles, and reviews to *American Literature, The Massachusetts Review, African American Review*, and a number of essay collections from the United States and the Caribbean.

RONE SHAVERS is assistant professor of English at the College of Saint Rose who writes in multiple genres. His collaborative critical projects include *Paper Empire: William Gaddis and the World System* (with Joseph Tabbi; University of Alabama Press, 2007); an e-casebook on author Lynne Tillman's *American Genius: A Comedy*, for *EBR: Electronic Book Review* (with Eric Dean Rasmussen); and a special issue of *Science Fiction Studies* devoted to the emergent literary and cultural genre known as Afro-Futurism (with Mark Bould).

K. MERINDA SIMMONS is assistant professor of religious studies at the University of Alabama. She is the author of *Changing the Subject: Writing Women Across the African Diaspora* (Ohio State University Press, 2014). She is coeditor (with Maha Marouan) of *Race and Displacement* (University of Alabama Press, 2013). Her areas of research and publication incorporate literary and religious studies with critical emphases in African diasporas, southern studies, gender theory, and feminist philosophy. She is currently conducting grant-funded research on "slave religion" in Southern U.S. port cities.

GREG THOMAS is associate professor of English at Tufts University. His books include *The Sexual Demon of Colonial Power: Pan-African Embodiment and Erotic Schemes of Empire* (Indiana University Press, 2007) and *Hip-Hop Revolution in the Flesh: Power, Knowledge and Pleasure in Lil' Kim's Lyricism* (Palgrave Macmillan, 2009). He is founder and former editor of the online journal *Proud Flesh* as well as coeditor (with LaMonda H. Stallings) of *Word Hustle: Critical Essays and Reflections on the Works of Donald Goines* (Black Classic Press, 2011). Currently he is at work on a study of the revolutionary writings of George L. Jackson, "the Dragon."

DANA A. WILLIAMS is professor of African American literature and Chair of the Department of English at Howard University. Her book *In the Light of Likeness—Transformed: The Art of Leon Forrest* (Ohio State University Press, 2005) is the only full-length study of Forrest. She has edited *Contemporary African American Fiction: New Critical Essays* (Ohio State University Press, 2009), *Humor, Irony, and Satire: Ishmael Reed Satirically Speaking* (Cambridge Scholars Publishing, 2007), and *August Wilson and Black Aesthetics* (with Sandra G. Shannon; Palgrave Macmillan, 2004). Her articles and reviews have appeared in *CLA Journal, Profession, Studies in American Fiction, African American Review*, and elsewhere. She is currently completing a book on Toni Morrison's editorship at Random House Publishing.

INDEX